Something for Everyone

150 Main-Dish Recipes for Families that include Vegetarians and Meat-Eaters

Carol Gelles

macmillan • usa

Dedicated to my mother and father

MACMILLAN
A Simon & Schuster Macmillan Company
1633 Broadway
New York, NY 10019

MACMILLAN is a registered trademark of Macmillan, Inc.

Library of Congress Cataloging-in-Publication Data

Gelles, Carol.
    Something for everyone : 150 main dish recipes for families that include vegetarians and
meat-eaters / Carol Gelles.
      p. cm.
    Includes index.
    ISBN 0-02-860996-4
    1. Entreés (Cookery) 2. Cookery, International. 3. Vegetarian
cookery. I. Title.
TX740.G39 1997   97-30068
641.8'2—dc21   CIP

ISBN: 0-02-861916-1

Manufactured in the United States of America

10 9 8 7 6 5 4 3 2 1

Book design by Nick Anderson

Acknowledgments

I think the concept for this book is truly brilliant. I can say that immodestly since the idea was not mine at all, but Emily Nolan's who was, at the time the book was conceived, an editor at Macmillan. I thank her and Justin Schwartz who suggested my name to Emily when she was looking for an author for this project, for their faith in my ability to make this concept into a reality. To Judith Weber, my agent, and David Weiser, who won the Name-this-Book contest.

For my friends and family who have been around for so many years; who have listened to me kvetch, tasted the recipes for this and my other books as well, and have always given great advice about the recipes as well as about life in general, and made me feel surrounded by love and affection, and don't generally mind that I not only write in long, run-on sentences, but that I also talk that way. There will never be enough thanks in the world to express my gratitude to you.

I hesitate to start naming names, since it's impossible not to exclude one or two people, but you know who you are and that you belong to this exceptional group of people; if I've left out your name, please forgive me. Thank you: Randy Kraft, Paula Rudolph-Minsky, Dori Jaffe, Sherry Gelles, Lorraine Klien, Nancy Jane Goldstein, Jesse Weissman, Erica Weissman, Leah Weissman, Myriam Abramowicz, Suefein, Steven Goldstein, Lisa Schachner, Bonnie Roche and to other members of the Shower Curtain Torah Study Group as well. Thanks!

Table of Contents

Introduction

Although vegetarianism is certainly on the rise in this country, the truth is, becoming a vegetarian is usually an individual, not a family decision. This creates a difficult situation in the kitchen: How do you cook for a family with two entirely different eating styles? Does the entire family have to give up meat because one member has decided to become a vegetarian? Does the vegetarian have to make due with side dishes or starve? Or is the family cook now saddled with cooking two entirely different meals? This book addresses the problem by providing recipes that limit the confusion and work involved in planning two separate menus, and allowing everyone at the table to have similar style meals.

Understanding and Dealing with a Divided Household

How well a family adjusts to vegetarianism depends partly on who made the initial decision. That member of the family who became the first—and possibly will remain the only—vegetarian, may determine how well the decision will be accommodated. For instance, if the first vegetarian is the family cook, the vegetarian(s) will be nicely

accommodated. In fact, the meat-eaters may have to learn to love vegetarian foods. If the first vegetarian is a child or teen, there might be a lack of support by other members of the family, especially the cook, who is the one most affected by this decision. In some instances, the vegetarian might have to fend for him/herself, surviving on the salad and/or side dishes served to the rest of the family. By providing recipes that yield entrées for both vegetarians and meat-eaters, it is my hope that both halves of the family can share meals together without hassles on either side of the table.

About the Book

Unlike my other books, which were written specifically for vegetarians, this book is written for families, or groups of people, which contain vegetarian and meat-eating individuals. I've tried to think of mealtime dynamics, envisioning a harried cook, pressured by a busy schedule and hungry people, trying to get something prepared that will please everyone. Therefore, most of these recipes are easy and quick, with serious consideration to a wide range of tastes. I have included recipes that children and teenagers will enjoy, emphasizing Italian, Mexican, and Chinese cuisine with universally loved recipes such as pizza, spaghetti and meatballs, tacos, burritos, chow mein, lo mein, and egg foo young. For more sophisticated palates, though, my Mediterranean and French recipes offer a nice variety of choices and flavors.

Structure, Structure, Structure

How to organize the recipes was one of my true challenges. I knew they could not be organized in the most common ways—by course, or type of meat—since all the dishes are entrées and only half of each recipe contains meat. Similarly, arranging by bean, grain, or tofu didn't make sense either. In the end, I found that what both recipe halves do have in common is flavor. So each chapter focuses on the predominate flavors of a country or region. It's also easy to choose a recipe by the flavor you're in the mood for—if you're in a spicy mood, experiment with the spicier fare in the Mexican or Asian chapters.

Menu Planning

When choosing a menu, use vegetarian dishes for courses other than the entrée. For example, if you are going to start with soup, don't choose one with a chicken or beef base. A vegetarian soup allows the entire family to have soup together. Many of the large soup companies make "vegetarian" soups, but don't necessarily announce them as such. For example: lentil, minestrone, and tomato soups are usually vegetarian. Vegetable (unless labeled "vegetarian"), split pea, and onion soups, as a general rule, are not vegetarian, but are are made with beef stock or seasoned with meat products. Read the labels. If there is no meat nor any type of animal product on the ingredient list, then it's a product that can be served to all members of the family. If you're planning to make soup from scratch, consult a vegetarian cookbook. The meat-eaters should not object just because the soup was made with vegetable broth instead of chicken or beef; in fact, they probably won't even notice the difference. Salads, side dishes and desserts are not usually a problem for the family to share.

Once you've selected your entrée, the rest of the menu should be fairly easy to build on. Since these chapters are divided by country, I suggest you plan the entire meal around that cuisine. For example, if you've chosen a recipe from the Mexican chapter, you may want to serve salsa and chips, or guacamole to start the meal, then serve rice and beans on the side. Recipes from the Far East always go well with white or brown rice. Italian foods just scream for salad and crusty bread.

How to Use This Book

The recipes are divided into three parts: the Base Recipe (which sometimes contains two parts: a sauce, dressing, filling, or marinade plus other ingredients), the vegetarian recipe, and the meat recipe. The end result is two different finished recipes, one containing meat and the other vegetarian, yet they both have the Base Recipe in common. IT IS VERY IMPORTANT when dividing the Base Recipe to be sure to divide any sauce or salad dressing evenly as well as the larger ingredients, unless directed otherwise.

Order of the Recipe

Although most of the recipes in this book are basically quick and easy to prepare, the fact that you are making two recipes at once can sometimes get a little confusing. It's best, of course, to read the recipe through entirely before beginning it to avoid any unnecessary surprises. In most cases, the Base Recipe is prepared first, followed by the vegetarian recipe and then the meat recipe. In some recipes, you must make both the vegetarian and meat recipes first, then proceed with the Base Recipe. For example, you need to make the two fillings for the strudel recipes, before you prepare the strudel layers.

Because it may not always be obvious which part of the recipe should be the starting point, I used the Recipe Tips to indicate when a recipe is best started somewhere other than with the Base Recipe. If you've skipped the headnotes, I've tried to indicate starting points in the recipes themselves.

Some of the recipes include ingredients that are already cooked, such as beans, grains, potatoes, corn, peas, etc. Be sure you have these ingredients cooked before you start any part of the recipe. For some ingredients, such as peas, corn, and beans, I usually use frozen (peas) or canned (corn and beans) since they are already prepared. In these instances, you don't have to cook them before adding them to the recipe. See *Ingredients* (page xi) for more about prepared ingredients.

The Base Recipe

The Base Recipe is the part that both completed dishes have in common. In the case of recipes that end up being extremely different, such as lentil burgers and meat loaf, the Base Recipe is simply the seasoning. In most other recipes, such as chili, the Base Recipe makes up practically the entire dish. Different ingredients are added in at the last minute to complete each version of the recipe. In some of the more complicated recipes, the Base Recipe contains a technique used in more than one recipe. Related recipes would include different fillings, for instance, for the strudels. Again, *it is important to remember that when dividing the Base Recipe, any sauce or salad dressing should be divided evenly as well.*

The Sub-recipes

The Vegetarian Recipe: This half of the recipe gives ingredients and instructions for finishing the vegetarian half of the Base Recipe. The section called *Totally Vegetarian* provides instructions for converting the whole recipe into a vegetarian one, omitting the meat (in case the whole group prefers the vegetarian version). If there are no instructions for *Totally Vegetarian*, simply double the vegetarian or meat recipe and use all of the Base Recipe to make 4 servings.

The Meat Recipe: This half of the recipe gives ingredients and instructions for finishing the meat-eater half of the Base Recipe. The section called *Totally con Carne* gives instructions for preparing the entire recipe with meat, omitting the vegetarian variation completely (in case the family vegetarians are out of town and the meat-eaters are hungry and want to have the whole thing their way). If there are no instructions for *Totally con Carne*, simply double the vegetarian or meat recipe and use all of the Base Recipe to make 4 servings.

Yields: I much prefer to have leftovers than to have anyone ever go hungry. Therefore, most of the portions are generous. When the recipe says "serves 2 to 3" it is describing extremely generous

portions for 2. In the instances when I'm not too sure about an appropriate portion size, I give fair warning in the introduction to the recipe. For example, in the quiche recipe I explain in the introduction to the recipe that the serving size allows half of a 6-inch quiche per person.

Using the Recipe When There is Only One Vegetarian or Meat-Eater

These recipes are written for four. They assume that half of the family is vegetarian. How do you use these recipes if only one person is a vegetarian? In many instances, you can prepare both recipes as written; serve the vegetarian his/her portion, then add the remaining vegetarian portion to the meat half of the recipe. For example: In the pasta salad recipe, adding some of the salad with beans to the portion with proscuitto will not adversely affect the meat recipe and will allow three people (or more, since this recipe has generous portions) to share the meat version of the meal. For recipes where the two halves are vastly different, you will have to use your judgment. One solution is to leave $3/4$ of the Base Recipe for the meat portion, and make only $1/2$ the amount of vegetarian recipe, and increase the meat, itself, by half. For example, in the Pasta Puttanesca/Broiled Tuna with Puttanesca Sauce recipe, reserve only $1/4$ of the Base Recipe sauce for the pasta and grill three tuna steaks instead of two, using the remaining $3/4$ of the Base Recipe sauce on the fish. The same method can be used with nearly any of the meat recipes. You can use a similar method to increase the vegetarian portion and decrease the meat-eaters' half.

Ingredients

Asparagus: Canned asparagus should never be used in these recipes. If you want to use frozen that is fine, but the canned are too mushy. Fresh asparagus are, of course, the first choice.

Beans: I use canned beans whenever possible. (Lentils, of course, don't come canned, only dried. That's okay because they don't require pre-soaking and they cook pretty quickly.) Canned beans save an enormous amount of time, and, even more important, planning. I feel that

Cooking Dried Beans:

Place 1 cup of beans in a stainless steel, glass, or enamel 2-quart pot, covered with 2-inches of water. Let stand overnight; then drain. Or, to quick soak the beans, bring the water to a boil over medium heat, boil 2 minutes. Turn off the heat, cover and let the beans stand 2 hours; drain.

Return the soaked beans to the pot and add 4 cups of cold UNSALTED water (adding salt to the water will severely retard the absorption of water, and in some cases the beans will never become tender). Bring the water to a boil over medium-high heat. Reduce heat and simmer, covered loosely, for the following times or until beans are tender when tasted:

Black beans	1 to 1^1/$_2$ hours
Butter beans	1 to 2 hours
Cannellini beans (white kidney)	1 to 1^1/$_2$ hours
Chickpeas beans (Garbanzo)	2 to 3 hours
Kidney beans	1 to 2 hours
Lentils (skip the soaking)	20 to 40 minutes
Pinto beans	1 to 2 hours

canned beans taste extremely good, although they are higher in sodium than homemade. (You can remove some of the salt by rinsing them before adding them to the recipes.) The quality varies from brand to brand, so try different ones until you find a personal preference (some I recommend are: S&W, Green Giant, and Goya). Good canned beans should be tender but not mushy, should not have much (if any) sludge at the bottom of the can, and certainly should not taste tinny like the can.

In case you want to cook beans from dried, I've provided some general cooking instructions for cooking 1 cup of dried beans. Remember, you have to allow enough time for the beans to soak and cook before you can cook the rest of the recipe you've chosen. (Start the day before if you're using the overnight soak.)

For me, the advantage of having beans ready for a last minute meal usually overrides any of the disadvantages of using canned beans.

Broth: I don't expect you to prepare the broth from scratch each time it is called for in a recipe. I assume you either will have homemade on hand or that you are using some form of store-bought broth. In the case of broth, homemade is really the best of all. I try to make a moderately sized batch and freeze it in 1-cup portions so I can just defrost however much is called for in a recipe (see page xii). Broth comes in cubes, powder, canned, jarred, and frozen. When I don't have time to make homemade, I usually "make" my broth from Knorr's vegetable cubes, a brand I find to have a pleasing flavor. There are many different brands and types of vegetable broth available in both supermarkets and health food stores. The costs and quality vary greatly from one to another. As with beans, you have to try different brands until you find the one that suits your taste.

If you would like to prepare homemade broth, a good recipe is below:

Corn: You can use fresh corn by husking it, then cutting the kernels from the cob using a sharp knife, then cooking until tender. I think this is a lot of work, so I usually use canned corn which is very good and doesn't need any cooking; just drain the liquid. Frozen corn can also be used. If it's going into a stew or dish that will be cooked, add it frozen and it will cook in the dish. If it's being used in a salad, or as a last minute ingredient, cook the frozen corn according to package directions.

Grains: When a recipe calls for cooked grains, I tend to prepare the grain the day before I plan to cook the recipe. Or, conversely, I sometimes look for a recipe that calls for a cooked grain that I already have on hand (this is especially true of leftover rice from the Chinese restaurant). A chart providing instructions for cooking 1 cup of dry grains is on page xiii.

Herbs: Herbs enhance the flavors in most recipes. Basil, parsley, dill, and cilantro are usually used fresh. Unless otherwise specified, other herbs used are dried.

Meat: Some of the meat recipes start with cooked meats.

Homemade Vegetable Broth

Leave the broth unsalted when you prepare it, then add salt to taste, after you've added it to the recipe. If your parsley root doesn't come with leaves, buy 1 bunch of fresh parsley for the recipe. If you can't find parsley root at all, substitute 1 small celery root (celeriac) or an additional parsnip.

10 cups water

5 medium carrots

5 large ribs celery, with leaves

2 medium leeks, light and dark green parts,
    coarsely chopped and rinsed thoroughly

2 medium parsnip

1 medium tomato

1 medium onion

2 small parsley roots (save the leaves)

2 cloves garlic

1 bay leaf

1 bunch fresh dill

1 bunch fresh parsley

(or saved tops of the parsley roots)

Place the water, carrots, celery, leeks, parsnip, tomato, onion, parsley roots, garlic, and bay leaf into a 6-quart pot. Bring to a boil over high heat. Reduce heat and simmer, covered, $1^1/_2$ hours.

Add the dill and parsley . Simmer, uncovered, 1 hour more. Place a large fine mesh strainer over a large bowl. Pour some of the broth and vegetables into the strainer. Using the bottom of a glass or any flat surface, gently press the vegetables in the strainer, until all the liquid has fallen into the bowl. Discard the pressed vegetables. Repeat with remaining broth and vegetables.

makes about 7 cups of broth

Beef: Most recipes call for boneless beef. Look for tender cuts of beef such as London broil, boneless sirloin, or, if you feel like being extravagant, club steak or filet mignon. Because the beef cooks only a short amount of time in most of these recipes, there's not enough cooking time to tenderize meat that is tough.

Some recipes call for cooked beef (see box, this page).

Ham: When I call for sliced ham, it is the kind you can buy in a delicatessen or the deli section of a supermarket. If the recipe calls for diced ham, I usually use a (pre-cooked) ham steak, or I have the deli slice boiled or baked ham $^1/_4$- to $^1/_2$-inch thick.

Chicken: I prefer to use white meat chicken in most recipes because it cooks faster than the dark meat. However, if you, or your family members, prefer dark meat, you can substitute skinless, boneless chicken thighs for the

Cooking Beef or Lamb

Preheat the broiler. Place 1-inch thick steak on a broiling pan. Sprinkle with black pepper, garlic powder, or other seasonings, if desired. Broil 4 to 6 inches from the heat for 3 to 4 minutes per side for medium-rare. Cook longer for well-done or less time for rare or very rare. Then salt, if desired.

breasts, but you may have to lengthen the cooking time (see box, page xiv).

Lamb: Lamb has such a distinctive flavor that there are no substitutes for ground lamb (even though you might be tempted to use a different ground meat). When a recipe calls for cooked lamb, I usually use lamb steaks—either

Cooking Grains

Bring the specified amount of water to a boil in a 2-quart saucepan, add 1 cup of the selected grain, return to a boil. Reduce heat and simmer, covered, specified amount of time (or until water is absorbed). Stir in salt, to taste, if desired.

grain	water	cooking time	yield
Pearl Barley	$2^1/_2$ cups	40 minutes	$3^1/_2$ cups
Bulgur	2 cups	20 minutes	3 cups
Couscous	$1^3/_4$ cups	2 minutes	$2^3/_4$ cups
Rice, white	2 cups	20 minutes	3 cups
Rice, converted white	$2^1/_4$ cups	20 minutes	$^3/_4$ cups
Rice, brown	$2^1/_4$ cups	45 minutes	$3^1/_2$ cups
Wheat Berries (whole grain wheat)	$2^1/_4$ cups	$1^3/_4$ hours	$2^1/_2$ cups
Wild Rice	2 cups	50 minutes	$3^1/_2$ cups

Cooking Chicken

poaching: In a 2- or 3-quart saucepan, bring to boil enough water to cover the skinless, boneless chicken breasts (you may want to add some of any of the following to the water: salt, white wine, bay leaf, thyme). Add the chicken and return to a boil. Reduce the heat and simmer about 7 minutes, or until the chicken is cooked through.

broiling/grilling: Heat the broiler or grill. If desired, first brush the chicken with olive oil, and/or sprinkle with any of the following: salt, black pepper, garlic powder, onion powder, paprika. Cook the skinless, boneless chicken breasts, 4 to 6 inches from the heat about 3 minutes per side or until chicken is cooked through.

microwaving: Season the chicken as suggested for Broiling/Grilling, if desired. Place 1 skinless and boneless chicken breast (about 8 to 12 ounces) onto a microwave-safe plate. Cover with plastic wrap, leaving a small edge uncovered to vent; microwave on high for 3 minutes. Turn the chicken over and re-cover; microwave on high 2 to 3 minutes longer, or until chicken is cooked through.

shoulder or leg. Try to find cuts with only a little bone that you can cut around (chops would work, but you'd need lots of them and the cost would be prohibitive).

Turkey: Ideally, you would have leftover cooked turkey to use in recipes calling for turkey. I really don't expect you to cook a whole turkey to get 1 cup of diced, cooked turkey meat. But if you don't have leftovers, fresh turkey cutlets are available in the meat case, generally found keeping company with the chicken parts. If you want to use turkey cutlets, you can cook them the same way as the skinless, boneless chicken breasts described above. If your market doesn't carry them, you can substitute chicken cutlets for the turkey.

Peas: Canned peas should never be used in these recipes. If you want to use frozen that is fine, but the canned are much too mushy. Fresh peas are, of course, the first choice.

Potatoes: Can be baked, microwaved, or boiled when the recipe calls for cooked potatoes. Unless otherwise specified, potatoes are always used peeled.

Cooking Potatoes

To microwave medium potatoes

Rinse potatoes and pierce with a fork in several places. Place on a paper towel in the microwave and cook on high, turning once:

1 potato	3 to 4 minutes
2 potatoes	5 to 6 minutes
3 potatoes	7 to 9 minutes
4 potatoes	9 to 12 minutes

To bake potatoes

Place the potatoes in a preheated 350°F oven and bake 40 minutes to 1 hour (depending on size), or until tender.

To boil potatoes

Peel, cut into 1 1/2-inch cubes. Cook in boiling water, over medium heat, 20 minutes or until tender when pierced with a fork; drain.

Tofu: Tofu is a high protein food made of soybean milk. It comes in the form of cakes which are white or creamy color when fresh and brown on the outside when baked or pressed. Tofu can be found in differing textures: firm, soft, or silken. Baked tofu is usually brown on the outside and the cakes are quite condensed (flat) and dense. They are much chewier and more flavorful than fresh tofu which tastes very bland by itself, but picks up the flavors of the other foods. Baked tofu can be found in the refrigerator case of most health food stores and some supermarkets. Flavored baked tofu, such as barbecue and Thai, can also be purchased. When I call for baked or pressed tofu in the recipes, however, I mean tofu without any added flavoring other than soy sauce. Fresh tofu can be found floating in water in the natural foods or produce stores, and packed in plastic in the refrigerator case of the produce or dairy section of most supermarkets.

Italian Ingredients

Pasta: Comes in many different sizes and shapes. Unless otherwise specified, I call for dried pasta. Below are examples of different sizes of pasta. You can use them interchangeably.
Long: spaghetti, linguine, fettucine, or angel hair
Medium: ziti, rigatoni, penne, radiatore, orchietto
Small: (which I keep on hand for soups): orzo, small shells, or small bowties

Sauces: There are many very good sauces available in supermarkets on the shelves or in the refrigerator case. As with beans and broth, try different brands until you find the ones you prefer. I like to keep a bottle or two of marinara sauce in my pantry at all times.

Mexican Ingredients

Herbs and Spices: The herbs and spices to keep on hand for Mexican cooking are fresh cilantro, ground cumin, and chili powder. You might also want to keep a packet or two of seasoned taco mix on hand.

Peppers: I use three different types of hot peppers in these recipes.

Fresh jalapeño peppers: These resemble large bullets with a stem on the top. They come in green and red, although green is more common. The greatest heat comes from the seeds and the ribs. When you are using fresh peppers, cut in half and discard the seeds before slicing or chopping. Also, wear rubber gloves and do not touch your eyes, nose, or mouth when handling fresh pepper. The oils can stay on your skin and irritate those sensitive places.

Canned chilies: These are fairly mild. They come whole or chopped, and can be found in most supermarkets.

Marinated jalapeños: These are packed in brine, and sold in jars. They can be bought whole or sometimes sliced. They are quite hot.

Salsa: There are lots of different salsas available for Mexican cooking. The most popular and easily available is a tomato-based sauce with chilies, some onion, and other stuff. There are many brands available in the supermarket. Some are in jars and others in the refrigerator case. They come in mild, medium, and hot. I find that mild is good to keep on hand in case my company doesn't tolerate too much heat. It's always easier to make dishes hotter for yourself by adding a touch of Tabasco, hot pepper sauce, or ground red pepper than to apologize for a meal that is prohibitively spicy to someone else. Salsa also comes as a green sauce, and you can find tomato salsa flavored with mango and other flavors. Find a brand that you like and keep it on hand.

You can easily make your own salsa, and it's usually better than any of the store-bought sauces. Here's a recipe for homemade salsa. If you don't have a food processor, you can mince all the ingredients by hand.

Homemade Salsa

2 cups tomato wedges

One 4-ounce can chopped chilies, undrained

$1/4$ cup chopped onion

2 tablespoons chopped, fresh cilantro

1 tablespoon fresh lime juice

2 cloves garlic, minced

$1/2$ teaspoon ground cumin

$1/4$ teaspoon salt, or to taste

$1/8$ teaspoon ground red pepper, optional

Place all the ingredients into a food processor. Cover and process until finely chopped. Let stand at least one hour to let the flavors blend. Refrigerate if you are not using immediately.

makes about $1^1/2$ cups

Mexican Sauces: In addition to salsa, there are enchilada and taco sauces available. They also come in a variety of hotnesses. As with salsa, I usually buy the mild and keep a can or two in my pantry.

Tortillas: Tortillas are the basis for many Mexican dishes. They come in corn and flour. You can find

them in the refrigerator case, or sometimes the freezer case, of your supermarket in 5-inch, 7-inch or 10-inch diameters. You can make excellent tortilla chips by cutting fresh tortillas into wedges and then frying them in oil until crisp.

Middle Eastern Ingredients

Spices: Curry powder, ground cumin, mint, ground turmeric, ground red pepper (cayenne), ground coriander

Tahini: Sauce made from ground sesame seeds

Asian Ingredients

Chili oil: Chili oil is a *very* spicy sesame oil. Its only purpose in a recipe is to add flavor and heat—lots of heat. It is not used to cook in, rather stirred into a recipe after cooking. If you don't like spicy foods, you can substitute sesame oil for some or all of the chili oil called for in any recipe.

Cornstarch: Cornstarch is the main thickening agent in Chinese cooking. Cornstarch is a white powder and you can find it in any supermarket, usually in the baking section. It must be stirred into cold or room temperature (not hot) liquid before adding to any recipe or it will not thicken. When a recipe using cornstarch comes to a boil, the sauce will turn from opaque to clear. That is when it has finished cooking. Cornstarch sauces will sometimes break down after they are cooled, so it's not unusual to find that last night's leftovers are no longer coated with thick sauce but one that has become watery. It perfectly okay to eat, but it won't have the same "mouthfeel" as when the sauce was thick.

Ginger: In these recipes, ginger is always used in its fresh form. Ginger is a root which has a light brown skin. The skin should have a nice sheen and should not be wrinkled (dull and wrinkled are the signs of old ginger). If the only "fresh" ginger available in your market is dull and wrinkled, it's still useable as long as it's not moldy, but try to find fresher ginger, if possible. Peel the ginger before chopping it for use in recipes.

Mirin (rice wine): This is a sweet wine. Although most recipes in this, and many other cookbooks, will give you the option of substituting dry sherry for the mirin, the mirin is far superior to sherry for this type of cooking. Since mirin is a cooking wine, by definition it contains salt. I find some brands to be unpleasantly salty and therefore always try to buy Kikkoman Aji-mirin, a brand I find to be more palatable.

Noodles: There are many different Asian noodles. Those made of wheat, such as lo mein noodles, are somewhere between spaghetti and egg noodles. Typically they are square or flat. Rice noodles are made from rice flour and are white. They are slightly chewier than wheat noodles. Bean threads cook up transparently and have a slippery mouth feel.

Chinese Sauces: There are a number of flavoring sauces used in this book. For the most part, they are very intensely flavored sauces that are used only in small amounts in recipes.
   Black bean: Very thick black sauce that is very salty
   Hoisin: Thick, dark brown sauce that has a sweet flavor
   Soy sauce: I use Kikkomon (or any Japanese soy sauce) in these recipes. This soy sauce is lighter and less salty than Chinese soy sauce (La Choy). Japanese soy sauce should be a staple in your pantry. Unless otherwise specified, when soy sauce is listed as an ingredient for a recipe in this book, I am referring to Japanese soy sauce. There are other types of soy sauce which you will find in an Oriental-food specialty store. Dark soy sauce is even darker and saltier than Chinese sauce. In a pinch, you can use Chinese soy sauce for a recipe which calls for dark soy sauce. I usually keep a bottle of La Choy on hand for those times I require dark soy sauce.

Sesame oil: Sesame oil is a highly-flavored, deep amber-colored (almost the color of pure maple syrup), oil. It is strictly a flavoring agent and is not used to cook foods in. It is usually added at the end of cooking the dish. If you like spicy foods, you can judiciously substitute chili oil for some or all of the sesame oil called for in any recipe.

Nutritional Content of the Recipes

I have made great efforts to include enough protein in the vegetarian recipes, without overdoing the amount of tofu or other health food specialty items (the meat recipes, obviously have adequate protein content). However, I have not gone out of my way to make these recipes low in fat, sodium, or calories.

If you are interested in cutting fat and calories (if you cut the fat, you will automatically reduce calories), here are some suggestions:

- Recipes which sauté ingredients can have the fat content reduced by half when using a non-stick skillet
- When choosing cheeses, look for the low-fat or nonfat varieties;
- When using eggs, try to substitute extra whites for the yolks (two egg whites can be

used as a whole egg) for example, make a two-egg omelet or scrambled eggs with 1 whole egg and 2 whites. Select nonfat or low-fat dairy products instead of whole milk ones. Use high-fat cheese only occasionally.

- When using milk, choose skim or low-fat instead of regular.

Similarly, if you are watching your sodium intake, you can simply omit salt whenever called for. Also be sure to buy salt-free bouillon, or make homemade, salt-free broth.

chapter one

American

Two Bean Chili & Chili con Carne

Serve this all-time favorite topped with sour cream or plain yogurt,
shredded Cheddar cheese and/or chopped onions.

BASE RECIPE

1$^1/_2$ tablespoons vegetable oil	$^1/_4$ teaspoon ground red pepper (cayenne)
1$^1/_2$ cups chopped onion	3 cups chopped tomato
$^1/_2$ cup chopped green bell pepper	1 cup beer
4 cloves garlic, minced	1 tablespoon molasses
3 tablespoons chili powder	$^1/_2$ teaspoon oregano
1 teaspoon ground cinnamon	1$^1/_2$ cups cooked (page xi) or canned,
$^1/_2$ teaspoon ground cumin	drained red kidney beans
$^1/_2$ teaspoon salt, or to taste	

In a 3-quart saucepan, heat the oil over medium-high heat. Add the onion, bell pepper, and garlic; cook, stirring, until softened, about 3 minutes. Stir in the chili powder, cinnamon, cumin, salt, and red pepper until absorbed. Add the tomatoes, beer, molasses, and oregano; bring to a boil. Stir in kidney beans; reduce heat and simmer, covered, 20 minutes. Uncover and simmer 20 minutes, stirring occasionally. Remove 2 cups of the Base Recipe from saucepan for the Chili con Carne recipe.

Two Bean Chili

1 cup cooked (page xi) or canned, drained
black beans

Add the black beans to the remaining portion
of the Base Recipe in the saucepan. Simmer
10–15 more minutes, stirring occasionally,
until beans are soft and chili is thick.

serves 2

Increase black beans to 1¹/₂ cups, and
use the entire Base Recipe.

Chili con Carne

¹/₂ pound ground beef

¹/₄ cup beer

3 tablespoons tomato paste

Salt, if desired

In a 2-quart saucepan, cook the ground beef
over medium-high heat, stirring with a wood-
en spoon to break up the beef into small
pieces, until no longer pink, about 3 minutes.
Add the reserved 2 cups of the Base Recipe to
the beef. Stir in the beer and tomato paste;
season with the salt. Cover and continue
cooking 10 to 15 minutes longer, stirring
occasionally.

serves 2

Omit the additional beer and tomato paste from
the Chili con Carne recipe. Increase the beef to 1
pound, and brown in the saucepan with the onion,
bell pepper, and garlic during the preparation of
the Base Recipe. Continue to cook according to the
Base Recipe directions.

Millet Corn Chili &
Beef and Corn Skillet Dinner

If you've never eaten millet, you may find this a nice introduction.

BASE RECIPE

2 teaspoons vegetable oil

$^3/_4$ cup chopped onion

2 cloves garlic, minced

1 tablespoon chili powder

One 8-ounce can tomato sauce

One 8-ounce can corn kernels, drained (liquid reserved)

$^1/_2$ teaspoon salt

$^1/_8$ teaspoon black pepper

In a 1-quart saucepan, heat the oil over medium-high heat. Add the onion and garlic. Cook, stirring, until softened, about 2 minutes. Stir in the chili powder. Stir in the tomato sauce, corn, salt, and black pepper. Bring to a boil; reduce heat and simmer, covered, 5 minutes. Set aside $^3/_4$ cup of the Base Recipe for the Beef and Corn Skillet Dinner recipe.

Millet Corn Chili

Reserved liquid from canned corn (see Base Recipe)

About 1 cup vegetable broth (page xii or store-bought)

2 teaspoons oil

$1/2$ cup millet (page xiii)

$1/2$ cup cooked (page xi) or canned, drained pinto or kidney beans

1 tablespoon chopped, fresh cilantro

Put the reserved corn liquid into a measuring cup. Add enough vegetable broth to make $1^1/4$ cups of liquid.

In a $1^1/2$ quart saucepan, heat the oil over medium-high heat. Add the millet and cook, stirring, until millet starts to brown and is making crackling noises, about 1 to 2 minutes. Add the broth mixture to the saucepan. Bring to a boil. Stir in the beans and the remaining Base Recipe. Return to a boil; reduce heat and simmer, covered, 25 minutes or until the liquid has been absorbed. Stir in the cilantro.

serves 2 to 3

Beef and Corn Skillet Dinner

$1/2$ pound ground beef

$1/3$ cup chopped green bell pepper

1 tablespoon tomato paste

$1/4$ teaspoon salt

Cook the beef and bell pepper in a medium skillet over medium-high heat, stirring, until beef is no longer pink, about 3 minutes. Stir in the reserved Base Recipe, tomato paste, and salt. Cook, stirring, until heated through, about 3 minutes.

serves 2

Barbecue Kidney Beans with Cornmeal Biscuits

Barbecue Kidney Beans and Kielbasa

You can use any kind of cooked sausage instead of the kielbasa, such as knockwurst, frankfurters, pepperoni, salami, or Italian sausage.

BASE RECIPE

1 tablespoon vegetable oil	2 tablespoons brown sugar
1¹/₂ cups chopped onion	1 tablespoon molasses
1 cup chopped green bell pepper	1 tablespoon distilled white vinegar
3 cloves garlic, minced	1 teaspoon anchovy-free Worcestershire sauce
3 cups cooked (page xi) or canned, drained kidney beans	1 bay leaf
	¹/₂ teaspoon mustard
³/₄ cup water	¹/₂ teaspoon salt
¹/₂ cup ketchup	¹/₄ teaspoon Tabasco
2 tablespoons tomato paste	

Preheat oven to 375°F.

In a 3-quart saucepan, heat the oil over medium-high heat. Add the onion, bell pepper, and garlic. Cook, stirring, until softened, about 2–3 minutes. Add the beans, water, ketchup, tomato paste, brown sugar, molasses, vinegar, Worcestershire sauce, bay leaf, mustard, salt, and Tabasco. Bring to a boil; reduce heat and simmer, uncovered, 20 minutes. Discard the bay leaf. Set aside half of the Base Recipe for the Barbecue Kidney Beans with Cornmeal Biscuits.

Barbecue Kidney Beans with Cornmeal Biscuits

$^1/_2$ cup all-purpose flour

$^1/_3$ cup cornmeal

1 teaspoon baking powder

$^1/_2$ teaspoon baking soda

$^1/_2$ teaspoon salt

$^1/_4$ cup shortening

6 tablespoons milk

In a large bowl stir together the flour, cornmeal, baking powder, baking soda, and salt. Using a pastry cutter or two knives, cut in the shortening until mixture resembles coarse cornmeal. Stir in the milk until mixture forms a soft dough. Place the reserved Base Recipe into a $1^1/_2$-quart casserole. Drop the muffin mixture over the top of the beans. Bake 25 minutes or until biscuits are baked and beans are heated through.

serves 2

Use a 3-quart casserole and all of the Base Recipe. Do not increase the biscuit recipe.

Barbecue Kidney Beans and Kielbasa

8 to 12 ounces sliced kielbasa

Stir the kielbasa into the Base Recipe remaining in the saucepan. Spoon into a 1-quart casserole. Bake for 15 to 20 minutes or until heated through.

serves 2

Double the Barbecue Kidney Beans and Kielbasa recipe and use all of the Base Recipe. Bake in a 2-quart casserole.

Barbecue Beans with Rice & Barbecue Salmon

BASE RECIPE

One 8-ounce can tomato sauce

2 tablespoons tomato paste

$1^1/_2$ tablespoons firmly packed brown sugar

$1^1/_2$ tablespoons distilled white vinegar

$1^1/_2$ teaspoons molasses

$^1/_2$ teaspoon anchovy-free Worcestershire sauce

$^1/_8$ teaspoon salt, or to taste

4 drops Tabasco sauce, or to taste

In a 1-quart saucepan, stir together the tomato sauce, tomato paste, brown sugar, vinegar, molasses, Worcestershire sauce, salt, and Tabasco over medium heat. Bring to a boil over high heat; reduce heat and simmer 7 minutes, stirring occasionally. Reserve $^1/_3$ cup of the sauce for the Barbecue Salmon recipe.

Barbecue Beans with Rice

2 teaspoons vegetable oil

$^1/_2$ cup chopped onion

$^1/_2$ cup finely chopped green bell pepper

$^1/_4$ cup water

$^3/_4$ cup cooked (page xi) or canned, drained red kidney beans

$^3/_4$ cup cooked (page xi) or canned, drained white kidney beans (canellini)

1 tablespoon chopped, fresh cilantro

$1^1/_2$ cups cooked white or brown rice

In a $1^1/_2$-quart saucepan, heat the oil over medium-high heat. Add the onion and bell pepper. Cook, stirring, until the vegetables are softened, about 2 minutes. Add the reserved Base Recipe and the water; boil. Add the beans and cilantro. Boil, reduce the heat and simmer, uncovered, 15 minutes, stirring occasionally. Serve over rice.

serves 2 to 3

Barbecue Salmon

8 to 12 ounces salmon fillet

Cooked rice

Preheat the broiler.

Place the fish in a baking or broiling pan lined with aluminum foil. Spread the reserved $^1/_3$ cup of Base Recipe over the fish. Broil until desired doneness, about 4 minutes. Serve with rice, if desired.

serves 2

Jambalaya with Beans & Jambalaya

BASE RECIPE

1 1/2 tablespoons vegetable oil

3/4 cup chopped onion

1/2 cup chopped celery

1/2 cup chopped green bell pepper

1/4 cup chopped scallion

1/4 cup chopped fresh parsley

3 cloves garlic, minced

One 14 1/2-ounce can whole, peeled tomatoes, undrained

One 8-ounce can tomato sauce

1 1/2 cups vegetable broth (page xii or store-bought)

1 bay leaf

1/4 teaspoon dried thyme

1 teaspoon salt

1/4 teaspoon black pepper

1/8 teaspoon ground red pepper

In a 2-quart saucepan, heat the oil over medium-high heat. Add the onion, celery, bell pepper, scallion, parsley, and garlic. Cook, stirring, until tender-crisp, about 2 to 3 minutes. Add the whole, peeled tomatoes, and break them up with the back of a spoon. Add the tomato sauce, broth, bay leaf, thyme, salt, and both black and red peppers; bring to a boil. Reduce the heat to medium-low and simmer, uncovered, 5 minutes. Reserve half of the Base Recipe for the Jambalaya recipe.

Jambalaya with Beans

1 cup cooked (page xi) or canned, drained red kidney beans

1/2 cup converted rice

1 1/2 teaspoons distilled white vinegar

Bring the Base Recipe remaining in the saucepan to a boil. Stir in the beans, rice, and vinegar. Return to a boil. Reduce heat and simmer, covered, 25 minutes or until rice is tender.

serves 2 to 3

Jambalaya

1/2 cup converted white rice

1/2 cup diced, cooked ham

1/2 cup (4 ounces) medium shrimp, peeled and deveined

In a 2-quart saucepan, bring the reserved Base Recipe to a boil. Add the rice; boil. Reduce heat and simmer, covered, 20 minutes, until most of the liquid is absorbed. Stir in the ham and shrimp, cook 5 minutes or until rice is tender and shrimp are done.

serves 2 to 3

Bean Gumbo & Chicken Gumbo

BASE RECIPE

1 tablespoon vegetable oil

$1^1/_2$ cups sliced, fresh okra

$^3/_4$ cup chopped onion

$^3/_4$ cup chopped celery

$^3/_4$ cup chopped green bell pepper

1 teaspoon chili powder

One 14 $^1/_2$-ounce can whole
  peeled tomatoes, with their juices

$^1/_4$ cup water

2 bay leaves

$^1/_2$ teaspoon dried oregano

$^1/_2$ teaspoon sugar

$^1/_4$ teaspoon dried basil

$^1/_4$ teaspoon dried thyme

$^1/_4$ teaspoon salt

$^1/_4$ teaspoon Tabasco sauce

In a 7-quart saucepan, heat the oil over medium-high heat. Add the okra, onion, celery, and bell pepper; cook, stirring, 3 to 5 minutes, until softened. Stir in chili powder. Add the tomatoes with their juices, breaking them up with the back of a spoon. Add the water, bay leaves, oregano, sugar, basil, and thyme; bring to a boil. Reduce heat to low and simmer, covered, 20 minutes. Stir in the salt and Tabasco. Discard the bay leaves. Remove 2 cups for the Chicken Gumbo recipe.

Bean Gumbo

$^3/_4$ cup cooked (page xi) or canned, drained
  kidney beans

$^1/_4$ cup chopped, fresh parsley

Add the beans and parsley to the remaining Base Recipe in the saucepan. Bring to a boil. Reduce heat and simmer 5 minutes, until okra is tender.

serves 2 to 3

Chicken Gumbo

$^1/_2$ to $^3/_4$ pound skinless, boneless chicken

1 tablespoon tomato paste

Cut the chicken into $^1/_2$-inch cubes. In a 2-quart saucepan, combine the chicken, tomato paste, and reserved Base Recipe. Cook over medium-high heat, stirring often, until the mixture boils. Reduce the heat to low and simmer 3 to 5 minutes, or until chicken is cooked through and okra is tender.

serves 2 to 3

New Mexico Bean Casserole & Albuturkey Casserole

I hope the citizens of Albuquerque will forgive my terrible pun.

BASE RECIPE

2 tablespoons vegetable oil

3 cups broccoli florets

1 cup chopped onion

$^3/_4$ cup chopped red bell pepper

2 cloves garlic, minced

2 tablespoons all-purpose flour

$^1/_2$ teaspoon ground cumin

$^3/_4$ cup vegetable broth
(page xii or store-bought)

1 cup shredded cheddar cheese

$^1/_3$ cup salsa (page xvi or store-bought)

2 tablespoons chopped, fresh cilantro

Preheat oven to 350°F. In a 3-quart saucepan, heat the oil over medium-high heat. Add the broccoli, onion, bell pepper, and garlic; cook, stirring, until softened, about 2–4 minutes. Stir in the flour and cumin. Stir in the broth. Cook, stirring, until mixture comes to a boil. Remove from heat, stir in the cheese, salsa, and cilantro. Remove $1^1/_3$ cups from the pot for the Albuturkey Casserole recipe.

New Mexico Bean Casserole

1 cup cooked (page xi) or canned, drained kidney beans

1 cup shredded Monterey Jack cheese

$^1/_4$ teaspoon anchovy-free Worcestershire sauce

$^3/_4$ cup coarsely crushed tortilla chips

In a 1-quart oven-proof casserole, stir together the beans, cheese, Worcestershire sauce, and remaining Base Recipe. Top with the chips. Bake for 20 minutes, or until heated through.

serves 2

Albuturkey Casserole

8 to 12 ounces skinless, boneless turkey or chicken

1 tablespoon vegetable oil

1 teaspoon chili powder

$^1/_4$ teaspoon salt

$^3/_4$ cup coarsely crushed tortilla chips

Cut the turkey into strips. In a large skillet, heat the oil over medium-high heat. Add the turkey; cook, stirring, until cooked through, about 3 minutes. Stir in the chili powder, salt, and reserved $1^1/_3$ cups of the Base Recipe. Spoon into a 1-quart oven-proof casserole. Sprinkle the chips over the casserole. Bake for 20 minutes, or until heated through.

serves 2

Mushrooms with Brown Rice and Butter Beans & Southwest Beef with Butter Beans

The portobello mushrooms make a great substitute for the beef since they have a satisfying, meaty texture. If you can't find them, try using shiitaki mushrooms instead.

BASE RECIPE

1 tablespoon olive oil

1 cup sliced onion

$1/2$ cup chopped green bell pepper

1 jalapeño pepper, seeded and minced

2 cloves garlic, minced

$11/2$ cups cooked (page xi) or canned, drained butter beans

In a large skillet, heat the oil over medium-high heat. Add the onion, bell and jalapeño peppers, and garlic. Cook, stirring, until softened, about 3 minutes. Remove mixture from the skillet and place in a medium bowl; stir in the butter beans. Reserve the skillet (unwashed) and $3/4$ cup of Base Recipe for the Mushrooms with Brown Rice and Butter Beans recipe.

Mushrooms with Brown Rice and Butter Beans

- 1 tablespoon vegetable oil
- 2 cups sliced portobello mushrooms (about 1 large mushroom)
- $1/4$ cup vegetable broth (page xii or store-bought)
- 1 cup cooked brown rice
- 2 tablespoons chopped, fresh parsley
- 1 teaspoon cider vinegar
- $1/4$ teaspoon salt

Heat the oil in the reserved skillet, add the mushrooms and cook over high heat until all the oil is absorbed. Add the broth to de-glaze the pan, scraping up any browned bits from the bottom with a wooden spoon.

When the mushrooms have softened and most of the liquid has evaporated, about 3 minutes, stir in the brown rice, parsley, vinegar, salt, and the reserved $3/4$ cup Base Recipe. Cook, stirring, until heated through.

serves 2

Southwest Beef with Butter Beans

- $1/2$ to $3/4$ pound boneless sirloin or London broil, sliced
- 1 teaspoon chili powder
- 1 tablespoon vegetable oil
- 2 tablespoons chopped, fresh cilantro
- $1/8$ teaspoon salt

Lightly coat the beef slices with the chili powder. In a medium skillet, heat the oil over medium-high heat. Add the beef and cook, stirring, about 2 to 3 minutes for rare, and 4 to 5 minutes for medium-rare, or to desired doneness. Add the cilantro, salt, and the remaining Base Recipe. Cook, stirring, until heated through, about 2 minutes.

serves 2

Spanish Omelet  Shrimp Creole

You can use frozen shrimp for this dish, but be sure to thaw and
drain them before adding them to the sauce.

BASE RECIPE

1 tablespoon vegetable oil

2 cups sliced onion

2 cups sliced green bell pepper

1 cup sliced red bell pepper

1 cup julienned celery

One 8-ounce can tomato sauce

$^1/_3$ cup chopped, fresh parsley

3 tablespoons water

$^1/_4$ teaspoon dried oregano

$^1/_4$ teaspoon dried thyme

$^1/_4$ teaspoon salt

$^1/_8$ teaspoon black pepper

In a large skillet, heat the oil over medium-high heat. Add the onion, green and red bell peppers, and celery; cook, stirring, until vegetables are softened, about 5 minutes. Add the tomato sauce, parsley, water, oregano, thyme, salt, and black pepper. Bring to a boil; reduce heat to low and simmer, uncovered, 5 to 7 minutes or until thickened. Reserve $1^1/_2$ cups of the Base Recipe for the Spanish Omelet.

Spanish Omelet

4 large eggs

2 large egg whites

2 tablespoons water

$^1/_4$ teaspoon salt, or to taste

2 tablespoons butter or margarine

In a medium bowl, beat eggs and egg whites with the water and salt. In a large skillet, melt the butter over medium-high heat. When hot, add the egg mixture. Cook, lifting edges with spatula while tilting skillet, to let uncooked portion flow to skillet bottom. Continue until egg mixture is cooked to desired doneness, about 3 minutes. Spoon the reserved Base Recipe onto half of the omelet. Fold other half over the filling. Slide onto serving plate. Cut in half to make two servings.

serves 2

Double the Spanish Omelet recipe and prepare two omelets using half of the Base Recipe in each.

Shrimp Creole

$^1/_2$ to $^3/_4$ pound large shrimp, peeled and de-veined

2 tablespoons dry white wine, dry vermouth, or water

$^1/_8$ teaspoon ground red pepper (cayenne)

$1^1/_2$ cups cooked long grain white rice, for serving

Add the shrimp, wine, and red pepper to the remaining Base Recipe in the skillet. Cook over medium-high heat until the shrimp are cooked through, about 4 minutes. Serve over the rice.

serves 2

Add $1^1/_4$ pounds shrimp, $^1/_4$ cup dry white wine, and $^1/_4$ teaspoon ground red pepper to all of the Base Recipe in the skillet. Cook until shrimp are cooked through, about 4 minutes.

Lentil Rice  Dirty Rice

The reason for the name "Dirty Rice" will become clear as soon as you prepare the recipe. To minimize your time spent in the kitchen, prepare both the Lentil Rice recipe and the Dirty Rice recipe while the Base Recipe is cooking.

BASE RECIPE

1¹/₃ cups water

1¹/₃ cups vegetable broth (page xii or store-bought)

1 cup converted white rice

1 tablespoon vegetable oil

¹/₂ cup finely chopped onion

¹/₂ cup finely chopped celery

¹/₂ cup finely chopped green bell pepper

¹/₄ cup chopped, fresh parsley

¹/₄ teaspoon black pepper

> **recipe tip:**
> *Cook the lentils before you start the Base Recipe.*

In a 2-quart saucepan, bring the water and broth to a boil. Add the rice and return to a boil. Reduce the heat and simmer, covered, until rice is tender and water is absorbed, 20 minutes. (Prepare the other two recipes now, while the rice cooks.)

In a large skillet, heat the oil over medium-high heat. Add the onion, celery, and bell pepper. Cook, stirring, about 3 minutes, until vegetables are softened. Add the cooked rice, parsley, and black pepper. Set aside half of the Base Recipe for the Dirty Rice.

Lentil Rice

2 teaspoons vegetable oil

1 cup finely chopped mushrooms

$^1/_4$ teaspoon dried sage leaves, crumbled

$^1/_4$ teaspoon dried thyme

$^1/_4$ teaspoon salt

1 cup cooked lentils (page xi)

In a small skillet, heat the oil over medium-high heat. Add the mushrooms; cook, stirring, until softened, about 2 minutes. Stir in the sage, thyme, and salt. Add the mushroom mixture to the remaining Base Recipe in the skillet. Add the lentils. Cook over medium heat, stirring, until heated through, about 3 minutes.

serves 2 to 3

Dirty Rice

2 slices bacon

6 ounces chicken liver, cut into small pieces

In a medium skillet, cook the bacon over medium-high heat 3 to 5 minutes, until crisp. Remove from skillet, drain on paper towels and crumble. Discard all but 1 tablespoon of the bacon fat from the skillet. Add the liver and cook, stirring and scraping up any browned bits in the skillet, 2 to 4 minutes, until desired doneness. Add the reserved Base Recipe and cook, stirring, 1 to 2 minutes, until heated through.

serves 2

Lentil Burgers & Meatloaf

Prepare meatloaf and place in oven before starting burgers.

BASE RECIPE

2 large eggs

³/₄ cup chopped onion

¹/₄ cup ketchup

¹/₄ cup plain dry bread crumbs

2 cloves garlic, minced

¹/₂ teaspoon anchovy-free Worcestershire sauce

Salt and pepper to taste

> **recipe tip:**
> *For a firmer burger, stir in an extra 1 to 2 tablespoons of bread crumbs to the lentil mixture when you add the Base Recipe.*

In a medium bowl, beat the eggs. Stir in the remaining ingredients. Reserve ¹/₂ cup of Base Recipe for the Lentil Burger recipe.

Lentil Burgers

1 cup cooked lentils (page xi)

3 tablespoons plain dry bread crumbs

3 tablespoons vegetable oil

2 hamburger buns, optional

In a medium bowl, mash the lentils slightly with a fork. Add the reserved ¹/₂ cup Base Recipe. Form the mixture into 2 patties. Coat the patties with bread crumbs. Heat the oil in a medium skillet over medium-high heat. Add the burgers and cook until browned on bottom, about 2 minutes. Turn and cook second side 2 minutes more. Serve on hamburger buns, if desired.

serves 2

Meatloaf

1 pound ground beef

2 tablespoons ketchup

1 tablespoon brown sugar

1 tablespoon apricot preserves

Preheat oven to 375°F. Add the beef to the bowl with the remaining Base Recipe. Mix until completely combined. Form into a 4 x 6-inch loaf. Place in a baking or loaf pan. In a small bowl, stir together the ketchup, sugar, and preserves; spread over the top of the meatloaf. Bake 35 minutes or until cooked through. (If making only the meat version, use all of the Base Recipe and bake 1 hour.)

serves 2 to 3

Feta-Stuffed Zucchini & Ham-Stuffed Zucchini

BASE RECIPE

4 medium zucchini (8 ounces each)

2 teaspoons vegetable oil

$^1/_2$ cup chopped onion

1 clove garlic, minced

$1^1/_2$ cups cooked brown rice

$^1/_2$ teaspoon salt

$^1/_4$ teaspoon black pepper

Preheat the oven to 350°F.

Cut each zucchini in half lengthwise. Scoop out the flesh, leaving $^1/_4$-inch of flesh lining the shells or "boats." Set the boats aside. Chop enough of the scooped-out flesh to measure $^3/_4$ cup.

In a medium skillet, heat the oil over medium-high heat. Add the onion and garlic and cook, stirring until softened, about 1 minute. Add the chopped zucchini; cook, stirring until tender, about 1 minute more. Stir in the brown rice, salt, and black pepper. Reserve half of the Base Recipe for the Feta-Stuffed Zucchini recipe.

Feta-Stuffed Zucchini

$^1/_4$ cup crumbled feta cheese

3 tablespoons chopped walnuts

2 tablespoons chopped, sun-dried tomatoes (packed in oil)

1 tablespoon dried currants

In a medium bowl, combine feta cheese, walnuts, sun-dried tomatoes, currants, and the reserved Base Recipe; mix well. Use the mixture to fill four of the zucchini boats evenly. Place the filled boats in a baking pan and bake until filling is cooked through and the boats are tender, about 25 minutes.

serves 2 to 3

Ham-Stuffed Zucchini

$^1/_4$ cup chopped, cooked ham

2 tablespoons chopped, fresh parsley

1 tablespoon snipped, fresh dill

In a medium bowl, combine the ham, parsley, and dill, and remaining half of the Base Recipe. Use to fill the remaining zucchini boats. Place the filled boats in a baking pan and bake until filling is cooked through and the boats are tender, about 25 minutes.

serves 2 to 3

Garbanzo Burgers & Fried Fish Cakes

If you cook the Garbanzo Burgers first, you can use the same skillet for the fish cakes;
otherwise, cook them in separate skillets.

BASE RECIPE

Sauce:
 3 tablespoons butter or margarine
 $1/3$ cup chopped scallion (white and green parts)
 $1/4$ cup all-purpose flour
 $3/4$ cup milk
 $1/4$ cup chopped, fresh parsley
 $1/8$ teaspoon black pepper

recipe tip:
Prepare the Base Recipe Sauce, then prepare the burgers and fish cakes. Return to the Base Recipe for breading and cooking instructions.

Breading:
 1 large egg
 1 tablespoon water
 $1/4$ cup all-purpose flour
 $1/2$ cup plain dry bread crumbs
 Vegetable oil, for frying

To prepare the sauce: In a $1^1/2$-quart saucepan, melt the butter over medium heat. Add the scallions and cook, stirring, until softened, about 30 seconds. Stir in the flour to form a paste. Slowly add the milk and cook, stirring, until smooth and the mixture comes to a boil, 3 to 4 minutes. Stir in the parsley and black pepper. Set aside $1/4$ cup of the Base Recipe Sauce for the Garbanzo Burgers.

To prepare the breading: In a medium bowl, beat the egg with the water. Place the flour on a piece of wax paper and the bread crumbs on another piece of wax paper.

(Prepare the Garbanzo Burgers and Fried Fish Cakes now.)

Coat all of the patties in flour, then dip in egg to coat, then in the bread crumbs. Pour the oil $1/8$-inch deep into a medium skillet. Heat the oil, over medium-high heat, until it bubbles when a few bread crumbs are tossed in. Add the garbanzo burger patties and cook, turning once, until browned on both sides, about 2 minutes. Then, cook the fish patties, turning once, until browned on both sides, about 2 minutes.

Garbanzo Burgers

1 cup cooked (page xi) or canned, rinsed chickpeas (garbanzo beans)

1 tablespoon plain dry bread crumbs

1 tablespoon chopped, fresh cilantro

$^1/_4$ teaspoon ground cumin

$^1/_8$ teaspoon salt

$^1/_8$ teaspoon ground red pepper (cayenne)

In a medium bowl, mash the chickpeas slightly with a fork. Stir in the bread crumbs, cilantro, cumin, salt, and red pepper. Stir in the $^1/_4$ cup reserved Base Recipe sauce. Form into 2 patties. Bread and cook as instructed in Base Recipe.

serves 2

totally Vegetarian

Double the Garbanzo Burgers recipe using $^1/_2$ cup of the Base Recipe.

Fried Fish Cakes

1 cup (about 8 ounces) flaked, cooked fish, such as flounder, tuna, cod, or salmon

2 tablespoons plain dry bread crumbs

$^1/_4$ teaspoon Worcestershire sauce

$^1/_8$ teaspoon salt

Stir the fish, 2 tablespoons of bread crumbs, Worcestershire sauce, and salt into the Base Recipe remaining in the saucepan. Let cool. Form into 2 patties. Bread and cook as instructed in Base Recipe.

serves 2

totally con Carne

Double both the Base Recipe Sauce and the Fried Fish Cake recipe.

Sloppy Josephines & Sloppy Joes

Serve this on hamburger buns, as is traditional, or use Kaiser rolls or any other sturdy bread that won't fall apart when lifted. Chili sauce is like chunky, tangier ketchup. If you don't have any, just use additional sauce—but the chili sauce is better.

BASE RECIPE

1 teaspoon vegetable oil

$^1/_2$ cup chopped onion

$^1/_2$ cup chopped green bell pepper

$^1/_2$ cup water

$^1/_2$ cup chili sauce

$^1/_4$ cup ketchup

2 teaspoons anchovy-free Worcestershire sauce

$^1/_4$ teaspoon salt

In a $1^1/_2$-quart saucepan, heat the oil over medium-high heat. Add the onion and bell pepper. Cook, stirring, until softened, about 2 minutes. Add the water, chili sauce, ketchup, Worcestershire sauce, and salt. Bring to a boil. Reduce heat and simmer for 2 minutes. Remove $^3/_4$ cup of the Base Recipe from the saucepan for the Sloppy Joe recipe.

Sloppy Josephines

1 cup cooked, coarse or medium grind bulgur (page xiii)

$^1/_2$ cup shredded Cheddar cheese

2 or 3 hamburger buns

Add the bulgur and cheese to the saucepan with remaining sauce. Simmer over low heat, stirring occasionally, until the cheese melts, about 1 to 2 minutes. Serve on buns.

serves 2 to 3

Sloppy Joes

$^1/_2$ pound ground beef

2 hamburger buns

In a 1-quart saucepan, brown the beef over medium-high heat until the beef is no longer pink, about 3 minutes. Pour off any fat. Add the reserved $^3/_4$ cup Base Recipe. Simmer, stirring occasionally, 10 minutes or until thickened. Serve on buns.

serves 2

Stir $2^1/_2$ cups bulgur and 1 cup shredded Cheddar into the total Base Recipe. Serves 4 to 6

Use 1 pound ground beef. Stir in entire Base Recipe. Serve on 4 buns.

Lentil Hash *&* Corned Beef Hash

BASE RECIPE

2 teaspoons vegetable oil

$^1/_2$ cup finely chopped onion

$^1/_2$ cup finely chopped green bell pepper

4 cups peeled, diced, cooked potatoes

$^1/_4$ teaspoon anchovy-free Worcestershire sauce

$^1/_4$ teaspoon salt

$^1/_4$ teaspoon black pepper

2 tablespoons milk or vegetable broth
 (page xii or store-bought)

In a large skillet, heat the oil over medium-high heat. Add the onion and bell pepper and cook, stirring, until softened, about 2 minutes. Remove from heat. Add the potatoes, Worcestershire sauce, salt, and black pepper. Stir in the milk or broth until absorbed. Reserve half of the Base Recipe for the Lentil Hash.

Lentil Hash

$^1/_2$ cup cooked lentils (page xi)

$^1/_4$ teaspoon salt

2 tablespoons vegetable oil

In a medium bowl, combine the lentils, salt, and the reserved Base Recipe. In a large skillet, heat the oil over medium-high heat. Add the lentil mixture and press into a pancake. Cook, over medium-high heat, about 5 minutes or until browned on bottom. Using a spatula, turn the hash over and cook about 3 minutes longer or until heated through.

serves 2

Double the lentils and salt and stir into the entire Base Recipe. Do not increase the oil.

Corned Beef Hash

$^1/_4$ pound chopped corned beef

2 tablespoons vegetable oil

Stir the chopped corned beef into the remaining Base Recipe. In a large skillet, heat the oil over medium-high heat. Add the hash and press it into a pancake. Cook about 5 minutes or until browned on bottom. Using a spatula, turn the hash over and cook about 3 minutes longer or until heated through.

serves 2

Double the amount of corned beef and stir into the entire Base Recipe. Do not increase the oil.

Mushroom-Filled Giant Popover

Beef-Filled Giant Popover

If you don't want to bother with the popovers, you can serve the fillings with rice or potatoes.

BASE RECIPE

2 large eggs

1 cup all-purpose flour

1 1/2 cups milk

1/2 teaspoon salt

1 1/2 tablespoons vegetable oil

recipe tip:
Prepare the fillings while the popovers are baking.

Preheat oven to 375°F.

In a medium bowl, beat the egg with the flour. Add the milk gradually, stirring, until the batter is smooth and lump-free. Stir in salt. Let the batter stand 10 minutes.

Pour half of the oil into each of two 1-quart oven-proof casseroles, and place them in the oven for 4 minutes. Add half of the batter to each of the dishes and bake for 20 minutes.

Meanwhile, prepare both the Mushroom-Filled Giant Popover and the Beef-Filled Giant Popover recipes.

Remove the popovers from the casseroles and fill each popover with one of the fillings.

Mushroom-Filled Giant Popover

1 tablespoon vegetable oil

3 cups coarsely chopped portobello mushrooms

$1/2$ cup finely chopped onion

2 cloves garlic, minced

1 tablespoon curry powder

$1/2$ cup chopped tomatoes

$1/2$ cup diced ($1/2$ inch), cooked potato

$1/2$ cup cooked peas

2 tablespoons water

$1/4$ teaspoon salt

In a 2-quart saucepan, heat the oil over medium-high heat. Add the mushrooms, onion, and garlic; cook, stirring, until softened, about 3 minutes. Stir in the curry powder. Add the tomatoes, potatoes, peas, water, and salt. Bring to a boil; reduce heat and simmer uncovered, 7 minutes, or until mixture is thickened. Spoon into one popover.

serves 2

Beef-Filled Giant Popover

$1/2$ pound ground beef

$1/2$ cup finely chopped onion

1 cup chopped tomato

1 tablespoon tomato paste

$1/2$ teaspoon dried oregano

$1/4$ teaspoon salt

$1/4$ teaspoon black pepper

$1/4$ cup cooked peas

In a medium skillet, cook the beef with the onion, over medium-high heat, until the beef is no longer pink, about 3 minutes. Add the tomato, tomato paste, oregano, salt, and black pepper. Cook, five minutes, stirring occasionally. Add the peas and cook, stirring, until heated through. Spoon into one popover.

serves 2

Cheesy Rice with Beans and Peas
& Cheesy Rice with Ham and Peas

Instead of using ham in the Cheesy Rice with Ham and Peas recipe, you can substitute 6 slices of cooked bacon, crumbled.

BASE RECIPE

2 teaspoons butter

$1/2$ cup finely chopped onion

$2^1/2$ cups water

$1^1/4$ cups converted white rice

$3/4$ cup cooked peas

$1/4$ cup chopped, fresh parsley

$3/4$ teaspoon salt

2 cups shredded Cheddar cheese

3 tablespoons grated Parmesan cheese

In a 2-quart saucepan, melt the butter over medium-high heat. Add the onion and cook, stirring, until softened, about 1 minute. Add the water and bring to a boil. Stir in the rice. Return to a boil; reduce the heat and simmer, covered, until liquid is absorbed, 20 minutes. Stir in the peas, parsley, and salt; simmer, covered, 5 minutes more. Stir in the cheese until melted, about 1 minute. Reserve $2^1/2$ cups for the Cheesy Rice with Ham and Peas recipe.

Cheesy Rice with Beans and Peas

$1/2$ cup cooked (page xi) or canned, rinsed kidney beans

Add the beans to the remaining Base Recipe in the saucepan. Cook over medium-high heat, stirring, until heated through, about 2 minutes.

serves 2 to 3

Cheesy Rice with Ham and Peas

$1/2$ cup diced, cooked ham

Combine the ham with the reserved Base Recipe. Heat if necessary.

serves 2 to 3

Not Franks and Beans

Franks and Beans

There are many brands of vegetarian frankfurters, which have a wide variety of tastes and textures. If you don't like the first brand you try, try another.

BASE RECIPE

$^1/_3$ cup water	1 tablespoon spicy, brown mustard
3 tablespoons firmly packed brown sugar	$^1/_2$ teaspoon salt, or to taste
2 tablespoons molasses	Two 10 $^1/_2$-ounce cans small white beans,
1$^1/_2$ tablespoons ketchup	drained and rinsed
1 tablespoon distilled white vinegar	2 tablespoons minced onion

In a 2-quart saucepan stir together the water, brown sugar, molasses, ketchup, vinegar, mustard, and salt. Stir in the beans and onion. Bring to a boil. Reduce heat and simmer, uncovered, 5 minutes. Remove 1 cup from the pot for the Franks and Beans recipe.

Not Franks and Beans

4 vegetarian frankfurters

Slice the frankfurters and add them to the pot with the remaining Base Recipe. Cook, uncovered, over medium heat, until the sauce has thickened, 5 minutes.

serves 2

Franks and Beans

4 frankfurters

Slice frankfurters. Combine the frankfurters and reserved Base Recipe in a 1$^1/_2$-quart saucepan. Cook over medium heat, uncovered, until sauce has thickened, 10 minutes.

serves 2

Almost Hot Dog Goulash & Hot Dog Goulash

This is an old family favorite. For the Hot Dog Goulash recipe, you can use salami or kielbasa instead of the frankfurters, if you prefer.

BASE RECIPE

1 tablespoon vegetable oil

1 cup chopped onion

1 tablespoon sweet Hungarian paprika

4 cups sliced, peeled potatoes

1³/₄ cups water

³/₄ teaspoon salt

¹/₄ teaspoon black pepper

In a 3-quart saucepan, heat the oil over medium-high heat. Add the onion and cook, stirring, until softened, about 2 minutes. Stir in the paprika until absorbed. Add the potatoes and stir to coat with the paprika. Stir in the water, salt, and black pepper. Bring to a boil. Reduce heat and simmer 10 minutes. Remove half of the mixture to a 1¹/₂ quart saucepan.

Almost Hot Dog Goulash

4 vegetarian frankfurters

Slice frankfurters and add to the remaining Base Recipe in the 3-quart saucepan. Cook over medium-high heat for 10 minutes, uncovered, until sauce has thickened.

serves 2

Hot Dog Goulash

4 frankfurters

Slice frankfurters and add to the reserved Base Recipe in the 1¹/₂-quart saucepan. Cook 10 minutes over medium-high heat, uncovered, until sauce has thickened.

serves 2

Mushroom Pita Pizza &
Pepperoni Pita Pizza

You can use any topping or toppings that you usually like on pizza on these pita pizzas, such as onion, peppers, meatballs, sausage, or even ham and pineapple.

BASE RECIPE

4 regular-size pita bread
6 tablespoons marinara or pizza sauce
$1^1/_3$ cups shredded mozzarella

Preheat the oven to 375°F. Place the pita breads on a large baking sheet. Top each with $1^1/_2$ tablespoons of sauce and spread, stopping $^1/_2$-inch from the edge of the pita breads. Sprinkle $^1/_3$ cup of the cheese over each of the pita breads. Sprinkle 2 of the pita breads with the mushroom topping and the remaining two pitas with the pepperoni topping. Bake 5 to 7 minutes or until the cheese is melted and the pita pizzas are heated through.

Mushroom Pita Pizza

$^1/_2$ cup sliced mushrooms
1 tablespoon olive oil

Brush the mushrooms lightly with olive oil. Use half of the mushroom mixture on each of 2 of the pita breads, as directed in the Base Recipe.

serves 2

Pepperoni Pita Pizza

One ounce thinly sliced pepperoni

Use half of the pepperoni on each of 2 of the pita breads, as directed in the Base Recipe.

serves 2

Fried Mozzarella and Zucchini
& Chicken Fingers
with Honey Mustard Dip

Use the breading ingredients for the cheese and zucchini before you use it for the chicken.
You can also fry the vegetables first then the chicken, or to save time, use two pots and
fry both at the same time.

BASE RECIPE

$^2/_3$ cup all-purpose flour

$^1/_2$ teaspoon salt

$^1/_8$ teaspoon black pepper

2 large eggs, beaten

2 tablespoons water

$1^1/_4$ cups plain or flavored dry bread crumbs

Oil for deep frying

recipe tip:

Prepare the Base Recipe bread-ing, then prepare both Fried Mozzarella and Zucchini and Chicken Fingers with Honey Mustard Dip recipes. Then fry both recipes according to the instructions given in the Base Recipe.

For the breading: On a piece of wax paper, stir together the flour, salt, and black pepper. In a medium bowl, beat the eggs with the water; set aside. Place the bread crumbs on another piece of wax paper.

Prepare Fried Mozzarella and Zucchini and Chicken Fingers with Honey Mustard Dip recipes.

For the frying: In a 3-quart saucepan, pour the oil to a depth of 2 inches and heat over high heat to 375°F, or until the oil bubbles when a few crumbs are tossed in. Carefully add the zucchini and mozzarella sticks, a few at a time, and cook until golden brown, about 3 minutes. Remove from the pot to drain. Repeat until all the zucchini and mozzarella are cooked. Then, carefully add the chicken strips, a few at a time, and cook until golden brown and cooked through, 3 minutes; drain. Repeat until all the chicken strips are cooked. Serve with their dipping sauces.

Fried Mozzarella and Zucchini

1 medium zucchini (8 ounces), cut into eighteen $^{1}/_{2}$ x 3-inch sticks

One 8-ounce package mozzarella sticks

1 cup marinara sauce (page 142) or store-bought

Using the mixture in the base recipe, dredge the zucchini and mozzarella sticks in the flour. Dip in the beaten egg, then coat with bread crumbs. If time allows, chill 1 hour. Fry according to Base Recipe. Warm the marinara sauce and serve as a dip with the zucchini and mozzarella sticks.

serves 2

Chicken Fingers with Honey Mustard Dip

$^{1}/_{2}$ to $^{3}/_{4}$ pound skinless, boneless chicken breasts, cut into $^{1}/_{2}$-inch strips, 3–4 inches long

$^{1}/_{2}$ cup yogurt

$^{1}/_{4}$ cup sour cream

3 tablespoons honey mustard

Using the mixture in the base recipe, dredge the chicken in the flour. Dip in the beaten egg, then coat with the bread crumbs. If time allows, chill 1 hour. Fry according to the Base Recipe. In a medium bowl, stir together the yogurt, sour cream, and honey mustard. Serve as a dip with the chicken strips.

serves 2

Stuffed Zucchini  Stuffed Flounder

BASE RECIPE

1 tablespoon olive oil

$^1/_2$ cup chopped zucchini (provided in the preparation
of the Stuffed Zucchini recipe)

$^1/_4$ cup finely chopped onion

1 clove garlic, minced

1 tablespoon all-purpose flour

$^1/_2$ cup vegetable broth (page xii or store-bought)

$^1/_2$ of a 10-ounce package chopped, frozen spinach,
thawed and squeezed dry

$^1/_4$ teaspoon thyme

$^1/_4$ teaspoon salt

$^1/_8$ teaspoon pepper

> **recipe tip:**
> *Prepare the zucchini boats
> as directed in the Stuffed
> Zucchini recipe before you
> start the Base Recipe. Bake
> both recipes at the same time.*

Preheat the oven to 350°F.

In a medium skillet, heat the oil over medium-high heat.

Add the zucchini, onion, and garlic. Cook, stirring, until softened, about 3 minutes.
Stir in the flour until absorbed. Stir in the broth and cook, stirring, until mixture
comes to a boil, about 3 minutes. Stir in the spinach, thyme, salt, and pepper. Reserve
half of the Base Recipe for the Stuffed Flounder recipe.

Stuffed Zucchini

2 medium zucchini

$^1/_2$ cup shredded Cheddar cheese

$^1/_4$ cup cooked corn kernels

1 tablespoon plain dry bread crumbs

$^1/_4$ cup chopped tomato

1 teaspoon melted butter

Cut the stem ends off of the zucchini and split them in half lengthwise. Using a spoon, scoop out most of the zucchini flesh, leaving $^1/_4$-inch thick shells. Chop the scooped-out flesh and set aside $^1/_2$ cup for use in preparing the Base Recipe. Add the cheese, corn, and tomato to the remaining Base Recipe in the skillet and stir until combined. Spoon the mixture into the zucchini shells. In a small bowl, stir together the bread crumbs and butter and sprinkle over the stuffed zucchini. Place in a 9-inch square pan. Bake until cooked through, 25 minutes.

serves 2

Stuffed Flounder

2 flounder fillets, 6 to 8 ounces each

2 tablespoons plain dry bread crumbs

2 teaspoons chopped, fresh dill

$^1/_4$ cup chicken or vegetable broth (page xii or store-bought)

2 tablespoons white wine, optional

Paprika

2 teaspoons butter, optional

Rinse the fillets and pat them dry.

In a medium bowl, combine the reserved Base Recipe with the bread crumbs and dill. Place half of the mixture on the thick end of each of the fillets. Roll to enclose the mixture. Place the stuffed fillets, seam side down, in an 8-inch loaf pan. Pour the broth and wine, if using, over the fish. Sprinkle the tops of the rolls with paprika and dot each with some of the butter. Cover the pan with aluminum foil and bake until cooked through, 25 minutes.

serves 2

Cornbread-Stuffed Eggplant
& Turkey-Stuffed Eggplant

Some cornbread stuffing mixes have meat products in them, such as chicken broth or beef broth.
Check the ingredients to be sure the cornbread mix is vegetarian.

∾◦◦◦◦◦◦◦◦◦◦◦◦◦◦◦◦◦◦◦◦◦◦

BASE RECIPE

1¼ cups vegetable broth (page xii or store-bought), divided

¼ cup white wine

½ teaspoon dried rosemary, crumbled

6 slices eggplant, ½-inch thick

2 teaspoons vegetable oil

½ cup chopped onion

½ cup chopped celery

1¼ cups cornbread stuffing mix

> **recipe tip:**
> *Prepare the Turkey-Stuffed Eggplant before the vegetarian version because the turkey stuffing takes longer to bake.*

Preheat the oven to 350°F.

In a large skillet, heat ½ cup of the broth, wine, and rosemary over medium-high heat; bring to a boil. Add the eggplant slices 2 at a time, and simmer 1 minute per side; remove from skillet. Repeat with the remaining eggplant slices. Once all of the eggplant is cooked, pour any remaining cooking liquid into a small bowl. Set aside.

Heat the oil in the same skillet over medium-high heat. Add the onion and celery; cook, stirring, until softened, about 2 minutes. Add the remaining ¾ cup of the broth and the reserved cooking liquid; bring to a boil. Remove from heat; add the stuffing mix and stir until liquid is absorbed. Set aside 1 cup for the Cornbread-Stuffed Eggplant recipe.

∾◦◦◦◦◦◦◦◦◦◦◦◦◦◦◦◦◦◦◦◦◦◦

Cornbread-Stuffed Eggplant

$1^1/_2$ teaspoons butter or vegetable oil

$^3/_4$ cup chopped apple

2 tablespoons raisins

2 tablespoons chopped, fresh parsley

Olive oil

In a medium skillet, melt the butter over medium-high heat. Add the apple and cook, stirring, until softened, about 2 minutes. Stir in the raisins, parsley, and the reserved 1 cup of Base Recipe. Place $^1/_3$ of the mixture down the center of each of the 3 eggplant slices. Roll up to enclose the filling. Place in a greased baking pan. Brush the tops of the rolls with olive oil. Bake for 25 minutes, or until filling is heated through.

serves 2 to 3

Turkey-Stuffed Eggplant

$^1/_2$ pound ground turkey

$^1/_8$ teaspoon ground poultry seasoning

$^1/_8$ teaspoon salt

$^1/_8$ teaspoon black pepper

Olive oil

Combine the ground turkey, poultry seasoning, salt, and black pepper. Add the remaining cornbread Base Recipe and combine. Place $^1/_3$ of the mixture down the center of each of the 3 eggplant slices. Roll up to enclose the filling. Place in a greased baking pan. Brush the tops of the rolls with olive oil. Bake 40 minutes, or until filling is cooked through.

serves 2 to 3

Wheat Berries with Seven Vegetables
Wheat Berries with Chicken

Wheat berries are also called whole grain wheat and can be found in your local health food stores. Be sure to cook them in unsalted water.

BASE RECIPE

1 tablespoon vegetable oil

1 cup chopped onion

2$^1/_2$ cups water

1 bay leaf

1 cup wheat berries

$^1/_3$ cup chopped, fresh parsley

3 tablespoons snipped, fresh dill

$^1/_2$ teaspoon salt

$^1/_4$ teaspoon black pepper

> **recipe tip:**
> *While the wheat berries are cooking, prepare the vegetarian and chicken recipes.*

In a 2-quart saucepan, heat the oil over medium-high heat. Add the onion and cook, stirring, until softened, about 2 minutes. Add the water and bay leaf; bring to a boil. Add the wheat berries; return to a boil. Reduce heat and simmer, covered, 1 hour and 45 minutes, or until tender.

While the wheat berries are cooking, prepare the vegetables and the chicken for the Wheat Berries with Seven Vegetables and Wheat Berries with Chicken recipes.

When the wheat berries are finished cooking, stir in the parsley, dill, salt, and black pepper. Reserve 1$^1/_4$ cups for the Wheat Berries with Seven Vegetables recipe.

Wheat Berries with Seven Vegetables

1 1/2 tablespoons vegetable oil

1/2 cup sliced leek, rinsed thoroughly

1/2 cup sliced carrot

1/2 cup sliced celery

1/2 cup sliced zucchini

1/2 cup sliced yellow squash

1/2 cup julienned parsnip

In a medium skillet, heat the oil over medium-high heat. Add the leek, carrot, celery, zucchini, yellow squash, and parsnip; cook, stirring, until tender crisp, about 2 to 4 minutes.

Combine the reserved Base Recipe with the cooked vegetables; cook over medium heat, stirring, until heated through, 2 minutes.

serves 2

Wheat Berries with Chicken

1 tablespoon vegetable oil

1/2 to 3/4 pound chicken, cubed

1 clove garlic, minced

In a medium skillet, heat the oil over medium-high heat. Add the chicken and garlic; cook, stirring, until chicken is cooked through, about 3 to 4 minutes.

Add the remaining Base Recipe and cook over medium heat, stirring, until heated through, 2 minutes.

serves 2

Macaroni and Cheese & Chicken Tetrazzini

When you are making the tetrazzini, if you have any cooked leftover chicken or turkey, just stir it into the skillet with the mushrooms instead of starting with raw.

BASE RECIPE

8 ounces elbow macaroni

3 tablespoons butter or margarine, divided

$1/4$ cup plain dry bread crumbs

3 tablespoons all-purpose flour

3 cups milk

$1/4$ teaspoon salt

$1/4$ teaspoon black pepper

> **recipe tip:**
> *You can prepare the crumb topping in a medium bowl by melting the butter in the microwave, if you like. Bake both dishes at the same time.*

Preheat the oven to 350°F.

Cook the macaroni according to package directions, drain.

In a small saucepan, melt 1 tablespoon of the butter; add the bread crumbs and stir to combine; set aside.

In a 4-quart saucepan melt the remaining 2 tablespoons of butter over medium heat; stir in the flour and cook until a paste is formed. Slowly stir in the milk, salt, and black pepper. Cook, stirring, until mixture comes to a boil. Add the macaroni, set aside $1^{1}/_{2}$ cups for the Chicken Tetrazzini recipe.

Macaroni and Cheese

2 cups shredded Cheddar

Stir the cheese into the remaining Base Recipe in the saucepan. Spoon the mixture into a 1$\frac{1}{2}$-quart casserole. Sprinkle half of the bread crumbs, reserved in the Base Recipe, over the top. Bake 25 minutes or until heated through and the bread crumbs have browned.

serves 3 to 4

Stir 3 cups of shredded Cheddar into the entire Base Recipe; bake in a 3-quart casserole.

Chicken Tetrazzini

1 tablespoon butter

1 cup sliced mushrooms

8 to 12 ounces skinless, boneless chicken or turkey breast, sliced $\frac{1}{2}$-inch thick

$\frac{1}{3}$ cup grated Parmesan cheese

$\frac{1}{8}$ teaspoon salt

In a large skillet, melt the butter over medium-high heat. Add the mushrooms and cook, stirring, until softened, about 2 minutes. Add the chicken and cook, stirring, until cooked through, about 4 minutes. Add the reserved Base Recipe, the Parmesan cheese, and salt; mix well. Spoon the mixture into a 1-quart casserole. Sprinkle the remaining half of the bread crumbs set aside in the Base Recipe over the top of the macaroni. Bake 25 minutes or until heated through and the bread crumbs have browned.

serves 2 to 3

Double the Chicken Tetrazzini recipe and use all of the Base Recipe; bake in a 3-quart casserole.

Baked Noodles Provençal & Cheddar Noodle Casserole

Either of these recipes can be made as meat or vegetarian. Just substitute 1 extra cup of broccoli for the ham from the Cheddar Noodle Casserole; conversely, you could add chopped ham to the Baked Noodles Provençal to make it into a meat dish.

BASE RECIPE

8 ounces broad egg noodles

One 8-ounce container cottage cheese

$^1/_2$ cup milk

2 large eggs, beaten

2 tablespoons melted butter

1 teaspoon salt

Preheat the oven to 350°F. Grease two $1^1/_2$-quart casseroles.

Cook the noodles according to the package directions; drain. While the noodles are cooking, place the cottage cheese, milk, eggs, butter, and salt into a food processor or blender; cover and blend until smooth.

In a large bowl, toss the noodles with the cottage cheese mixture. Reserve half of the Base Recipe for the Cheddar Noodle Casserole.

Baked Noodles Provençal

1 tablespoon olive oil

1 cup chopped onion

2 cups chopped eggplant

1 cup chopped zucchini

1 cup chopped tomato

$1/2$ teaspoon dried rosemary, crumbled

$1/8$ teaspoon dried thyme

In a large skillet, heat the oil over medium-high heat. Add the onion; cook, stirring, until softened, 1 minute. Add the eggplant and zucchini; cook, stirring, until softened, about 5 minutes. Add the tomato, rosemary, and thyme; cook, stirring, until softened, about 5 minutes more. Remove from heat; add the reserved Base Recipe to the skillet. Toss to combine. Spoon into a $1^1/_2$-quart casserole. Bake until heated through, 30 minutes.

serves 2 to 3

Double the Baked Noodles Provençal recipe and use with entire Base Recipe. Spoon into greased 3-quart casserole.

Cheddar Noodle Casserole

2 cups cooked, chopped broccoli

1 cup chopped ham

1 cup shredded Cheddar cheese

$1/2$ teaspoon Worcestershire sauce

In a medium bowl, add the broccoli, ham, Cheddar, and Worcestershire sauce to the reserved Base Recipe. Toss to combine. Spoon into a prepared casserole. Bake until heated through, 30 minutes.

serves 2 to 3

Double Cheddar Noodle Casserole recipe and toss it with the entire Base Recipe. Spoon into a greased 3-quart casserole.

chapter two

Eastern European

Mushrooms Stroganoff with Dilled Noodles &

Beef Stroganoff with Dilled Noodles

This recipe is perfect when you are looking for an elegant meal you can serve to guests.
Serve both dishes over the Dilled Noodles.

BASE RECIPE

$^1/_2$ cup sour cream

1 teaspoon Dijon mustard

$^1/_4$ teaspoon salt, or to taste

$^1/_8$ teaspoon black pepper

3 tablespoons butter

$1^1/_2$ pounds portobello mushrooms,
   thickly sliced (about 10 cups)

$^1/_4$ cup minced onion

2 tablespoons all-purpose flour

$^1/_2$ cup vegetable broth (page xii or store-bought)

recipe tip:

Prepare the Beef Stroganoff before cooking the Base Recipe. Have the water boiling for the noodles before starting the Base Recipe and cook noodles while you prepare Base Recipe.

In a small bowl, stir together the sour cream, mustard, salt, and black pepper; set aside.

In a large skillet, melt the butter over medium-high heat. Add the mushrooms and onion and cook, stirring, until soft, about 5 minutes. Stir in the flour until absorbed. Stir in the broth and cook, stirring, until broth boils, about 3 minutes. Add the sour cream mixture. Set aside 1 cup of the Base Recipe for the Beef Stroganoff recipe. The remaining Base Recipe is the Mushrooms Stroganoff, which is served over the Dilled Noodles.

Dilled Noodles

3 cups extra wide noodles

1 tablespoon butter

2 tablespoons snipped, fresh dill

Salt, to taste

Cook the noodles according to package directions; drain. Toss the noodles with the butter until the butter has melted and the noodles are coated. Add the dill and toss. Season with the salt. Serve half of the noodles topped with the remaining Base Recipe and serve the other half topped with the Beef Stroganoff.

serves 2

Use the entire Dilled Noodles recipe and increase the Base Recipe by $1/2$.

Beef Stroganoff with Dilled Noodles

$1/2$ pound sirloin, filet mignon or other tender cut of boneless beef, cut into $1/8$ to $1/4$-inch thick strips

1 tablespoon all-purpose flour

$1 1/2$ tablespoons butter

Salt, to taste

In a small bowl, toss the beef strips in the flour until coated; set aside. Melt the butter in a large skillet over medium-high heat. Add the beef and cook, stirring, for 4 minutes for medium-rare, or until cooked to desired doneness. Stir in the reserved Base Recipe and cook, stirring, until heated through, about 2 minutes. Serve over the reserved half of the Dilled Noodles.

serves 2

Double the Beef Stroganoff recipe and use all the Base Recipe. Serve over the Dilled Noodles, if desired.

Mushroom Sauerbraten & Instant Sauerbraten

Make the gingerbread crumbs either by placing the cookies in a plastic bag and smashing them with something heavy, or by using a food processor or blender.

BASE RECIPE

1 tablespoon vegetable oil

1 cup chopped onion

1 cup vegetable broth (page xii or store-bought)

2 tablespoons red wine vinegar

3 tablespoons gingersnap cookie crumbs

1 tablespoon brown sugar

1 tablespoon ketchup

$1/8$ teaspoon black pepper

In a 2-quart saucepan, heat the oil over medium-high heat. Add the onion and cook, stirring, until softened, about 3 minutes. Add the broth and vinegar; bring to a boil; add the cookie crumbs, brown sugar, ketchup, and black pepper. Return to a boil; reduce heat and simmer 10 minutes. Set aside 1 cup for the Mushroom Sauerbraten.

Mushroom Sauerbraten

$1^1/2$ tablespoons vegetable oil

6 cups sliced portobello mushrooms (about 12 ounces)

2 tablespoons dry red wine

2 to 3 cups cooked egg noodles

In a large skillet, heat the oil over medium-high heat. Add the mushrooms and cook, stirring, until softened, 3 to 4 minutes. Add the wine and reserved 1 cup Base Recipe and cook, stirring, until mixture comes to a boil, about 3 minutes. Serve over the noodles.

serves 2

Instant Sauerbraten

$1/2$ pound ground beef

2 tablespoons gingersnap cookie crumbs

1 tablespoon ketchup

2 teaspoons brown sugar

$1/8$ teaspoon salt

2 to 3 cups cooked egg noodles

In a medium bowl, combine the beef, cookie crumbs, ketchup, brown sugar, and salt. Form into 1-inch balls. Add the meatballs to the remaining Base Recipe in the saucepan. Bring to a boil, reduce heat and simmer, uncovered, until meatballs are cooked through, 10 minutes. Serve over the noodles.

serves 2

Roasted Red Pepper and Lentils & Lentils with Kielbasa

Since the red peppers constitute a dominant flavor, I like to roast my own (see page 168), but you can use jarred ones from the supermarket if you are in a pinch. Don't substitute pimientos, however, for the roasted red peppers, because they are packed in brine.

BASE RECIPE

- 1 tablespoon olive oil
- 1 cup chopped onion
- 3 cups diced ($1/2$-inch) zucchini
- 2 cloves garlic, minced
- 3 cups cooked lentils (page xi)

- $1/4$ cup chopped, fresh parsley
- $1/2$ teaspoon dried oregano
- $1/4$ teaspoon dried rosemary, crumbled
- $1/4$ teaspoon salt
- $1/8$ teaspoon black pepper

In a large skillet heat the oil over medium-high heat. Add the onion, zucchini, and garlic. Cook, stirring, until softened, about 2 minutes. Stir in the lentils, parsley, oregano, rosemary, salt, and black pepper. Set aside $1^1/2$ cups for the Lentils with Kielbasa recipe.

Roasted Red Pepper and Lentils

- $1/2$ cup sliced, roasted red bell peppers
- $1/4$ cup sliced scallion, white and green parts
- 1 teaspoon soy sauce

Add the bell peppers, scallion, and soy sauce to the remaining Base Recipe in the skillet. Cook over medium-high heat, stirring, until heated through, 2 to 3 minutes.

serves 2

Lentils with Kielbasa

- $1^1/2$ cups sliced kielbasa

In a $1^1/2$-quart saucepan, combine the kielbasa with the reserved $1^1/2$ cups of Base Recipe. Cook over medium-high heat, stirring, until heated through, about 3 minutes.

serves 2

Barley and Dilled Lima Beans
Liver, Bacon, and Barley

I use chicken liver for this recipe but you can use calf or steer liver instead.

BASE RECIPE

1 tablespoon vegetable oil

1 cup chopped onion

$^1/_3$ cup chopped green bell pepper

1 cup vegetable broth (page xii or store-bought)

$^3/_4$ cup water

$^3/_4$ cup pearl barley

$^1/_4$ teaspoon salt

$^1/_4$ teaspoon black pepper

In a 2-quart saucepan, heat the oil over medium-high heat. Add the onion and bell pepper; cook, stirring, until softened, about 2 minutes. Add the broth and water; bring to a boil. Add the barley; return to a boil. Reduce heat and simmer, covered, 45 minutes. Stir in the salt and black pepper. Reserve $1^1/_4$ cups for the Liver, Bacon, and Barley recipe.

Barley and Dilled Lima Beans

$^1/_4$ cup vegetable broth
(page xii or store-bought)

1 tablespoon water

One 10-ounce package frozen lima beans

$1^1/_2$ tablespoons snipped, fresh dill

1 teaspoon butter

In a $1^1/_2$-quart saucepan, bring the broth and water to a boil. Add the lima beans; return to a boil. Reduce heat to medium and cook, uncovered, 7 to 10 minutes or until the liquid has almost completely evaporated. Stir in the dill and butter. Add to the remaining Base Recipe in the saucepan. Cook, stirring, until heated through.

serves 2

Liver, Bacon, and Barley

4 strips bacon

$^3/_4$ cup chopped apple

$^1/_2$ pound liver, cut into bite-sized pieces

2 tablespoons chopped, fresh parsley

In a medium skillet, cook the bacon over medium-high heat until crisp, about 3 minutes. Drain on paper towels; crumble. Remove all but 1 tablespoon of the bacon fat from the skillet. Add the apple to the skillet and cook over medium heat, stirring, until softened, 1 to 2 minutes. Remove the apple from the skillet; set aside. Add the liver to the skillet and cook, stirring, until cooked to desired doneness, 3 to 5 minutes. Add the reserved Base Recipe, apple, crumbled bacon, and parsley. Cook, stirring, until heated through.

serves 2

Kasha and Lentils *&* Kasha and Chicken

Kasha is toasted buckwheat. You can buy it whole or ground three ways: coarse, medium, and fine. I like either whole or coarse kasha for this recipe. The egg keeps the grains separated.

BASE RECIPE

1 large egg

$3/_4$ cup coarse kasha (page xiii)

1 tablespoon oil

1 cup chopped onion

$1^2/_3$ cups vegetable broth (page xii or store-bought)

$1/_4$ teaspoon black pepper

In a medium bowl, beat the egg. Stir in the kasha until coated. In a 2-quart saucepan, heat the oil over medium-high heat. Add the onion and cook, stirring, until onion is transparent. Add the kasha and cook, stirring, until grains are separate and egg has dried. Add the broth and black pepper. Reduce heat and simmer, covered, until broth has been absorbed, 12 to 15 minutes. Remove $1^1/_2$ cups of the Base Recipe from saucepan for the Kasha and Chicken recipe.

Kasha and Lentils

1 cup cooked lentils (page xi)

$^1/_3$ cup chopped walnuts

Stir the cooked lentils and walnuts into the Base Recipe in the saucepan. Cook over medium heat until heated through.

serves 2

Kasha and Chicken

$^1/_2$ pound skinless, boneless chicken cutlets

1 tablespoon olive oil

1 clove garlic, halved

With a mallet or rolling pin, pound the chicken cutlets between two pieces of waxed paper until $^1/_2$-inch thick. Heat the oil with the garlic over medium-high heat. Remove the garlic from the skillet. Add the chicken to the skillet. Cook, turning once, until the chicken is cooked through. Remove from the skillet and cut into bite-sized pieces. Return them to skillet and add the reserved $1^1/_2$ cups Base Recipe. Cook, stirring, over medium heat until heated through.

serves 2

Spinach Strudel & Seafood Strudel

If there are any leftovers, they can be refrigerated. They will become noticeably soggy,
but will crisp up again when heated in a 350°F oven for 20 to 25 minutes.
Use this Base Recipe for strudel instructions.

BASE RECIPE

6 phyllo sheets (12 x 17 inches each),
    thawed according to package directions, if frozen

2 to 3 tablespoons melted butter,
    margarine, or vegetable oil

5 tablespoons plain dry bread crumbs or crushed cornflakes

> **recipe tip:**
> *Prepare the fillings before you*
> *prepare the Base Recipe.*

Preheat the oven to 350°F. Grease a baking sheet.

Prepare both the Spinach Strudel and Seafood Strudel filling recipes.

Remove the thawed phyllo sheets from the package. (Reseal the package to prevent drying.) Place 1 sheet on a work surface with the long edge parallel to the edge of the surface. Brush lightly with the butter and sprinkle with 2 teaspoons of the crumbs. Place the next phyllo sheet on top of the first and brush with butter and sprinkle with crumbs, as before. Repeat with third sheet. Fold in half. Repeat with remaining 3 sheets so that you end up with two phyllo "stacks" that are approximately 2 inches by 6 inches, placed on your work surface with the long side closest to you. Spoon the fillings onto the phyllo stacks, and then fold the two short edges over the filling. Then, starting with the long edge nearest you, fold the phyllo up over the filling, encasing it, and then roll up the rest of the stack (but not too tightly or the phyllo may burst). The finished product will look like a neat log. Place the strudel seam side down on a baking sheet and brush the top with the any remaining butter. Bake 30 to 40 minutes, or until golden. Cut into thick slices to serve.

Spinach Strudel

2 teaspoons vegetable oil

$^1/_3$ cup chopped onion

1 clove garlic, minced

1 tablespoon all-purpose flour

$^1/_2$ cup vegetable broth
  (page xii or store-bought)

One 10-ounce package chopped, frozen
  spinach, thawed and squeezed dry

1 tablespoon plain dry bread crumbs

$^1/_4$ teaspoon dried oregano

$^1/_4$ teaspoon salt, or to taste

$^1/_8$ teaspoon black pepper

$^1/_3$ cup feta cheese, crumbled

In a medium skillet, heat the oil over medium-high heat. Add the onion and garlic and cook, stirring, until softened, about 2 minutes. Stir in the flour until absorbed. Add the broth and cook, stirring, until mixture comes to a boil and is thick, about 3 minutes. Remove the skillet from the heat and stir in the spinach, bread crumbs, oregano, salt, and black pepper. Add the cheese, toss until combined. See page 52 for instructions on filling and folding the strudel.

serves 2 to 3

Seafood Strudel

$^1/_2$ cup water

1 bay leaf

$^1/_4$ teaspoon dried thyme

$^1/_4$ pound scallops

$^1/_4$ pound medium shrimp, peeled and deveined

1 tablespoon butter

$^1/_4$ cup sliced leek (white and light green
  parts only), rinsed thoroughly

$1^1/_2$ tablespoons all-purpose flour

2 tablespoons white wine

1 tablespoon heavy cream

1 tablespoon plain dry bread crumbs

1 tablespoon chopped, fresh parsley

$^1/_8$ teaspoon salt

In a 1-quart saucepan, bring the water, bay leaf, and thyme to a boil. Add the scallops and shrimp; simmer until the shrimp and scallops are opaque, 2 to 3 minutes. Discard the bay leaf. Place a strainer over a small bowl and strain the seafood mixture; set aside, reserving $^1/_3$ cup of the cooking liquid.

In a $1^1/_2$-quart saucepan, melt the butter over medium-high heat. Add the leek and cook, stirring, until softened, about 1 minute. Stir in the flour until absorbed. Stir in the seafood and the reserved $^1/_3$ cup cooking liquid, wine, and heavy cream. Cook, stirring, until mixture comes to a boil. Stir in the bread crumbs, parsley, and salt. Let cool 20 minutes before filling the strudel (see page 52 for instructions).

serves 2 to 3

Wild Rice Strudel

Wild Rice–Chicken Strudel

I like to serve this with a puréed vegetable soup to start, then a tossed salad on the side (something with Belgium endive or radiccio is always nice). I then serve a fruity dessert, like a Tart Tartan or something with lemon, for a grand meal.

BASE RECIPE

For the Filling:

2 tablespoons butter or margarine

$1/2$ cup sliced leek, rinsed thoroughly

2 cups sliced white mushrooms

2 tablespoons all-purpose flour

$1/2$ cup vegetable broth (page xii or store-bought)

1 cup cooked Uncle Ben's™ White and Wild rice mix or cooked wild rice

$1/4$ cup chopped, fresh parsley

$1/8$ teaspoon salt

$1/8$ teaspoon black pepper

> **recipe tip:**
> *Do not prepare the strudel leaves until both fillings are prepared and you are ready to fill them.*

For the strudel recipe, see page 52.

Preheat the oven to 350°F. Grease a baking sheet.

In a large skillet, melt the butter over medium-high heat. Add the leeks and cook, stirring, until softened, about 30 seconds. Add the mushrooms and cook, stirring, until softened, about 2 to 3 minutes. Add the flour, stirring until absorbed. Add the broth and cook, stirring, until mixture comes to a boil, 3 minutes. Stir in the rice, parsley, salt, and black pepper. Reserve $1/2$ cup of the Base Recipe for the Wild Rice–Chicken Strudel recipe.

(Prepare both filling recipes now.)

See page 52 for instructions on filling and folding the strudel.

Wild Rice Strudel

1 teaspoon vegetable oil

$^3/_4$ cup fresh or frozen asparagus pieces ($^3/_4$-inch long)

2 tablespoons grated Parmesan cheese

In a medium skillet, heat the oil over medium-high heat. Add the asparagus and cook, stirring, until softened, about 1 minute. Add the Parmesan cheese and the remaining Base Recipe. See page 52 for instructions on filling, folding, and baking the strudel.

serves 2

totally Vegetarian

Triple the Wild Rice Strudel recipe and use all of the Base Recipe. Use this to fill 2 strudels.

Wild Rice—Chicken Strudel

2 teaspoons vegetable oil

4 ounces skinless, boneless chicken breast, sliced

$^1/_3$ cup chopped walnuts

1 teaspoon soy sauce

In a medium skillet, heat the oil over medium-high heat. Add the chicken, cook, stirring, until cooked through, about 5 minutes. Add the walnuts, soy sauce, and the reserved Base Recipe. See page 52 for instructions on filling, folding, and baking the strudel.

serves 2

totally con Carne

Increase the chicken to 8 ounces and use 1 cup of the Base Recipe. Make two strudels from this mixture. Serve any remaining Base Recipe on the side.

Cabbage and Potato Strudel
Corned Beef and Cabbage Strudel

The Base Recipe is an Irish potato dish, called Colcannon. You can use it as a side dish on a day you don't feel like making strudel.

BASE RECIPE

2 cups peeled, cubed all-purpose potatoes

1¹/₂ tablespoons butter or margarine

2 cups chopped cabbage

¹/₃ cup finely chopped onion

¹/₄ cup milk or vegetable broth (page xii or store-bought)

¹/₄ teaspoon salt, or to taste

¹/₈ teaspoon black pepper

recipe tip:
Do not prepare the strudel leaves until both fillings are prepared and you are ready to fill them.

For the strudel recipe, see page 52.

Preheat the oven to 350°F. Grease a baking sheet.

In a 2-quart saucepan, cook the potatoes in enough water to cover the potatoes by 1-inch. Bring to a boil over high heat. Reduce heat to medium high and cook 15 to 20 minutes or until potatoes are fork tender; drain and return the potatoes to the pot. Add the milk or broth, salt, and black pepper to the potatoes. Mash with fork until desired consistency, set aside.

Melt the butter over medium-high heat in a medium skillet. Add the cabbage and onion. Cook, stirring, until cabbage has wilted, 4 minutes. Add cabbage mixture to the mashed potatoes, stir until combined. Reserve ³/₄ cup of the Base Recipe for the Corned Beef and Cabbage filling.

Prepare both the Cabbage and Potato filling and the Corned Beef and Cabbage filling recipes.

See page 52 for instructions on filling and folding the strudel.

Cabbage and Potato Strudel

1 teaspoon vegetable oil

$^1/_3$ cup coarsely shredded carrot

1 tablespoon chopped, fresh parsley

$^1/_8$ teaspoon salt

In a small skillet heat the oil over medium high heat. Add the carrots and cook, stirring, until softened, about 1 to 2 minutes. Add the parsley, salt, and the remaining Base Recipe; stir.

See page 52 for instructions on filling, folding, and baking the strudel.

serves 2

Corned Beef and Cabbage Strudel

$^1/_4$ pound corned beef, chopped

Combine the corned beef and the reserved Base Recipe; mix well. See page 52 for instructions on filling, folding, and baking the strudel.

serves 2

Cheese Strudel &
Cheese and Salmon Strudel

You can substitute canned, drained salmon or fresh, cooked salmon for the smoked.

BASE RECIPE

2 large eggs

Two 8-ounce packages farmer cheese

2 tablespoons grated Parmesan cheese

2 tablespoons all-purpose flour

3 tablespoons chopped, fresh parsley

$1/8$ teaspoon black pepper

> **recipe tip:**
> *Do not prepare the strudel leaves until both fillings are prepared and you are ready to fill them.*

For the strudel recipe, see page 52.

Preheat the oven to 350°F. Grease a baking sheet.

In a medium bowl, beat the eggs. Stir in the cheeses and flour until combined. Add the parsley and black pepper. Reserve half the Base Recipe for the Cheese Strudel.

(Prepare the Cheese Strudel and the Cheese and Salmon Strudel fillings now.)

See page 52 for instructions on filling and folding the strudel.

Cheese Strudel

3 tablespoons finely chopped, sun-dried tomatoes, packed in oil

$1/4$ cup shredded Swiss cheese

Stir the sun-dried tomatoes and Swiss cheese into the reserved Base Recipe. See page 52 for instructions on filling, folding, and baking the strudel.

serves 2

Cheese and Salmon Strudel

$1/4$ cup chopped smoked salmon

1 tablespoon snipped, fresh dill

1 teaspoon grated lemon rind

Stir the smoked salmon, dill, and lemon rind into the remaining Base Recipe. See page 52 for instructions on filling, folding, and baking the strudel.

serves 2

chapter three

Asian

Vegetable Chow Mein

& Shrimp Chow Mein

The color of this version of chow mein is slightly darker than what you might find at a Chinese restaurant. The color comes from the soy sauce, which traditional chow mein does not use.

BASE RECIPE

1 cup vegetable broth (page xi or store-bought)

1¹/₂ tablespoons cornstarch

1 tablespoon soy sauce

1 tablespoon mirin (rice wine) or dry sherry

1 teaspoon sugar

1¹/₂ tablespoons vegetable oil

1¹/₂ cups thickly sliced (¹/₄ inch) onion

1 cup sliced celery

2 cloves garlic, minced

4 cups sliced Chinese cabbage or bok choy

1 cup fresh mung bean sprouts

recipe tip:
Cook the snow peas and mushrooms for the Vegetable Chow Mein recipe first, using the same wok or large skillet you are going to use for the Base Recipe. Remove the vegetables from the wok, then prepare the Base Recipe.

In a medium bowl, stir together the broth, cornstarch, soy sauce, mirin, and sugar; set aside. In a wok or large skillet, heat the vegetable oil over high heat. Add the onion, celery, and garlic; cook stirring, until tender-crisp, about 3 minutes. Add the Chinese cabbage and bean sprouts; cook, stirring, until softened, about 1 minute. Add the sauce and cook, stirring, until thickened, about 2 minutes. Set aside 1¹/₂ cups for the Shrimp Chow Mein recipe.

Vegetable Chow Mein

1 tablespoon vegetable oil

2 cups sliced mushrooms

1 cup snow peas

In a wok or large skillet, heat the vegetable oil over high heat. Add the mushrooms and snow peas and cook, stirring until tender-crisp, about 2 to 3 minutes. Remove the vegetables from the skillet; set aside and proceed with the Base Recipe.

Add the mushroom mixture to the remaining Base Recipe in the wok or large skillet and cook, stirring, until heated through, about 2 minutes.

serves 2

Shrimp Chow Mein

$1/2$ pound large shrimp, peeled and de-veined

1 teaspoon mirin (rice wine) or dry sherry

$1/2$ teaspoon soy sauce

1 tablespoon vegetable oil

In a medium bowl, stir together the shrimp, mirin, and soy sauce; let stand 5 minutes. In a medium skillet, heat the oil over high heat. Add the shrimp and cook, stirring, 2 to 3 minutes, until shrimp is cooked through. Add the reserved Base Recipe and cook, stirring, 1 to 2 minutes, until heated through.

serves 2

Vegetable Egg Foo Yung
Egg Foo Yung with Chicken

Some people serve this without the sauce, but I really think the sauce is important. This recipe doesn't hold together the way an omelet would, so don't expect to be able to turn it in one piece. The end result, once you've added the sauce, is a lot like scrambled eggs.

BASE RECIPE

1 tablespoon vegetable oil

1 cup sliced ($^1/_4$ inch) onion

1 cup thinly sliced celery

1 tablespoon minced ginger

6 eggs, beaten

1 tablespoon mirin (rice wine) or dry sherry

2 teaspoons soy sauce

recipe tip:

Prepare the Vegetable Egg Foo Yung and Egg Foo Yung with Chicken recipes before the Base Recipe.

Sauce:

1 cup vegetable broth (page xi or store-bought)

1 tablespoon cornstarch

1 teaspoon soy sauce

1 teaspoon vegetable oil

$^1/_2$ cup sliced leek (white and light green parts only), rinsed thoroughly

$^1/_2$ cup cooked green peas

In a wok or large skillet, heat the oil over high heat. Add the onion, celery, and ginger; cook, stirring, until tender-crisp, about 3 minutes. Set aside.

In a medium bowl, beat the eggs with the mirin and soy sauce.

Stir in the onion mixture. Reserve half for the Vegetable Egg Foo Yung recipe.

To prepare the sauce:
In a small bowl, stir together the vegetable broth, cornstarch, and soy sauce. Set aside.

Heat the oil in a $1^1/_2$-quart saucepan over medium-high heat. Add the leek and cook, stirring, about 1 minute, until softened. Add the soy sauce mixture and peas. Cook, stirring, until mixture comes to a boil and is thickened. Divide the Base Recipe sauce in half.

Vegetable Egg Foo Yung

1 cup bean sprouts

1 cup coarsely chopped snow peas

1¹/₂ tablespoons vegetable oil

Cook the bean sprouts and snow peas in boiling water, about 1 minute, until just tender-crisp; drain. In a medium bowl, combine the sprouts and snow peas with the reserved Base Recipe.

In a large skillet, heat the oil over high heat; add the Base Recipe and vegetable combination (but not the sauce). Cook over medium-high heat, lifting edges with a spatula while tilting the skillet to let the uncooked portion flow to the bottom. Continue until egg mixture is cooked to desired doneness. Stir in half of the Base Recipe sauce.

serves 2

Double the Vegetable Egg Foo Yung recipe and use all the Base Recipe.

Egg Foo Yung with Chicken

1 cup diced, cooked chicken (page xiv)

¹/₂ teaspoon soy sauce

1¹/₂ tablespoons vegetable oil

Add the chicken and soy sauce to the remaining Base Recipe in the bowl. Heat the oil in a large skillet over high heat. Add the Base Recipe (but not the sauce). Cook over medium-high heat, lifting the edges with a spatula while tilting the skillet to let the uncooked portion flow to the bottom. Continue until egg mixture is cooked to desired doneness. Stir in the remaining Base Recipe sauce.

serves 2

Double the chicken and use all the Base Recipe.

Cantonese Vegetables with Almonds
& Chicken with Chinese Vegetables

This is a dish—with its crunchy celery, water chestnuts and rich flavored almonds—
I really loved as a kid.

BASE RECIPE

$^1/_3$ cup water

$^1/_4$ mirin (rice wine) or dry sherry

$1^1/_2$ tablespoons soy sauce

1 tablespoon cornstarch

2 tablespoons vegetable oil

3 cups diced ($^1/_2$-inch pieces) celery

2 cups coarsely chopped onion

3 cloves garlic, minced

One 8-ounce can whole water chestnuts, drained and quartered

One 8-ounce can bamboo shoots, drained and diced

In a small bowl, stir together the water, mirin, soy sauce, and cornstarch; set aside.

Heat the oil in a wok or large skillet over high heat. Add the celery, onion, and garlic; cook, stirring, about 4 minutes, until tender-crisp. Add the water chestnuts and bamboo shoots; cook, stirring, about 2 minutes, until heated through. Add the soy sauce mixture and cook, stirring, about 2 minutes, until thickened. Set aside $^1/_3$ of Base Recipe for the Chicken with Chinese Vegetables recipe.

Cantonese Vegetables with Almonds

$^1/_2$ cup coarsely chopped almonds

Preheat the oven to 350°F.

Place the almonds on a baking sheet and toast them in the oven for 10 minutes; set aside.

Add the almonds to the remaining Base Recipe in the wok. Cook, stirring, until heated through.

serves 2 to 3

Chicken with Chinese Vegetables

1 tablespoon oil

$^1/_2$ pound skinless, boneless chicken breasts, cut into $^3/_4$-inch cubes

One 8-ounce can sliced mushrooms, drained

Heat the oil in a medium skillet over medium-high heat. Add the chicken and cook, stirring, about 4 minutes, or until cooked through.

Add the reserved Base Recipe and the mushrooms. Cook over medium-high heat, stirring, until heated through, about 2 minutes.

serves 2 to 3

Sweet and Sour Tofu & Sweet and Sour Pork

I know that a lot of people love pineapple in their Sweet and Sour dishes. If you do, use juice-packed canned pineapple chunks, drain them well, and add them to the skillet after you've added the sauce. You can also substitute pineapple juice for some of the water.

BASE RECIPE

$^1/_2$ cup water

$^1/_4$ cup white vinegar

$^1/_4$ cup sugar

3 tablespoons ketchup

$1^1/_2$ tablespoons soy sauce

1 tablespoon cornstarch

2 tablespoons vegetable oil

1 tablespoon ginger, minced

2 cloves garlic, minced

3 cups red and/or green bell pepper, cut into 1-inch chunks

1 cup cubed (1-inch) onion

Hot cooked rice, for serving

recipe tip:
Prepare the tofu and pork cubes before you prepare the Base Recipe. If you fry the tofu before the pork, you can use the same saucepan oil.

In a small bowl, stir together the water, vinegar, sugar, ketchup, soy sauce, and cornstarch; set aside.

In a wok or large skillet, heat the oil over high heat. Add the ginger and garlic and cook, stirring, 10 seconds. Add the bell peppers and onion. Cook, stirring, until tender-crisp, about 3 minutes. Add the soy sauce mixture and cook, stirring, until mixture comes to a boil and has thickened. Reserve half of the mixture for the Sweet and Sour Pork recipe.

Sweet and Sour Tofu

2 teaspoons mirin (rice wine) or dry sherry

1 teaspoon soy sauce

Two 4-ounce cakes tofu, cut into 1-inch cubes

3 tablespoons cornstarch

Vegetable oil for frying

In a medium bowl, stir together the mirin and soy sauce. Add the tofu and let stand 5 minutes, tossing once. Pour off any marinade that has not been absorbed. Dredge the tofu cubes in the cornstarch.

In a 2-quart saucepan, pour the oil to a depth of 2 inches and heat over medium-high heat to 360°F or until it bubbles when one tofu cube is tossed in. Fry the tofu cubes, a few at a time, turning once, until crispy on the outside, about 3 minutes. Remove the tofu from the oil and drain on paper towels.

Add the fried tofu to the remaining half of the Base Recipe in the skillet and cook, over high heat, until mixture is heated through. Serve with rice.

serves 2

Sweet and Sour Pork

$1/2$ pound boneless pork, cut into 1-inch cubes

$1^1/_2$ tablespoons cornstarch

Vegetable oil for frying

Dredge the pork in the cornstarch. In a 2-quart saucepan, heat the oil over medium high heat to 360°F or until oil bubbles when a small piece of pork is thrown in. Fry the pork, a few cubes at a time, until brown and cooked through, about 4 to 5 minutes. Remove from the oil and drain on paper towels.

Place the reserved Base Recipe into a medium skillet. Add the fried pork cubes and cook, over high heat, until mixture is heated through. Serve with rice.

serves 2

Moo Shu–Style Vegetables
Moo Shu–Style Pork

Moo Shu vegetables are usually served with a dollop of hoisin sauce and in a pancake, rolled up like a fajita. Instead of making moo shu pancakes, you can do what I do; roll them up using store-bought egg roll skins. Otherwise, I serve them unwrapped, with rice on the side. Hoisin sauce, a sweet brown sauce, is available in Asian-food markets or in the Asian-food section of the supermarket.

BASE RECIPE

1 cup vegetable broth (page xii or store-bought)

1 tablespoon soy sauce

2 tablespoons mirin (rice wine) or dry sherry

1^1/$_2$ tablespoons hoisin sauce

^{1}/$_2$ teaspoon sugar

4 teaspoons cornstarch

2 tablespoons vegetable oil

1 cup sliced mushrooms

^{1}/$_2$ cup scallion, cut into 1^1/$_2$-inch pieces (white and green parts)

1 tablespoon minced ginger

3 cloves garlic, minced

3 cups shredded, Chinese cabbage or bok choy

2 cups shredded, green cabbage

1 cup julienned carrots

Hoisin sauce, for serving

Egg roll wrappers, for serving, if desired

In a small bowl, blend the broth, soy sauce, mirin, hoisin sauce, and sugar. Add cornstarch and stir until smooth. In a wok or large skillet, heat the oil over high heat. Add the mushrooms, scallion, ginger, and garlic. Cook, stirring, until softened, about 3 minutes. Add the Chinese and green cabbage, and carrots. Cook stirring, until tender-crisp. Add the soy sauce mixture. Cook, stirring, until sauce is thickened. Set aside half of the Base Recipe for the Moo Shu–Style Pork recipe.

Moo Shu-Style Vegetables

2 teaspoons vegetable oil

1 egg, beaten

$^1/_2$ cup diced, baked or pressed tofu

Heat the oil in a medium skillet over medium-high heat. Add the egg, and cook, stirring constantly, until dry. Remove the egg from the skillet and let cool. Finely dice the egg. Combine the diced egg and tofu with the remaining Base Recipe in the skillet. Cook over medium heat, stirring, until heated through. Serve with the hoisin sauce and egg roll wrappers, if using.

serves 2

Moo Shu-Style Pork

$^1/_2$ pound boneless pork loin, julienned or cut into very thin strips

2 teaspoons cornstarch

1 tablespoon vegetable oil

Toss the pork with the cornstarch until lightly dusted with cornstarch. Heat the oil in a medium skillet over high heat. Add the pork and cook, stirring until cooked through, about 3 to 4 minutes. Stir in the reserved half of the Base Recipe. Cook, stirring, until heated through. Serve with the hoisin sauce and egg roll wrappers, if using.

serves 2

Eggplant with Five Flavors & Pork with Five Flavors

Five-fragrance powder, sometimes called five-spice powder or blend, is a ground blend of Eastern spices. It is an extremely potent flavoring agent. One of the primary spices in the mix is anise, which has a strong licorice flavor. If you are not fond of licorice, this recipe may not be for you.

BASE RECIPE

$1/4$ cup water

3 tablespoons mirin (rice wine) or dry sherry

1 tablespoon honey

1 tablespoon ketchup

1 tablespoon soy sauce

1 tablespoon cornstarch

$1/4$ teaspoon five-fragrance powder

1 tablespoon vegetable oil

1 tablespoon ginger, minced

2 cloves garlic, minced

$1/2$ cup chopped ($1^1/2$-inch) scallion (green and white parts)

In a small bowl, stir together the water, mirin, honey, ketchup, soy sauce, cornstarch, and five-fragrance powder; set aside. In a wok or large skillet, heat the oil over high heat. Add the ginger and garlic and cook, stirring, 10 seconds. Add the scallion. Cook, stirring, until tender-crisp, about 1 minute.

Stir in the soy sauce mixture and cook until it comes to a boil and thickens. Reserve half the Base Recipe for the Eggplant with Five Flavors.

Eggplant with Five Flavors

1 tablespoon vegetable oil

5 cups cubed eggplant

$^1/_3$ cup water

In a wok or large skillet, heat the oil over high heat. Add the eggplant and cook, stirring, until oil is absorbed. Add water and cook, stirring until eggplant is cooked through, about 3 minutes.

Stir in the reserved Base Recipe and cook, stirring, until mixture is heated through.

serves 2

Pork with Five Flavors

1 tablespoon vegetable oil

2 cups cubed, red bell pepper

2 cups cubed eggplant

$^1/_2$ pound ground pork

In a wok or large skillet, heat the oil over high heat. Add the bell pepper and cook, stirring, until tender-crisp, about 2 minutes. Add the eggplant and cook, stirring, until softened, about 2 minutes. Add the pork and cook, stirring, until cooked through and no longer pink, about 3 minutes.

Stir in the remaining Base Recipe and cook, stirring, until the mixture is heated through.

serves 2

Tofu with Green Beans

Beef with Green Beans

This dish is only faintly spicy. For real Szechuan fans, feel free to double the amount of crushed red pepper flakes. If you can get Chinese long beans, you can substitute them for the green beans called for here.

BASE RECIPE

$1/2$ cup vegetable broth (page xii or store-bought)

2 tablespoons mirin (rice wine) or dry sherry

1 tablespoon soy sauce

1 tablespoon cornstarch

1 teaspoon sugar

$1^1/2$ tablespoons vegetable oil

2 cloves garlic, minced

$1^1/4$ pounds whole green beans, ends trimmed

2 cups scallions, cut into 2-inch pieces

$1/2$ cup thinly sliced red bell peppers

$1/4$ teaspoon crushed red pepper, to taste, optional

In a small bowl, stir together the broth, mirin, soy sauce, cornstarch, and sugar; set aside. In a wok or large skillet, heat the oil over high heat. Add the garlic and cook, stirring, 10 seconds. Add the green beans, scallions, bell peppers, and crushed red pepper. Cook, stirring, until tender-crisp, about 4 minutes. Stir in the soy sauce mixture and cook until it comes to a boil and thickens. Reserve half of the mixture for the Beef with Green Beans recipe.

Tofu with Green Beans

Two 4-ounce cakes tofu, cut into 1-inch cubes

1 tablespoon plum sauce

1 teaspoon soy sauce

Add the tofu to the Base Recipe remaining in the skillet. Stir in the plum sauce and soy sauce and cook over medium-high heat, stirring, until heated through.

serves 2

Beef with Green Beans

$^1/_2$ to $^3/_4$ pound tender cut of boneless beef, such as sirloin, or London broil

1 tablespoon cornstarch

1 tablespoon vegetable oil

$^1/_4$ cup vegetable broth (page xii or store-bought)

Cut the beef into $^1/_4$-inch-thick slices. Toss the beef in the cornstarch until it is lightly coated. In a medium skillet, heat the oil over medium-high heat. Add the beef and cook, stirring, until the beef is cooked through, about 3 minutes. Add the reserved Base Recipe and the broth to the skillet with the beef, cook, stirring, until heated through.

serves 2

Eggplant with Tofu & Eggplant with Sliced Chicken

Don't be lazy—be sure to peel the eggplant. Otherwise the dish will have a different texture.
Look for chili oil in the Asian-food section of your supermarket.

BASE RECIPE

Marinade:
$1/2$ cup water

$1^1/2$ tablespoons soy sauce

2 tablespoons mirin (rice wine) or dry sherry

1 tablespoon black bean sauce

1 teaspoon sugar

1 tablespoon cornstarch

> **recipe tip:**
> *Marinate the tofu and chicken while you prepare the rest of the Base Recipe.*

Vegetables:
2 tablespoons vegetable oil

1 tablespoon minced ginger

2 cloves garlic, minced

6 cups peeled, cubed eggplant ($1/2$-inch pieces)

1 cup cubed red bell pepper (1-inch pieces)

$1/2$ cup scallion, cut into 2-inch pieces

1 teaspoon chili oil

To prepare the marinade:
In a medium bowl, stir together the water, soy sauce, mirin, black bean sauce, and sugar. Place 1 tablespoon of marinade into each of two bowls; set aside. Stir the cornstarch into the remaining marinade; set aside.

To prepare the vegetables:
In a wok or large skillet, heat the oil over high heat. Add the ginger and garlic and cook, stirring, 10 seconds. Add the eggplant, bell pepper, and scallion. Cook, stirring, until softened, about 4 minutes. Stir in the reserved cornstarch-marinade mixture and cook until thickened, about 2 minutes. Stir in the chili oil. Remove half of the Base Recipe from the skillet for the Eggplant with Sliced Chicken recipe.

Eggplant with Tofu

2 cups cubed tofu

Add the tofu into one of the bowls with the reserved marinade, let stand 10 minutes, tossing once or twice. Add tofu and any unabsorbed marinade into the remaining Base Recipe in the skillet. Cook over medium heat, stirring, until heated through, about 2 minutes.

serves 2

Place 2 tablespoons of the unthickened Base Recipe marinade into one bowl; add 4 cups of cubed tofu. Continue with Eggplant with Tofu recipe using all of the Base Recipe.

Eggplant with Sliced Chicken

$^1/_4$ pound skinless, boneless chicken, cut into $^1/_4$-inch strips

1 tablespoon vegetable oil

Add the chicken into one of the bowls with the reserved marinade, let stand 10 minutes, tossing once or twice. Heat the oil in a medium skillet, over medium-high heat. Add the chicken and cook, stirring, about 3 minutes, until no longer pink. Add the reserved Base Recipe to the skillet; cook, stirring, until heated through, about 2 minutes.

serves 2

Place 2 tablespoons of the Base Recipe marinade (without the constarch) into one bowl; add $^1/_2$ pound of sliced chicken. Continue with Eggplant with Sliced Chicken recipe, using all of the Base Recipe.

Szechuan Vegetables with Tofu & Garlic Beef

I like to order this dish when I go out to Chinese restaurants.
It is sometimes called Szechuan Beef or Garlic Beef.

BASE RECIPE

$1/2$ cup vegetable broth (page xii or
  store-bought) or water

2 tablespoons mirin (rice wine)
  or dry sherry

1 tablespoon cornstarch

1 tablespoon soy sauce

2 tablespoons vegetable oil

1 tablespoon minced ginger

3 cloves garlic, minced

$1/4$ teaspoon crushed red pepper
  flakes, or to taste

3 cups julienned celery

3 cups julienned carrot

1 cup julienned scallion

In a small bowl, stir together the broth, mirin, cornstarch, and soy sauce; set aside.

In a wok or large skillet, heat the oil over high heat. Add the ginger, garlic, and red pepper; cook, stirring, 10 seconds. Add the celery, carrots, and scallion; cook, stirring until softened, about 4 minutes. Add the soy sauce mixture and cook, stirring, until it comes to a boil and thickens, about 3 minutes. Remove half of the Base Recipe from the wok for the Garlic Beef recipe.

Szechuan Vegetables with Tofu

1 cup julienned, baked or pressed tofu

1 teaspoon sesame oil

Add the tofu to the Base Recipe remaining in the skillet. Cook over medium heat, stirring, until heated through. Stir in the sesame oil.

serves 2

Garlic Beef

2 teaspoons vegetable oil

$1/2$ pound boneless sirloin, London broil, or
  other tender cut of beef, julienned

In a medium skillet, heat the oil over medium-high heat. Add the beef and cook, stirring, until desired doneness, 3-5 minutes for medium rare. Add the reserved Base Recipe and cook, stirring, until heated through.

serves 2

Szechuan Broccoli with Tofu
& Shredded Chicken with Broccoli

You can substitute thinly sliced broccoli stems for some of the florets.

BASE RECIPE

$^1/_2$ cup vegetable broth (page xii
  or store-bought)

3 tablespoons mirin (rice wine)
  or dry sherry

1 tablespoon ketchup

1 tablespoon soy sauce

1 tablespoon cornstarch

1 tablespoon vegetable oil

1 tablespoon minced ginger

1 tablespoon garlic, minced

$^1/_4$ teaspoon crushed red pepper

4 cups broccoli florets

1 cup cubed red bell pepper

(1-inch pieces)

In a medium bowl, stir together the broth, mirin, ketchup, soy sauce, and cornstarch; set aside. In a wok or large skillet, heat the vegetable oil over high heat. Add the ginger, garlic, and crushed red pepper, cook stirring, 30 seconds. Add the broccoli and bell pepper; cook stirring, until tender-crisp, about 3 minutes. Add the soy sauce mixture and cook, stirring, until thickened, about 1 minute. Reserve $1^1/_2$ cups Base Recipe from the wok for the Shredded Chicken with Broccoli recipe.

Szechuan Broccoli with Tofu

2 firm tofu cakes (5–6 ounces each), diced

Stir the tofu into the Base Recipe remaining in the wok. Cook over high heat, stirring, until heated through, about 1 minute.

serves 2

Shredded Chicken with Broccoli

8 ounces skinless, boneless chicken breast

1 tablespoon vegetable oil

2 teaspoons hoisin sauce

Cut the chicken into thin ($^1/_4$-inch) strips. In a medium skillet, heat the oil over medium-high heat. Add the chicken and cook, stirring, until cooked through, about 3 minutes. Stir in the hoisin sauce. Stir in the reserved Base Recipe. Cook, stirring, until heated through.

serves 2

Hunan Green Beans with Tofu
Hunan Green Beans with Pork

You can add $1/4$ to $1/2$ teaspoon chili oil when you add the walnuts, if you would like to increase the heat in this dish.

BASE RECIPE

$1/2$ cup vegetable broth (page xii or store-bought)

2 tablespoons mirin (rice wine) or dry sherry

2 tablespoons hoisin sauce

1 tablespoon ketchup

1 tablespoon sugar

1 tablespoon cornstarch

2 tablespoons vegetable oil

4 cloves garlic, minced

1 tablespoon minced ginger

$1^1/2$ pounds whole green beans

1 cup sliced red bell pepper

$1/2$ cup chopped walnuts

recipe tip:
Marinate and cook the pork before you prepare the Base Recipe.

In a small bowl, stir together the broth, mirin, hoisin, ketchup, sugar, and cornstarch; set aside. In a wok or large skillet, heat the oil over high heat. Add the garlic and ginger and cook, stirring, 10 seconds. Add the green beans and bell peppers. Cook, stirring, until tender-crisp, about 4 minutes.

Stir in the sauce mixture and cook until mixture comes to a boil and sauce is thickened. Stir in the walnuts. Remove half of the mixture from the skillet for the Hunan Green Beans with Pork recipe.

Hunan Green Beans with Tofu

6 ounces baked or pressed tofu, thinly sliced

$^1/_4$ cup sliced scallion (white and green parts)

Add the tofu and scallions to the Base Recipe still in the wok and cook over high heat, stirring, until heated through.

serves 2

Hunan Green Beans with Pork

$^1/_2$ to $^3/_4$ pound boneless pork loin

2 teaspoons soy sauce

$^1/_2$ teaspoon hoisin sauce

1 tablespoon vegetable oil

Cut the pork into thin slices. In a medium bowl, combine the pork, soy sauce, and hoisin sauce; let stand 5 minutes.

In a medium skillet, heat the oil over medium high heat. Add the pork and cook, stirring, until the pork is completely cooked through, about 4 minutes. Add the reserved Base Recipe, cook, stirring, until heated through.

serves 2

Fried Rice-a-Roni™ & Shrimp Fried Rice-a-Roni™

Not exactly an "authentic" fried rice, but tasty, nevertheless. If you don't want to use shrimp, you can substitute ¹/₂ cup diced, cooked ham, chicken, or pork.

BASE RECIPE

2 tablespoons vegetable oil

1 package Rice-a-Roni™ Fried Rice mix (6.2-ounces), seasoning packet reserved

1 cup chopped onion

2 cups water

One 16-ounce can straw mushrooms, drained

One 8-ounce can water chestnuts, drained and chopped

1 cup fresh mung bean sprouts

¹/₂ teaspoon soy sauce

In a large skillet, heat the oil over medium heat.

Add the fried rice mix and onion; cook, stirring, until the vermicelli is lightly browned. Add the water and the reserved seasoning packet. Bring to a boil. Reduce heat and simmer, covered, until rice is tender, 15 minutes. Stir in the mushrooms, water chestnuts, bean sprouts, and soy sauce. Cover and continue to simmer 5 minutes longer. Set aside half of the mixture for the Shrimp Fried Rice-a-Roni™ recipe.

Fried Rice-a-Roni™

2 large eggs

2 tablespoons chopped scallion

1 tablespoon vegetable oil

$^1/_2$ cup baby corn, cut into pieces

Beat eggs in a medium bowl; add the scallion.

In a medium skillet, heat the oil over medium-high heat. Add the egg mixture and cook, stirring occasionally, until egg is set and cooked through, about 1 minute. Remove the egg from the pan and chop. Add the egg mixture and the baby corn to the remaining Base Recipe in the skillet. Cook over medium heat, stirring, until heated through, about 1 minute.

serves 2

Shrimp Fried Rice-a-Roni™

$^1/_2$ pound large shrimp

Peel and de-vein the shrimp. In a medium skillet, add the reserved Base Recipe and the shrimp. Cook over medium heat, stirring, until the shrimp are pink and cooked through, about 3 minutes.

serves 2

Curried Fried Rice & Curried Pork Fried Rice

This is one of my favorite uses for leftover rice from a Chinese restaurant. Of course, you don't have to wait to have leftover rice since it does not take much time to cook some rice yourself.

BASE RECIPE

2 tablespoons vegetable oil

1 cup chopped onion

1 cup chopped celery

2 cloves garlic, minced

1 tablespoon curry powder

$2^1/_2$ cups cooked rice (white or brown)

$^1/_4$ teaspoon salt, or to taste

$^1/_8$ teaspoon black pepper

$^1/_2$ cup cooked peas

2 tablespoons chopped, fresh cilantro

In a large skillet, heat the oil over medium-high heat. Add the onion, celery, and garlic; cook, stirring, until softened, about 2 to 3 minutes. Stir in the curry. Add the rice, salt, and black pepper; cook, stirring, until heated through. Stir in the peas and cilantro. Remove 2 cups of the Base Recipe for the Curried Pork Fried Rice recipe.

Curried Fried Rice

1 cup diced, baked or pressed, or savory tofu

$^1/_2$ cup chopped, blanched snow peas

$^1/_4$ cup chopped peanuts

Add the tofu, snow peas, and peanuts to the Base Recipe remaining in the skillet. Cook, stirring, until heated through.

serves 2

Curried Pork Fried Rice

$^1/_4$ to $^1/_2$ pound boneless pork cutlet, cut into $^1/_2$-inch cubes

1 teaspoon soy sauce

1 tablespoon vegetable oil

In a medium bowl, toss the pork with the soy sauce; let stand 10 minutes. In a medium skillet, heat the oil over medium-high heat. Add the pork and cook, stirring, until cooked through about 4 minutes. Add the reserved 2 cups of Base Recipe and cook, stirring, until heated through.

serves 2

Lo Mein & Shrimp Lo Mein

This is my dad's absolute favorite Chinese recipe. You can use any vegetables you like in it—broccoli, string beans, or even corn. These, however, are just the ones that Dad and I like.

BASE RECIPE

3 tablespoons soy sauce

3 tablespoons mirin (rice wine)
  or dry sherry

8 ounces dry lo mein noodles
  or thin spaghetti

2 tablespoons vegetable oil

1 cup julienned carrots

1 cup julienned celery

2 cloves garlic, minced

1 cup scallion cut into $1^1/_2$ inch pieces
  (both white and green parts)

In a small bowl, stir together the soy sauce and mirin; set aside.

Cook the noodles according to package directions, drain; set aside.

In a wok or large skillet, heat the oil over high heat. Add the carrots, celery, and garlic. Cook, stirring, until tender-crisp, about 2 minutes. Add the scallion and cook, stirring, about 30 seconds more. Add the noodles and toss to combine. Add the soy sauce mixture and cook, stirring, until noodles are coated and heated through, about 2 minutes. Remove half of the Base Recipe from the skillet for the Shrimp Lo Mein recipe.

Lo Mein

Two 4-ounce cakes baked or pressed tofu, diced
($^1/_4$ inch)

Add the tofu to the remaining Base Recipe in the skillet. Cook over high heat, stirring, until heated through, about 1 minute.

serves 2

Shrimp Lo Mein

$^1/_3$ pound small shrimp

Peel and de-vein the shrimp. In a medium saucepan, cook the shrimp in boiling water until pink and cooked through, 1 to 3 minutes; drain. Return to saucepan and add the reserved Base Recipe to the shrimp. If necessary, cook, stirring, until heated through.

serves 2

Broccoli Rabe with Rice Noodles
& Beef with Broccoli Rabe

Broccoli rabe looks like broccoli florets on long, thin, leafy stems and has a slightly bitter flavor. The florets, stems, and leaves are used in cooking. If you can't find broccoli rabe, you can substitute regular broccoli. The black bean sauce is a thick, salty, paste found in Asian-food specialty stores, or in the Asian-food section of your supermarket.

BASE RECIPE

4 to 6 dried shiitaki mushrooms

$^3/_4$ cup boiling water

3 tablespoons mirin (rice wine) or dry sherry

2 tablespoons water

1 tablespoon dark soy sauce

1 tablespoon cornstarch

2 teaspoons black bean sauce

2 tablespoons vegetable oil

1 tablespoon minced ginger

3 cloves garlic, minced

5 cups broccoli rabe florets and thinly sliced stems

One 16-ounce can baby corn, drained

$^1/_2$ teaspoon chili oil

recipe tip:
Prepare the rice noodles while the mushrooms are soaking and before you cook the broccoli rabe in the Base Recipe.

In a small bowl, soak the mushrooms in the boiling water for 5 minutes. Remove the mushrooms from the water, reserving the soaking water. Chop the mushrooms, discarding the tough stems. Set the chopped mushrooms aside for the Broccoli Rabe with Rice Noodles recipe.

Add the mirin, water, soy sauce, cornstarch, and black bean sauce to the soaking water; set aside.

In a wok or large skillet, heat the vegetable oil over high heat. Add the ginger and garlic, cook, stirring, 30 seconds. Add the broccoli rabe and cook, stirring, until tender-crisp, about 3 minutes. Add the soy sauce mixture and cook, stirring, until thickened. Add the baby corn and chili oil. Set aside 1 cup for the Beef with Broccoli Rabe recipe.

Broccoli Rabe with Rice Noodles

2 ounces dry, thin rice noodles

Cook the noodles according to package directions. Drain and set aside. Add the noodles to the skillet with the chopped mushrooms and remaining Base Recipe. Cook, stirring, until heated through.

serves 2

Beef with Broccoli Rabe

$^1/_2$ pound tender cut of boneless beef, such as sirloin, or London broil, thinly sliced

1 teaspoon soy sauce

1 tablespoon cornstarch

1 tablespoon vegetable oil

2 tablespoons water

In a medium bowl, combine the beef and soy sauce; let stand 5 minutes.

Toss the beef in the cornstarch to coat.

In a medium skillet, heat the vegetable oil over high heat. Add the beef and cook, stirring, until the beef is cooked through, 2 to 3 minutes. Add the reserved Base Recipe and water and cook over medium heat, stirring, until heated through, 2 minutes.

serves 2

Noodles with Peanut Sauce

& Peanut Noodles with Chicken

If you can't find lo mein noodles, angel hair pasta is fine. You can make this dish spicier by adding extra chili oil. I prefer rice vinegar in this recipe, but if you don't have any, cider vinegar will be fine.

BASE RECIPE

8 to 10 ounces dry lo mein noodles or angel hair noodles

$2/3$ cup smooth peanut butter

$1/4$ cup dark soy sauce

$1/4$ cup mirin (rice wine) or dry sherry

1 tablespoon rice or cider vinegar

2 tablespoons sugar

$1/4$ teaspoon chili oil

$1/2$ small clove garlic, minced

$1/3$ cup sliced scallion

> **recipe tip:**
> *Cook and cool the chicken before you start the Base Recipe*

Cook noodles according to package directions. Drain and rinse under cold water until cool; set aside.

Place the peanut butter, soy sauce, mirin, vinegar, sugar, chili oil, and garlic into a blender or food processor fitted with a steel blade. Cover and process until thoroughly combined. In a large bowl, toss the cooked noodles with sauce and scallions. Reserve half of the Base Recipe for the Noodles with Peanut Sauce recipe.

Noodles with Peanut Sauce

$^3/_4$ cup diced ($^1/_4$-inch) baked or pressed tofu

1 cup mung bean sprouts

In a large bowl, combine the tofu and bean sprouts with the reserved half of the Base Recipe. Toss to combine.

serves 2

Peanut Noodles with Chicken

1 tablespoon vegetable oil

8 to 12 ounces skinless, boneless chicken breast

1 cup julienned cucumber

Heat the oil in a large skillet over medium heat. Add the chicken and cook, turning once, until lightly brown and cooked through, about 6 minutes. Remove the chicken from the pan to cool.

When the chicken is cool enough to handle, slice into strips. Add the chicken and cucumber to the noodles remaining in the bowl, toss to combine.

serves 2 to 3

Vegetables with Pan Fried Noodles & Chicken with Pan Fried Noodles

I love the crispy bed of noodles in this dish. However if you want a lighter version, skip frying the noodles and just serve them cooked. Look for straw mushrooms in cans in the Asian-food section of your supermarket. If you can't find them there, canned button mushrooms can be substituted.

BASE RECIPE

6 ounces lo mein noodles or thin spaghetti

$^1/_4$ cup vegetable oil

2 cups shredded cabbage

2 cups thinly sliced bok choy or Chinese cabbage

1 cup thinly sliced celery

1 cup julienned carrot

1 cup chopped onion

1 jalapeño pepper, thinly sliced

2 cloves garlic, minced

$1^1/_2$ tablespoons soy sauce

Cook the noodles according to package directions; drain well so that no water is clinging to the noodles.

Heat 2 tablespoons of the oil in a large skillet. Add half of the noodles to the skillet and cook, undisturbed, until browned on bottom, about 2 minutes. Turn with spatula and cook on second side until crispy. Remove the noodles from the oil and drain on paper towels. Repeat with the remaining 2 tablespoons of oil and the remaining noodles.

Pour off all but 1 tablespoon of the oil from the skillet. Add the cabbage, bok choy, celery, carrot, onion, jalapeño pepper, and garlic to the skillet. Cook, stirring, until tender-crisp, about 4 to 5 minutes. Stir in the soy sauce. Remove $1^1/_2$ cups of the Base Recipe from the skillet for the Chicken with Pan Fried Noodles recipe.

Vegetables with Pan Fried Noodles

$^1/_2$ cup straw mushrooms

$^1/_2$ cup sliced water chestnuts

Add the mushrooms and water chestnuts to the remaining Base Recipe in the skillet. Cook over high heat, stirring, until heated through. Serve over one of the noodle nests.

serves 2

Chicken with Pan Fried Noodles

$^1/_2$ pound skinless, boneless chicken breast, cut into thin strips

2 teaspoons hoisin sauce

1 tablespoon vegetable oil

$^1/_2$ teaspoon sesame oil

In a medium bowl, combine the chicken and hoisin sauce, stir to mix. In a wok or large skillet, heat the oil. Add the chicken and cook, stirring, until cooked through, 3 to 4 minutes. Add the reserved Base Recipe and sesame oil; cook, stirring, until heated through. Serve over one of the noodle nests.

serves 2

Asian Noodles with Broccoli
& Asian Noodles with Chicken

I like to use lo mein noodles which are square, but if you can't find them, thin spaghetti will do. Lo mein noodles are available in Asian markets or in the Asian-food section of your supermarket.

BASE RECIPE

8 ounces dry lo mein noodles or thin spaghetti

$3/4$ cup vegetable broth (page xii or store-bought)

2 tablespoons mirin (rice wine) or sherry

2 tablespoons soy sauce

1 tablespoon cornstarch

1 teaspoon sugar

2 tablespoons vegetable oil

2 tablespoons minced ginger

3 cloves garlic, sliced thinly

3 cups sliced bok choy

1 cup sliced onion

1 cup sliced celery

1 cup julienned carrot

recipe tip:

Prepare the Asian Noodles with Broccoli and Asian Noodles with Chicken recipes to the point where you add the Base Recipe, before starting to cook the Base Recipe.

Cook the noodles according to package directions; drain and set aside.

In a medium bowl, stir together the broth, mirin, soy sauce, cornstarch, and sugar; set aside.

In a wok or large skillet, heat the oil over high heat. Add the ginger and garlic; cook, stirring, 10 seconds. Add the bok choy, onion, celery, and carrot; cook, stirring, until vegetables are tender-crisp, about 3 minutes. Stir in the soy sauce mixture. Cook, stirring, until mixture comes to a boil. Add the noodles and toss. Reserve half of the Base Recipe for the Asian Noodles with Broccoli recipe.

Asian Noodles with Broccoli

$^1/_2$ cup slivered almonds

1 tablespoon vegetable oil

4 cups broccoli florets

$^1/_4$ teaspoon crushed red pepper flakes, optional

Preheat the oven to 350°F. Place the almonds on a baking sheet and bake until lightly toasted, about 10 minutes.

In a large skillet, heat the oil over high heat. Add the broccoli and red pepper flakes, if using, and cook, stirring, until tender-crisp, about 3 minutes. Add the almonds and the reserved Base Recipe to the broccoli mixture in the skillet. Cook over medium-high heat, stirring, until heated through.

serves 2 to 3

Asian Noodles with Chicken

8 ounces skinless, boneless chicken breast

1 teaspoon soy sauce

1 tablespoon vegetable oil

Slice the chicken into thin, $^1/_4$ inch strips. In a medium bowl, toss the chicken with the soy sauce.

In a large skillet, heat the oil over high heat. Add the chicken and cook, stirring, until cooked through, about 2 minutes. Add the remaining Base Recipe to the chicken in the skillet and cook, stirring, until heated through.

serves 2 to 3

Tofu Tempura & Shrimp Tempura

Some of the vegetables I like for tempura are thinly sliced carrots, sweet potatoes, or butternut squash; whole green beans; and strips of bell peppers. You can use other vegetables as well, such as eggplant, scallions, broccoli, and cauliflower. Seltzer is added to the batter to make it light and gives a crispy finish.

BASE RECIPE

Dipping Sauce:

2 tablespoons water

1¹/₂ tablespoons soy sauce

1 tablespoon mirin (rice wine) or dry sherry

1 teaspoon thinly sliced scallion

1 teaspoon ginger, minced

1 teaspoon sugar

1 clove garlic, minced

> **recipe tip:**
> *You can fry the shrimp and vegetables in two different pots, or fry the vegetables and tofu first, then cook the shrimp in the same oil.*

Tempura:

³/₄ cup all-purpose flour

2 tablespoons cornstarch

1 egg yolk

1 cup seltzer or club soda

4 cups assorted cut-up vegetables (see headnote, above)

Vegetable oil, for deep frying

To prepare the dipping sauce:

In a small bowl, stir together the water, soy sauce, mirin, scallion, ginger, sugar, and garlic. Let stand 1 hour for the flavors to blend.

To prepare the tempura batter:

In a medium bowl or on a piece of wax paper, stir together the flour and cornstarch, set aside. In a medium bowl, lightly beat the egg yolk. Stir in the seltzer until just combined. Combine the flour with the egg mixture, using a pastry cutter in an up-and-down motion (there will be lumps).

To cook the tempura:

In a 3-quart pot, pour the oil to a depth of 2 inches and heat over medium-high heat to 375°F (a small piece of tempura will rise to the surface after 10 seconds). Dip several of the assorted vegetables in the tempura batter. Carefully add the vegetables to the hot oil and cook, turning once, until golden brown, about 3 minutes. Drain on paper towels. Repeat with remaining vegetables, being careful not to overcrowd the pot and allowing the oil temperature to return to 375°F between batches.

Serve half of the vegetables and the dipping sauce with each of the tempura recipes.

Tofu Tempura

Two 4-ounce cakes tofu

2 teaspoons soy sauce

Cut the tofu into 1-inch cubes. Put in a medium bowl with the soy sauce and let stand 10 minutes, tossing once or twice; drain.

Dip the tofu in the tempura batter. Carefully add the tofu to the hot oil and fry, turning once, if necessary, until crispy and cooked through, about 2 minutes.

serves 2

Shrimp Tempura

$1/2$ pound jumbo shrimp

Peel and de-vein the shrimp, leaving the tail intact. Dip the shrimp into the batter. Carefully add the shrimp to the hot oil and fry, turning once, if necessary, until crispy and cooked through, about 2 minutes.

serves 2

Ants Climbing a Tree with TVP
& Ants Climbing a Tree

An odd name for a delicious dish, but hey, I didn't name it—this is a translation of the Chinese. You can find black bean sauce (thick and very salty) in the Asian-food section of your supermarket. Texturized Vegetable Protein (TVP) can be purchased in any health food store.

BASE RECIPE

1/2 cup sliced (1/2-inch) scallion	1 teaspoon chili oil
3 tablespoons soy sauce	1 teaspoon sugar
3 tablespoons mirin (rice wine) or dry sherry	1/4 teaspoon ground ginger
1 tablespoon sesame oil	12 ounces lo mein noodles or thin spaghetti

In a medium bowl, combine the scallion, soy sauce, mirin, sesame oil, chili oil, sugar, and ginger; set aside.

Cook the noodles according to package directions; drain. Return noodles to the pot and toss with soy sauce mixture. Reserve half of the Base Recipe for the Ants Climbing a Tree recipe.

Ants Climbing a Tree with TVP

1/4 cup TVP

1/4 cup hot vegetable broth (page xi or store-bought)

2 teaspoons black bean sauce

1 teaspoon soy sauce

In a medium bowl combine the TVP, broth, black bean sauce, and soy sauce, let stand 10 minutes until TVP has absorbed the liquids. Add the TVP mixture to the Base Recipe still in the pot. Cook over medium heat, stirring, until heated through.

serves 2 to 3

Ants Climbing a Tree

1/2 pound ground pork

1 1/2 teaspoons soy sauce

1 teaspoon black bean sauce

In a large skillet, cook the pork over medium high heat until no longer pink, about 3 minutes. Stir in the soy sauce and black bean sauce. Add the reserved Base Recipe noodles and cook, stirring, until heated through.

serves 2 to 3

Tofu Teriyaki & Chicken Teriyaki

*I fried the tofu in this recipe to add a crispiness that gives
a nice contrast to the soft tofu texture.*

BASE RECIPE

2 tablespoons soy sauce

$^1/_4$ cup sake, mirin (rice wine), or dry sherry

1 tablespoon thinly sliced scallion

$1^1/_2$ teaspoons sugar

$1^1/_2$ teaspoons minced ginger

> **recipe tip:**
> *Fry the tofu while the chicken is broiling.*

In a medium bowl, combine the soy sauce, sake, scallion, sugar, and ginger. Set aside 3 tablespoons of the Base Recipe for the Chicken Teriyaki.

Tofu Teriyaki

Two 4-ounce cakes firm tofu

$^1/_4$ cup cornstarch

Vegetable oil, for deep frying

Cut the tofu into 1-inch cubes. In a medium bowl, toss the tofu with the remaining Base Recipe. Let stand 10 minutes, turning occasionally; drain. Toss the cubes in the cornstarch to coat.

Pour the oil into a 2-quart saucepan to a depth of 2-inches. Heat over medium-high heat to 375°F, or until oil bubbles when a small piece of tofu is dropped in. Carefully add the tofu cubes, a few at a time, into the oil. Cook, turning once if necessary, until tofu turns a slightly tan color, about 2 minutes. Remove from skillet and drain on paper towels.

serves 2

Chicken Teriyaki

$^1/_2$ to $^3/_4$ pound skinless, boneless chicken breast, cubed

Preheat the broiler.

In a medium bowl, toss the chicken cubes in the reserved Base Recipe, let stand 10 minutes, turning occasionally. String the chicken onto four 8-inch metal skewers. Broil the skewers, brushing occasionally with any remaining marinade, until completely cooked, 3 to 4 minutes per side.

serves 2

Asian Tofu & Asian Salmon

If you can't find fresh salmon, this recipe is just as delicious on many other types of fish.
Try it on swordfish, tuna, halibut, or any other firm fleshed fish.

BASE RECIPE

$1/4$ cup chopped scallion

2 tablespoons soy sauce

2 tablespoons mirin (rice wine) or dry sherry

1 tablespoon minced ginger

1 tablespoon sugar

1 teaspoon sesame oil

1 tablespoon vegetable oil

2 cloves garlic, minced

1 cup snow peas

1 cup sliced red bell pepper

1 cup mung bean sprouts

One 16-ounce can straw mushrooms

recipe tip:
Prepare the marinade, then marinate and cook the tofu and salmon before you sauté the vegetables in the Base Recipe.

In small bowl, stir together the scallion, soy sauce, mirin, ginger, sugar, and sesame oil. Reserve 2 tablespoons of the marinade.

In a large skillet, heat the vegetable oil over high heat. Add the garlic and cook, stirring, 10 seconds. Add the snow peas and bell peppers. Cook, stirring, until vegetables are tender-crisp, about 2 minutes. Add the remaining marinade, bean sprouts, and straw mushrooms. Cook, stirring, until vegetables are heated through. Reserve half of the vegetables for the Asian Salmon.

Asian Tofu

Two 4-ounce cakes tofu

3 tablespoons cornstarch

Vegetable oil for deep frying

Cut each cake of the tofu into 4 pieces. Marinate them in a medium bowl with 1 tablespoon of the reserved marinade for at least 10 minutes; drain. Toss the tofu in the cornstarch to coat.

Pour the oil to the depth of $1^{1}/_{2}$ to 2 inches in a $1^{1}/_{2}$-quart saucepan. Heat the oil over medium-high heat, to 375°F, or until oil bubbles when a little cornstarch is thrown in. Fry tofu, a few cubes at a time, until slightly brown and crispy, about 4 to 5 minutes. Remove the tofu from the oil and drain on paper towels. Repeat with the remaining tofu. Stir the fried tofu into the remaining Base Recipe still in the skillet. Cook over medium-heat until heated though.

serves 2

Double the Asian Tofu recipe and serve
with all of the Base Recipe.

Asian Salmon

$^{3}/_{4}$ to 1 pound salmon fillet

Place the salmon in a medium bowl with 1 tablespoon of the reserved Base Recipe marinade; let stand 10 minutes, turning once.

Preheat the broiler.

Broil the salmon on a baking pan, for 5 minutes or to desired doneness. Serve with the reserved Base Recipe.

serves 2

Double the Asian Salmon recipe using both tablespoons of the Base Recipe marinade and serve
it with all of the Base Recipe vegetables.

Sukiyaki & Beef Sukiyaki

Sukiyaki Bean threads and dried shiitaki mushrooms can be purchased in Asian markets or sometimes in the ethnic ingredients sections of your local supermarket. If you can't find dried shiitaki mushrooms, you can substitute fresh, just skip the soaking instruction.

BASE RECIPE

3^1/$_2$ ounce package bean threads

^{1}/$_2$ cup boiling water

6 dried shiitaki mushrooms

^{1}/$_3$ cup vegetable broth (page xii or store-bought)

^{1}/$_4$ cup dark soy sauce

^{1}/$_4$ cup mirin (rice wine) or sherry

2 tablespoons sugar

1 tablespoon vegetable oil

5 to 6 scallions, cut into 2-inch lengths

12 ounces fresh spinach, rinsed thoroughly

1 cup thinly sliced carrot

One 8-ounce can sliced bamboo shoots, drained

> **recipe tip:**
> *Prepare the marinade in the Base Recipe, then marinate the tofu before you prepare the rest of the Base Recipe.*

In a medium bowl, soak bean threads in boiling water to cover for 15 minutes or until softened; drain and set aside.

While the bean threads are soaking, combine the mushrooms and ^{1}/$_2$ cup boiling water in a small bowl and let stand for 5 minutes; drain, reserving the soaking liquid. Halve the mushrooms, discarding the tough stems; set aside.

In a medium bowl, stir together the broth, soy sauce, mirin, sugar, and reserved soaking liquid; set aside 1 tablespoon of sauce for marinating the tofu.

In a large skillet, heat the oil over high heat. Add the scallion and cook, stirring, 30 seconds. Remove ^{1}/$_2$ of the scallions to a second large skillet, pushing them to one side of the skillet. Add half of the vegetables and noodles to each of the skillets; placing each item into a separate section of the skillet. Pour half of the soy sauce mixture into each skillet.

Sukiyaki

Two 4-ounce cakes tofu (preferably firm silken; see page xv)

Cut the tofu into ¹/₄-inch slices. Place the tofu and the tablespoon of reserved Base Recipe soy sauce mixture in a bowl and let marinate at least 5 minutes.

Add tofu to one of the skillets. Cook, covered, over high heat, until vegetables are tender-crisp, about 5 minutes.

serves 2 to 3

Reserve 2 tablespoons of the Base Recipe soy sauce mixture to marinate the tofu. Increase the tofu to 3 cakes.

note:
You will still need both skillets to accommodate all the vegetables.

Beef Sukiyaki

8 ounces tender cut of boneless beef, such as sirloin, or London broil, thinly sliced

Add the beef to one of the skillets. Cook, covered, on high heat, until vegetables are tender-crisp and beef is cooked through, about 5 minutes.

serves 2

Double the Beef Sukiyaki recipe, and use all of the Base Recipe.

note:
You will still need both skillets to accommodate all the vegetables.

Tofu Nasi Goreng & Nasi Goreng with Shrimp

Although the name may sound unfamiliar, this is really just a recipe for Indonesian fried rice.

BASE RECIPE

2 large eggs

2 tablespoons vegetable oil, divided

$^3/_4$ cup chopped onion

2 cloves garlic, minced

3 cups cooked rice

$^1/_2$ cup cooked peas

$^1/_3$ cup sliced scallion (white and green parts)

$1^1/_2$ tablespoons soy sauce

1 tablespoon molasses

$^1/_4$ teaspoon crushed red pepper flakes

Beat the eggs in a medium bowl. In a large skillet, heat 1 tablespoon of the oil over high heat. Add the eggs and cook, stirring, until fully set. Remove the eggs from skillet; chop and set aside.

Heat the remaining tablespoon of oil in the skillet over medium-high heat. Add the onion and garlic and cook, stirring, until softened, about 2 minutes. Add the chopped egg, rice, peas, scallion, soy sauce, molasses, and red pepper. Cook, stirring, until heated through. Reserve half of the Base Recipe in the skillet for the Tofu Nasi Goreng.

Tofu Nasi Goreng

$^1/_2$ cup finely diced, baked or pressed tofu

2 tablespoons chopped, fresh cilantro

Stir the tofu and cilantro into the remaining Base Recipe in the skillet. Cook, stirring, over medium heat, until heated through.

serves 2

Nasi Goreng with Shrimp

$^1/_2$ pound small shrimp, peeled and de-veined

1 teaspoon soy sauce

2 teaspoons vegetable oil

1 clove garlic, minced

1 tablespoon water

In a medium bowl, combine the shrimp with soy sauce and let stand 10 minutes.

In a medium skillet, heat the oil over high heat. Add the shrimp and garlic, cook, stirring, until shrimp is cooked through, about 2 minutes. Add the reserved Base Recipe and the water and cook, stirring, until heated through, about 2 minutes.

serves 2

Tofu Satay

Chicken Satay

You can find satay in Indonesia, Thailand, and Vietnam, and possibly other countries in that region. Although satays vary from country to country, they all use a peanut-based sauce.

BASE RECIPE

Marinade:
- 2 tablespoons soy sauce
- 1 tablespoon sugar
- 1 tablespoon lime juice
- 2 cloves garlic, minced

Satay sauce:
- $^2/_3$ cup water
- $^1/_2$ cup smooth peanut butter
- 3 tablespoons soy sauce
- 3 tablespoons brown sugar
- 1 tablespoon lime juice
- 3 cloves garlic, minced
- $^1/_2$ teaspoon curry powder
- $^1/_4$ teaspoon ground red pepper (cayenne)

> **recipe tips:**
> *When basting raw chicken with sauce, do not re-use the same sauce for serving. Avoid cross-contamination by setting aside 3 tablespoons of the satay sauce for basting the chicken. Serve the remaining sauce at the table. Prepare the marinade and marinate the chicken and tofu. While they are marinating, prepare the satay sauce.*

To prepare the marinade:

In a small bowl, stir together the soy sauce, sugar, lime juice, and garlic. Reserve 2 tablespoons for the Chicken Satay recipe.

To prepare the satay sauce:

In a blender, combine the water, peanut butter, soy sauce, brown sugar, lime juice, garlic, curry powder, and red pepper. Cover and blend until smooth. Place the peanut butter mixture in a 1-quart saucepan and bring to a boil. Reduce the heat to low and simmer 5 minutes. Set aside 3 tablespoons for the Chicken Satay recipe and 3 tablespoons for the Tofu Satay recipe. Place the remaining sauce in a small serving bowl.

Tofu Satay

2 tablespoons water

2 cakes tofu, cut into 1-inch cubes

Add the water to the remaining Base Recipe marinade. Add the tofu and let stand at least 10 minutes, stirring occasionally.

Preheat the broiler.

String the tofu onto four 8-inch metal skewers and brush generously with the reserved Base Recipe satay sauce. Broil 6-inches from the heat, 3 minutes per side or until tofu is golden and glazed. Brush once with more Base Recipe satay sauce when you turn the skewers. Serve the skewers with any unused Base Recipe satay sauce on the side.

serves 2

totally *Vegetarian*

Double the Tofu Satay recipe and use with all of the Base Recipe marinade and satay sauce.

Chicken Satay

$1/2$ to $3/4$ pound skinless, boneless chicken breast, cubed

In a medium bowl, toss the chicken cubes with the reserved 2 tablespoons of the Base Recipe marinade , let stand 10 minutes tossing occasionally. Prepare the Base Recipe satay sauce.

Preheat the broiler.

String the chicken onto four 8-inch metal skewers. Place in baking pan. Spoon a little of the reserved Base Recipe satay sauce over each of the chicken skewers. Broil 6-inches from the heat for 3 minutes. Turn skewers and spoon more of the Base Recipe satay sauce onto the second side of the chicken. Broil 3 minutes longer or until chicken is cooked through. Serve with the unused Base Recipe satay sauce.

serves 2

totally *con Carne*

Double the Chicken Satay recipe and use all of the Base Recipe marinade and satay sauce.

Coriander Vegetable Kebobs
Coriander Beef Kebobs

This recipe is based on a popular street food in Thailand called Beef Heaven. You can use any combination of vegetables for these (and any of the following kebobs), but I found these to be particularly good matches with the sweet/salty marinade. Serve these skewers with brown or white rice on the side. With this dish, I especially like a short grain white rice, that cooks up sticky.

BASE RECIPE

2 tablespoons coriander seeds

3 tablespoons soy sauce

3 tablespoons packed brown sugar

1 tablespoon molasses

$1/4$ teaspoon black pepper

2 (any color) bell peppers, cut into $1^1/_2$ inch chunks

2 medium onions, quartered

Preheat the broiler.

Place the coriander seeds into a plastic bag. Using a meat pounder or the bottom of a heavy skillet, pound the seeds until crushed.

In a medium bowl, stir together the crushed seeds, soy sauce, brown sugar, molasses, and black pepper. Divide this mixture into two medium bowls. Place half of the bell peppers and onions into each bowl. Set aside one of the bowls for the Coriander Beef Kebobs recipe.

Coriander Vegetable Kebobs

1 zucchini, cut into eight 1-inch pieces

8 white mushrooms

Toss the zucchini and the mushrooms in one of the bowls containing Base Recipe. Let stand at least 10 minutes. String the vegetables alternately on four 8-inch metal skewers. Brush the skewers with any remaining marinade. Place the skewers on a greased broiling tray. Broil 4-inches from heat source, about 3 minutes. Turn, cook second side, about 3 minutes, until cooked through.

serves 2

totally Vegetarian

Double the Coriander Vegetable Kebobs recipe and use all the Base Recipe. String vegetables on 8 skewers.

Coriander Beef Kebobs

$1/2$ pound tender cut of boneless beef, such as sirloin, or London broil, cut into 1-inch cubes

1 tablespoon molasses

Toss the beef with the reserved bowl of Base Recipe. Let stand at least 10 minutes. String the beef alternately with the bell peppers and onions on each of four 8-inch skewers. Brush the skewers with any remaining marinade. Place the skewers on a greased baking tray. Broil 4-inches from heat source, about 2 to 3 minutes, until browned. Turn, cook second side until cooked to desired doneness, about 3 minutes for medium-rare.

serves 2

totally con Carne

Use 1 pound of beef and toss with 2 tablespoons of the Base Recipe plus 1 tablespoon of molasses. Use all the vegetables from the Base Recipe to string with the beef. Use 8 skewers.

Polynesian Vegetarian Kebobs
Polynesian Chicken Kebobs

Seitan is available in most health food stores. It comes in a plastic container packed in either a mild soy sauce or water. It has a chewy, "meaty" texture and a pretty neutral flavor. You can grill these kebobs, if you prefer. Serve these pretty kebobs over rice.

BASE RECIPE

¹/₃ cup pineapple juice

2 tablespoons brown sugar

1 tablespoon ketchup

1 tablespoon minced ginger

1 tablespoon cider vinegar

2 teaspoons soy sauce

1 large green bell pepper

1 large onion

Eight 1¹/₂-inch cubes fresh pineapple (about ¹/₂ of a pineapple)

recipe tip:

Prepare the coating, then the Coconut Tofu and Coconut Shrimp recipes. Return to the Base Recipe for frying instructions.

In a medium bowl combine the juice, brown sugar, ketchup, ginger, vinegar, and soy sauce. Reserve 3 tablespoons of the marinade.

Preheat the broiler.

Cut the bell pepper in half, through the stem. Discard the stem, seeds, and any ribs. Cut each half into 4 pieces. Peel the onion. Cut into 8 wedges.

Place the pineapple and all of the vegetables into the bowl with the remaining marinade and toss to coat. Let marinate at least 10 minutes.

Set aside half the marinated pineapple and vegetables for the Polynesian Vegetarian Kebob recipe, reserving any marinade as well.

Polynesian Vegetarian Kebobs

One 8-ounce container seitan (wheat gluten), drained

Cut the seitan into cubes. Toss with $1^{1}/_{2}$ tablespoons of the reserved marinade and let stand at least 10 minutes.

String the seitan and the reserved vegetables and pineapple alternately onto four 8-inch metal skewers. Broil the kebobs, brushing occasionally with the marinade, until vegetables are cooked through, about 2 to 3 minutes per side.

serves 2

Polynesian Chicken Kebobs

$^{1}/_{2}$ to $^{3}/_{4}$ pound skinless, boneless chicken, cubed

Toss with $1^{1}/_{2}$ tablespoons of the marinade and let stand at least 10 minutes.

String the chicken and the remaining vegetables and pineapple alternately onto four 8-inch metal skewers. Broil the skewers, brushing occasionally with the marinade, until vegetables are cooked through, about 2 to 3 minutes per side.

serves 2

Coconut Tofu & Coconut Shrimp

You can use chicken strips instead of shrimp, and seitan (wheat gluten, available in health food stores) instead of tofu. Dip and cook the vegetarian version before dipping the shrimp. That way, you can use the same bowl for the batter as well as the the same oil for frying.

BASE RECIPE

1 large egg, beaten

6 tablespoons milk

2 teaspoons water

$1/2$ cup all-purpose flour

1 tablespoon cornstarch

$1/4$ teaspoon salt

Two 3 $1/2$-ounce cans shredded,
   sweetened coconut (about 2$2/3$ cups)

Vegetable oil for frying

Prepare the batter: In a medium bowl, combine the egg, milk, and water. Stir in the flour, cornstarch, and salt. Place the coconut on a plate or piece of waxed paper. Set aside.

Prepare the Coconut Tofu and Coconut Shrimp recipes.

For frying: In a 3-quart saucepan, pour the oil to the depth of 2 inches and heat over high heat to 375°F or until the oil bubbles when a few crumbs are tossed in. Dip the tofu into the batter and then into the coconut. Carefully add the tofu, a few pieces at a time, to the hot oil and fry until golden, about 2 minutes. Repeat until all the tofu is fried. Dip the shrimp into the batter and then into the coconut. Carefully add the shrimp, a few pieces at a time, to the hot oil and fry until cooked through, 2 minutes.

Coconut Tofu

2 to 3 cakes tofu

1 tablespoon soy sauce

Cut the tofu into 1-inch cubes and place in a medium bowl with the soy sauce. Toss gently to coat the tofu, let stand 10 minutes, tossing occasionally. Follow frying directions in Base Recipe.

serves 2

Double the Coconut Tofu and use all of the Base Recipe.

Coconut Shrimp

$1/2$ pound large shrimp

Peel and de-vein shrimp. Follow the frying directions in the Base Recipe.

serves 2

Double the shrimp and use all of the Base Recipe.

chapter four

French

Cheese Omelet  Western Omelet

If you don't like your omelets with runny egg, cook your omelet until almost done, then place under a preheated broiler for a minute to cook the top of the omelet.

BASE RECIPE

8 large eggs

4 large egg whites

2 tablespoons water

$1/4$ teaspoon salt, or to taste

2 tablespoons butter or margarine, divided

> **recipe tip:**
> *Prepare both the cheese and western fillings before you start cooking the Base Recipe.*

In a medium bowl, beat the eggs and egg whites with the water and salt. Melt 1 tablespoon of the butter in a large, slope-sided skillet over medium-high heat. When hot, add one half of the egg mixture. Cook, lifting the edges with a spatula, tilting the skillet to let the uncooked portion flow to the skillet bottom. Cook the egg mixture to desired doneness. Spoon the western filling onto one side of the omelet. Fold other side over the filling. Slide onto a serving plate. Repeat with the remaining butter and egg mixture, using the cheese filling. Cut each omelet in half to make two servings.

Cheese Omelet

1 cup shredded cheese (any type of cheese that you like, such as Swiss, Cheddar, Fontina, Gouda, Colby, etc.)

Use to fill the omelet as directed in the Base Recipe.

serves 2

Western Omelet

2 teaspoons vegetable oil

$1/4$ cup chopped onion

$1/4$ cup chopped green bell pepper

$1/2$ cup diced ham ($1/4$-inch pieces)

$1/8$ teaspoon black pepper

In a small skillet, heat the oil over medium high heat. Add the onion and bell pepper; cook, stirring until softened, 2 to 3 minutes. Add the ham and black pepper, remove from heat. Use to fill the omelet as directed in the Base Recipe.

serves 2

Bell Pepper Piperade
Bell Peppers with Chicken

Bell pepper stir-fry mix should be available in the freezer case of your local supermarket.

BASE RECIPE

1 tablespoon olive oil

One 10-ounce bag frozen, bell pepper stir-fry mix

2 cups chopped portobello mushrooms

$^1/_2$ teaspoon dried oregano

$^1/_4$ teaspoon dried basil

In a large skillet, heat the oil over high heat. Add the stir-fry mixture and the mushrooms. Cook, stirring, until vegetables are cooked through, about 5 minutes. Stir in the oregano and basil. Place the vegetables in a strainer set over a bowl, to reserve the liquid for the Bell Peppers with Chicken recipe. Set aside $^3/_4$ cup of the Base Recipe vegetables for the Bell Pepper Piperade recipe.

Bell Pepper Piperade

3 large eggs

2 large egg whites

$^1/_4$ teaspoon salt, or to taste

$^1/_8$ teaspoon black pepper

1 tablespoon butter or margarine

In a large bowl, beat the eggs and egg whites with the salt and black pepper. Stir in the reserved Base Recipe. Melt the butter in a large skillet over medium-high heat. Add egg mixture and cook, stirring gently, until eggs begin to set, about 2 minutes, continue cooking to desired doneness.

serves 2

Bell Peppers with Chicken

8 to 12 ounces skinless, boneless chicken, cut into $^1/_2$-inch strips

1 tablespoon olive oil

2 cloves garlic, minced

$1^1/_2$ teaspoons Dijon mustard

In a small bowl, toss the chicken with the olive oil and garlic. Let stand 5 minutes. In a medium skillet, cook the chicken over medium-high heat until cooked through, 3 to 5 minutes. Add the remaining Base Recipe, reserved liquid, and mustard; cook, stirring, until liquid has reduced by half, about 5 minutes.

serves 2

Broccoli Quiche & Quiche Lorraine

To streamline the time I spend in the kitchen, I used 3-inch, frozen, unbaked tart shells for this recipe (6-inch tart shells work well, too). You can also purchase pre-made pastry dough in the refrigerated section of your supermarket, and fit it into your own tart shells. This makes putting these quiches together a snap. Of course, if you want, you can always use your favorite pastry recipe to make homemade dough. Whichever you choose, this recipe makes eight 3-inch quiches or four 6-inch quiches.

BASE RECIPE

Eight 3-inch frozen tart shells (or four 6-inch tart shells)
2 large eggs
1 cup milk
$1/4$ teaspoon salt
$1/8$ teaspoon black pepper

Preheat the oven to 425°F.

Defrost the tart shells for 15 minutes, if frozen. If using homemade, fit the pastry into eight 3-inch tart shells for four 6-inch ones) and crimp the edges, if necesary.

To prevent the crusts from rising, use pie weights or dried beans to weigh down the crusts. Bake the crusts for l0 minutes; remove the weights from the pastry when cool. Reserve half of the crusts for the Broccoli Quiche.

In a medium bowl, beat the eggs; stir in milk, salt, and black pepper. Reserve half of the egg mixture for the Broccoli Quiche recipe.

Broccoli Quiche

1 tablespoon butter

$^1/_2$ cup sliced leek (white and light green parts only), rinsed thoroughly

1 cup broccoli florets

$^1/_3$ cup shredded Cheddar cheese

Reduce oven temperature to 350°F.

In a medium skillet over medium-high heat, melt the butter. Add the leeks, and cook until softened, about 1 minute. Add the broccoli and cook, stirring, until slightly softened, about 2 minutes more.

In a medium bowl, combine the cheese and broccoli mixture. Divide the broccoli mixture evenly among the reserved Base Recipe pie crusts. Fill the crusts evenly with the reserved Base Recipe.

Bake the quiches until knife inserted in center comes out clean, 40 to 50 minutes. Cool on rack 5 minutes before slicing.

serves 2

Double the Broccoli Quiche recipe and spoon
evenly into all of the Base Recipe crusts;
fill all crusts using equal amounts of the
total Base Recipe.

Quiche Lorraine

$^1/_2$ cup diced or thinly sliced ham

$^1/_2$ cup shredded Swiss cheese

Reduce oven temperature to 350°F.

Combine the ham and cheese in a small bowl. Divide the ham mixture evenly among the remaining Base Recipe pie crusts. Divide the remaining Base Recipe evenly between the pie shells.

Bake the quiches until a knife inserted in center comes out clean, 40 to 50 minutes. Cool on rack 5 minutes before slicing.

serves 2

Double the Quiche Lorraine recipe and spoon
evenly into all of the Base Recipe crusts;
fill all crusts using equal amounts of the
total Base Recipe.

Zucchini Quiche & Sausage Quiche

Although I used Italian sausage in this recipe, you can substitute breakfast sausage links for the Italian, if you prefer. A big green salad and crusty bread rounds out this meal nicely. The serving portion for this recipe is a little small; if you've got a hungry crowd you may want to double the recipe.

BASE RECIPE

Two 6-inch frozen pie crusts, or pastry for two 6-inch crusts

$1^1/_2$ teaspoons butter or margarine

$^1/_3$ cup sliced leek (white and light green part), rinsed thoroughly

2 large eggs

1 cup milk

2 tablespoons fresh chopped basil

$^1/_4$ teaspoon dried oregano

$^1/_8$ teaspoon black pepper

Preheat the oven to 425°F.

Defrost the pie crusts for 15 minutes, if frozen. If using homemade, fit the pastry into two 6-inch pie shells and crimp the edges.

To prevent the crusts from rising, use pie weights or dried beans to weigh down the crusts. Bake the crusts for 10 minutes, removing the weights from the pastry when cool.

In a medium skillet over medium-high heat, melt the butter; add leeks; cook until softened, about 1 minute.

In a medium bowl, beat the eggs. Stir in the milk, basil, oregano, and black pepper. Add the leek. Reserve half of the Base Recipe for the Zucchini Quiche recipe.

Zucchini Quiche

$^1/_2$ cup shredded Swiss cheese

$^1/_2$ cup coarsely shredded zucchini

$^1/_8$ teaspoon salt

Reduce oven temperature to 350°F. Toss the cheese and zucchini together; place in bottom of one of the pie crusts. Season with salt. Pour the reserved half of the Base Recipe into the pie crust.

Bake the quiche until knife inserted in center comes out clean, 50 to 60 minutes. Cool on rack 5 minutes before slicing.

serves 2

Sausage Quiche

$^1/_4$ pound Italian sweet or hot sausage, casing removed, if necessary

$^1/_2$ cup shredded Fontina or Swiss cheese

Reduce oven temperature to 350°F.

Cook the sausage in a medium skillet, over medium-high heat until cooked through and no longer pink, about 4 minutes. Drain off any fat.

Place the sausage in the bottom of one pie crust, add the cheese. Pour the remaining half of the Base Recipe into the crust.

Bake the quiche until a knife inserted in center comes out clean, 50 to 60 minutes. Cool on rack 5 minutes before slicing.

serves 2

Strata Provençal & Monte Cristo Strata

A strata is somewhere between a bread pudding and a crustless quiche. I like to serve the Monte Cristo Strata with cranberry sauce or cranberry relish on the side.

BASE RECIPE

1/4 cup butter

8 slices white bread, cut into 1-inch cubes (about 4 1/2 cups cubes)

4 large eggs

1 1/2 cups milk

1/4 cup chopped, fresh parsley

1/4 cup grated Parmesan cheese

1/2 teaspoon salt, or to taste

1/8 teaspoon black pepper

Preheat the oven to 350°F. Grease two 1-quart casseroles.

Place 2 tablespoons of the butter in each casserole and place them in the oven to melt, about 7 minutes.

Add half of the bread to each casserole and toss until coated with butter.

In a medium bowl, beat together the eggs, milk, parsley, Parmesan, salt, and black pepper. Divide the egg mixture in half. Pour one half of it over the bread in each casserole and toss. Let stand for 30 minutes, tossing once or twice.

Strata Provençal

1 tablespoon olive oil

$^1/_2$ cup chopped onion

$^1/_3$ cup chopped red bell pepper

1 clove garlic, minced

$1^1/_2$ cups finely diced ($^1/_4$ inch) eggplant

$^1/_4$ teaspoon dried rosemary, crumbled

$^1/_8$ teaspoon dried thyme

In a medium skillet, heat the oil over medium-high heat. Add the onion, bell pepper, and garlic, cook, stirring until softened, about 2 minutes. Add the eggplant and cook, stirring, until softened, about 2 minutes. Stir in the rosemary and thyme. Add the vegetable mixture to one of the Base Recipe casseroles, stir gently to combine. Bake 1 hour or until a knife inserted in the center comes out clean.

serves 2

Double the Strata Provençal recipe and use all of the Base Recipe. Bake 1 hour and 15 minutes in one 2-quart casserole until a knife inserted in center comes out clean.

Monte Cristo Strata

$^1/_2$ cup cooked ham, cut into julienne strips

$^1/_2$ cup cooked turkey, cut into julienne strips

Add the ham and turkey mixture to the remaining Base Recipe casserole. Stir gently to combine. Bake 1 hour or until a knife inserted in the center comes out clean.

serves 2

Double the Monte Cristo Strata recipe and use all of the Base Recipe. Bake 1 hour and 15 minutes in one 2-quart casserole until a knife inserted in center comes out clean.

Spinach-Cheese Roulade & Roulade with Beef

You can use Boursin, or any other garlicky cream cheese–based spread in the vegetarian version.

BASE RECIPE

$^1/_4$ cup butter

$^1/_4$ cup flour

1 cup milk

6 large eggs, separated

$^1/_3$ cup plain yogurt

1 teaspoon salt

2 large egg whites

recipe tip:
Prepare the fillings while the Base Recipe is baking.

Preheat oven to 375°F. Grease a 15 $^1/_2$×10 $^1/_2$×1-inch jelly roll pan. Line the bottom of the pan with wax paper and generously grease the waxed paper; dust generously with flour.

In a medium saucepan, melt the butter over medium-high heat. Stir in the flour until smooth. Slowly add the milk, stirring constantly, and cook until mixture comes to a boil and thickens to make a white sauce, about 4 minutes.

In a large bowl, beat the egg yolks lightly. Gradually stir in the white sauce. Beat in the yogurt and salt.

In a separate large bowl, using clean beaters, beat all of the egg whites until stiff but not dry. Fold the egg whites into the egg yolk mixture. Spread into the prepared pan. Bake 25 minutes, or until puffed and golden brown. Remove the roulade from the oven; do not turn off the oven.

Turn out the roulade onto a piece of aluminum foil and peel off the waxed paper from the bottom of the roulade. Cut the roulade into half to form two $7^3/_4$ x $10^1/_2$-inch pieces. Using two spatulas, place each roulade piece onto a sheet of aluminum foil. Spread each half with one of the fillings. Roll, jelly roll style into a log. Wrap the roulade log in the aluminum foil to secure. Place each roulade on a baking sheet and bake until heated through, 20 minutes.

Spinach-Cheese Roulade

1 cup shredded Swiss cheese

$^1/_2$ cup garlic-herb cream cheese

One 10-ounce package chopped, frozen spinach, thawed and squeezed dry

In a small bowl, stir together both of the cheeses and the spinach to blend. Spread over one of the roulades.

serves 2

Double the Spinach-Cheese recipe.
Do not cut the roulade in half, but spread over entire roulade.

Roulade with Beef

$^1/_2$ pound ground beef

2 tablespoons flour

$^1/_2$ cup milk

$^1/_2$ cup shredded Swiss cheese

3 tablespoons chopped, fresh dill

$^1/_2$ teaspoon salt

In a medium skillet, brown the beef over medium heat, until no longer pink, about 3 minutes. Stir in the flour. Add the milk and cook, stirring, until mixture comes to a boil and thickens. Stir in the cheese, dill, and salt. Spread over one of the roulades.

serves 2

Double the Beef recipe. Do not cut the roulade in half, but spread over entire roulade.

Root Vegetable Crêpes & Seafood Crêpes

When preparing the crêpes, your skillet must be quite hot or the crêpes will stick to it and not come out well. You can keep the finished crêpes in a warm (200°F) oven while you fill and roll the others. You can prepare the crêpes ahead of time and reheat them at 350°F for 12 minutes.

BASE RECIPE

Crêpes:
1 1/3 cups milk
1 cup plus 1 tablespoon all-purpose flour
2 large eggs
3 tablespoons melted butter or margarine
1 teaspoon salt
Oil or melted butter

recipe tip:
Prepare the crêpe fillings while the crêpe batter rests.

Place all the ingredients into a blender or food processor fitted with a steel blade. Cover and process until smooth. Let stand 30 minutes. Prepare both the Root Vegetable filling and the Seafood filling.

Prepare the Crêpes:
Heat a 10-inch slope-sided skillet over medium heat, until a drop of water dances across the surface before evaporating. Brush the skillet lightly with oil or butter. Pour 1/4 cup batter into the skillet and immediately tilt and rotate the pan, so that a thin layer of batter spreads over the bottom. Cook until the top of the crêpe is no longer wet and shiny, and the bottom is lightly browned, about 30 seconds. Gently turn the crêpe, and cook the second side a few seconds until lightly browned. Remove the crêpe from the skillet and place on wax paper to cool. Repeat until all the crêpe batter is used, making 12 crêpes. Stack the crêpes with wax paper between each layer.

Use six of the crêpes for the Root Vegetable Crêpes and six for the Seafood Crêpes. Place about 2 tablespoons of the filling down the center of each of six crêpes. Roll to enclose. Serve immediately.

Root Vegetable Crêpes

1¹/₂ tablespoons butter

¹/₂ cup sliced leek (white and light green parts only), rinsed thoroughly

1 cup julienned carrot

1 cup julienned rutabaga (yellow turnip)

1 cup julienned sweet potato

1¹/₂ tablespoons all-purpose flour

¹/₂ cup vegetable broth (page xii or store-bought)

2 tablespoons half and half

³/₄ cup shredded Swiss cheese

2 teaspoons sherry

¹/₈ teaspoon black pepper

In a medium skillet, melt the butter over medium-high heat. Add the leek, cook, stirring until softened, about 1 minute. Add the carrot, rutabaga, and sweet potato; cook, stirring, until tender, about 5 minutes. Stir in the flour until absorbed. Stir in the broth and half and half. Cook, stirring, until mixture comes to a boil. Stir in the Swiss cheese, sherry, and black pepper. Cook, stirring, until heated through. Fill as instructed in Base Recipe.

serves 2

Seafood Crêpes

¹/₃ cup water

3 tablespoons white wine or additional water

1 tablespoon fresh lemon juice

1 bay leaf

¹/₄ pound scallops

¹/₄ pound salmon fillet (skin removed)

¹/₄ pound codfish fillet (skin removed)

1 tablespoon butter

¹/₃ cup sliced leek (white and light green parts only), rinsed thoroughly

1¹/₂ tablespoons all-purpose flour

2 tablespoons half and half

1 tablespoon snipped, fresh dill

¹/₈ teaspoon salt

¹/₂ cup shredded Swiss cheese

In a 1-quart saucepan, bring the water, wine, lemon juice, and bay leaf to a boil over medium-high heat. Add the seafood; boil. Reduce heat and simmer 4 minutes or until cooked through. Discard bay leaf. Set aside, reserving ¹/₂ cup of the cooking liquid. When cool, break up the fish pieces into large chunks; set aside.

In a 1¹/₂-quart saucepan, melt the butter over medium heat. Add the leek and cook, stirring, until softened, about 1 minute. Stir in the flour. Add the reserved liquid; cook, stirring, until mixture comes to a boil. Stir in the half and half, dill, and salt. Add the cheese and cooked seafood. Cook, stirring, until heated through and the cheese has melted, about 3 minutes. Fill as instructed in Base Recipe.

serves 2

Mushroom and Broccoli Crêpes
Chicken and Broccoli Crêpes

BASE RECIPE

1 recipe crêpes (page 122)

5 cups broccoli florets

$1^1/_2$ tablespoons butter

$^1/_2$ cup sliced leek (white and light green parts only),
  rinsed thoroughly

$1^1/_2$ tablespoons all-purpose flour

$^3/_4$ cup vegetable broth (page xii or store-bought)

2 tablespoons water

3 tablespoons Boursin or similar garlic & herb cheese

$^1/_8$ teaspoon salt

recipe tip:
While the crêpe batter is resting, prepare the remaining Base Recipe and crêpe fillings.

Prepare the Crêpe Recipe on page 122. While batter is resting, use a 2-quart saucepan to cook the broccoli in boiling water until tender, about 3 minutes; drain. Melt the butter in a 3-quart saucepan over medium-high heat. Add the leek and cook, stirring, until softened, about 1 minute. Stir in the flour. Stir in the broth and water. Cook, stirring, until mixture comes to a boil.

Add the Boursin and salt; cook, stirring, until Boursin is melted. Stir in the broccoli until heated through. Remove 1 cup for the Chicken and Broccoli Crêpes recipe.

Prepare the Crêpes:

Heat a 10-inch slope-sided skillet over medium heat, until a drop of water dances across the surface before evaporating. Brush the skillet lightly with oil or butter. Pour $^1/_4$ cup batter into the skillet and immediately tilt and rotate the pan, so that a thin layer of batter spreads over the bottom. Cook until the top of the crêpe is no longer wet and shiny, and the bottom is lightly browned, about 30 seconds. Gently turn the crêpe, and cook second side a few seconds until lightly browned. Remove the crêpe from the skillet and place on wax paper to cool. Repeat until all the crêpe batter is used, making 12 crêpes. Stack the crêpes with wax paper between each layer.

Serve six of the crêpes filled with the Mushroom and Broccoli Filling and the remaining six crêpes filled with the Chicken and Broccoli Filling.

Mushroom and Broccoli Crêpes

1 tablespoon butter

2 cups chopped mushrooms

$^1/_2$ cup shredded Swiss cheese

2 tablespoons chopped, fresh parsley

In a medium skillet melt the butter over medium-high heat. Add the mushrooms and cook, stirring, until softened, about 3 minutes. Stir in the cheese, parsley, and the remaining Base Recipe. Use to fill six of the crêpes and serve at once.

serves 2

Chicken and Broccoli Crêpes

1 tablespoon butter

1 tablespoon minced shallot

$^3/_4$ pound skinless, boneless chicken breast, thinly sliced

In a medium skillet melt the butter over medium-high heat. Add the shallot and cook, stirring, until softened, about 10 seconds. Add the chicken and cook, stirring, until cooked through, about 3 minutes. Stir in the reserved Base Recipe. Use to fill six of the crêpes and serve at once.

serves 2

Tortellini with Creamy Leek Sauce & Coquilles St. Jacques

This is a rich, delicious dish I tend to save for company. I like to serve the vegetarian recipe with filled, fresh pasta, but you can substitute 6 ounces of dried pasta, such as penne or rigatoni.

BASE RECIPE

2 tablespoons butter

$^1/_2$ cup sliced leeks, rinsed thoroughly

2 tablespoons all-purpose flour

1 cup vegetable broth (page xii or store-bought)

3 tablespoons heavy cream

$^1/_8$ teaspoon black pepper

In a 1$^1/_2$-quart saucepan, melt the butter over medium-high heat. Add the leeks and cook, stirring, until softened, about 1 minute. Stir in the flour. Add the broth, cream, and pepper; cook, stirring until mixture comes to a boil and thickens, about 3 minutes. Reserve $^1/_2$ cup for the Coquille St. Jacques recipe.

Tortellini with Creamy Leek Sauce

12 ounces fresh or frozen cheese tortellini or ravioli

1 tablespoon butter

1 cup coarsely chopped wild mushrooms, such as portobello or shiitaki

1 tablespoon water

3 tablespoons grated Parmesan cheese

2 tablespoons chopped, fresh parsley

$^1/_4$ teaspoon salt

Cook the tortellini according to package directions; drain. While the pasta is cooking, melt the butter in a 2-quart saucepan over medium-high heat. Add the mushrooms and cook, stirring, until softened, about 2 minutes. Stir in the water, scraping up any browned bits from the bottom.

Stir in the remaining Base Recipe, the cheese, parsley, and salt. Add the cooked pasta and cook, stirring, until heated through, about 2 minutes.

serves 2

Double the Tortellini with Creamy Leek Sauce recipe. Use all of the Base Recipe, adding $^1/_2$ cup of half-and-half.

Coquilles St. Jacques

1 cup water

2 tablespoons white wine

1 bay leaf

$^1/_8$ teaspoon thyme

$^1/_2$ to $^3/_4$ pound bay scallops

$^1/_3$ cup coarsely shredded Swiss cheese

$^1/_8$ teaspoon black pepper

Preheat the broiler.

In a 1-quart saucepan, bring the water, wine, bay leaf, and thyme to a boil. Add the scallops and return to a boil. Reduce heat and simmer until scallops turn opaque, about 3 minutes, drain. Remove and discard the bay leaf.

Stir the scallops into the reserved $^1/_2$ cup Base Recipe. Stir in the cheese and black pepper.

Place the scallop mixture in scallop shells or a shallow small casserole. Place under broiler, and broil until slightly browned on top and the cheese is melted, about 2 minutes.

serves 2

Double the Coquilles St. Jacques recipe and use 1 cup of the Base Recipe.

Eggplant with Apples and Leeks
Chicken with Apples and Leeks

This is very nice when served on a bed of wild rice or a wild rice pilaf.
Any variety of apple will work nicely in this recipe.

BASE RECIPE

1 tablespoon butter or margarine

2 cups peeled, coarsely chopped apple

1 cup sliced leek (white and light green parts only), rinsed thoroughly

$1/2$ teaspoon dried rosemary, crumbled

$1/8$ teaspoon dried thyme

In a large skillet melt the butter over medium high heat. Add the apple, leek, rosemary, and thyme. Cook, stirring, until softened, about 5 minutes. Set aside half of the mixture for the Chicken with Apples and Leeks recipe.

Eggplant with Apples and Leeks

1 tablespoon olive oil

4 cups diced eggplant

3 tablespoons water

2 tablespoons white wine or additional water

$^1/_4$ cup chopped, dried apricots

$^1/_4$ cup chopped cashews

2 tablespoons raisins

1 tablespoon honey

1 tablespoon balsamic vinegar

$^1/_8$ teaspoon salt

$^1/_8$ teaspoon black pepper

In a large skillet, heat the oil over medium-high heat. Add the eggplant and cook, stirring, until the oil is absorbed, 1 minute. Add the water and wine; cook, stirring, until liquid is absorbed, 3 to 4 minutes. Stir in the remaining Base Recipe, apricots, cashews, raisins, honey, vinegar, salt, and black pepper. Cook, stirring, until heated through, about 2 minutes.

serves 2

Chicken with Apples and Leeks

1 tablespoon butter or margarine

$^1/_2$ to $^3/_4$ pound skinless, boneless chicken breast, cubed

1 tablespoon all-purpose flour

$^1/_2$ cup chicken or vegetable broth (page xii or store-bought)

1 tablespoon heavy cream

$^1/_8$ teaspoon salt

In a 1 $^1/_2$-quart saucepan, melt the butter over medium-high heat. Add the chicken and cook, stirring, until cooked through, about 3 minutes. Stir in the flour. Add the broth and cook, stirring, until mixture comes to a boil. Stir in the remaining Base Recipe, cream, and salt. Cook, stirring, until heated through.

serves 2

Eggplant Stew  Chicken Stew

*You can substitute 2 cups of wild mushrooms—such as porcini, shiitaki, portobello, or cremini—
for 2 cups of the white mushrooms for a more intense flavor.*

BASE RECIPE

1 tablespoon butter or margarine

1 cup sliced leek (white and light green parts only), rinsed thoroughly

3 cloves garlic, minced

4 $^1/_2$ cups sliced white mushrooms

3 cups coarsely chopped tomatoes

2 tablespoons white wine

1 bay leaf

$^1/_4$ teaspoon thyme

$^1/_4$ teaspoon salt

$^1/_2$ cup pitted, sliced black olives

$^1/_4$ cup chopped, fresh parsley

> **recipe tip:**
> *Prepare the Chicken Stew
> before the Eggplant Stew.*

In a 3-quart saucepan, melt the butter over medium-high heat. Add the leeks and garlic; cook, stirring until softened, about 1 minute. Add the mushrooms and cook, stirring, until softened, about 3 minutes. Add the tomatoes and cook, stirring, until mixture comes to a boil. Stir in the wine, bay leaf, thyme, and salt. Return to a boil; reduce heat and simmer, uncovered, 10 minutes. Remove and discard the bay leaf. Stir in olives and parsley. Remove 1 cup for the Chicken Stew recipe.

Eggplant Stew

4 cups cubed eggplant

$^1/_2$ teaspoon sugar

Add the eggplant and sugar to the remaining Base Recipe still in the saucepan. Bring to a boil; reduce heat and simmer, covered, 20 minutes, until eggplant is tender.

serves 2

totally *Vegetarian*

Double the Eggplant Stew recipe and use all of the Base Recipe.

Chicken Stew

2 to 4 chicken legs, thighs, and/or drumsticks

2 tablespoons all-purpose flour

1 tablespoon butter or margarine

Dredge the chicken legs in the flour. In a medium skillet, melt the butter over medium-high heat. Add the chicken and cook, until browned on all sides, about 6 minutes. Add the reserved 1 cup of the Base Recipe to the chicken. Simmer, covered, 25 minutes or until chicken is cooked through.

serves 2 to 3

totally *con Carne*

Double the Chicken Stew recipe and use 2 cups of the Base Recipe.

Ratatouille Polenta Pie
Ratatouille Stuffed Chicken Breast

For an easier vegetarian recipe, prepare the ratatouille and just serve it over cooked polenta or couscous, instead of preparing the "pie." I use instant polenta, which can be found in supermarkets and gourmet shops.

BASE RECIPE

2 tablespoons olive oil

1 cup coarsely chopped onion

$1/_2$ cup cubed red bell pepper

$1/_2$ cup cubed green bell pepper

3 cloves garlic, minced

3 cups cubed (1-inch) eggplant

1 cup sliced zucchini or yellow squash

3 cups peeled tomato wedges (4-6 tomatoes)

$1/_3$ cup chopped, fresh parsley

1 tablespoon dry vermouth or water

$1/_4$ teaspoon dried rosemary, crumbled

$1/_4$ teaspoon dried thyme

$1/_4$ teaspoon salt, to taste

$1/_8$ teaspoon black pepper

r e c i p e   t i p :

To peel a tomato easily, lightly cut an X into the skin. Drop the tomato into boiling water for 30 seconds, then place the tomato into an ice water bath. The skin should slip off immediately. Prepare the polenta according to package directions while the Base Recipe is simmering for 20 minutes.

Preheat oven to 350°. In a large skillet, heat the oil over medium-high heat. Add the onion, both bell peppers, and the garlic. Cook, stirring, 1 minute. Add the eggplant and zucchini, cook, stirring, until softened, 4 minutes. Add the tomatoes, parsley, vermouth, rosemary, thyme, salt, and black pepper. Bring to a boil, stirring frequently. Reduce heat and simmer, stirring occasionally, 20 minutes. Reserve $2/_3$ cup of the Base Recipe for the Ratatouille Stuffed Chicken Breast.

Ratatouille Polenta Pie

$^1/_2$ cup plain dry bread crumbs

1 tablespoon melted butter or margarine

$^1/_2$ cup finely shredded Swiss cheese

2 tablespoons grated Parmesan cheese

1 cup cooked polenta (coarsely ground cornmeal)

Generously grease a 7-inch springform pan. In a medium bowl stir together the bread crumbs and butter until completely combined. Add both Swiss and Parmesan cheeses, mix well; set aside. Spread the polenta over the bottom of the pan. Spread the remaining Base Recipe over the polenta. Sprinkle with the bread crumb mixture and pat to form a crust. Bake 30 minutes or until topping is browned and pie is heated through.

serves 2 to 3

Use all the Base Recipe in the filling; increase the cooked polenta to $1^1/_2$ cups and use an 8-inch springform pan.

Ratatouille Stuffed Chicken Breast

3 tablespoons fresh bread crumbs

Two 6-ounce skinless, boneless chicken breast halves

1 tablespoon olive oil

1 tablespoon fresh lemon juice

1 tablespoon dry white wine

1 clove garlic, minced

$^1/_8$ teaspoon dried rosemary, crumbled

$^1/_8$ teaspoon paprika

$^1/_8$ teaspoon salt

In a medium bowl, stir together the reserved $^2/_3$ cup of the Base Recipe and the bread crumbs. Cut a pocket into each of the chicken breasts. Place half of the ratatouille mixture into each of the pockets. Secure with toothpicks. In a small bowl, stir together the oil, lemon juice, wine, garlic, rosemary, paprika, and salt. Place the stuffed chicken breasts into an 8-inch square baking pan. Brush both sides of the stuffed breast with the wine mixture. Bake for 40 minutes, brushing occasionally with additional wine mixture.

serves 2

Double the Ratatouille Stuffed Chicken Breast recipe. Serve any additional ratatouille spooned over the chicken breasts, using $1^1/_3$ cups of the ratatouille to fill the breasts.

Parsnip, Potatoes, and Leeks Au Gratin
Chicken with Potatoes and Leeks

You can use shredded Swiss or Jarlsberg instead of the Gruyère.

BASE RECIPE

$^1/_4$ cup plain dry bread crumbs

1 tablespoon melted butter or margarine

6 cups peeled, sliced baking potatoes

2 tablespoons butter

$1^1/_2$ cups sliced leek (white and light green parts only),
  rinsed thoroughly

1 clove garlic, minced

3 tablespoons all-purpose flour

$1^3/_4$ cups milk

1 cup shredded Gruyère cheese

3 tablespoons grated Parmesan cheese

$^1/_4$ teaspoon salt

$^1/_8$ teaspoon black pepper

Preheat oven to 350°F. In a medium bowl, combine the bread crumbs and the melted butter and toss to combine. Reserve half for the Chicken with Potatoes and Leeks recipe. In a large pot of boiling water, cook the potatoes until tender, 5 to 7 minutes; drain.

In a $1^1/_2$-quart saucepan, melt the 2 tablespoons of butter over medium-high heat. Add the leeks and garlic; cook, stirring, until softened, about 1 minute. Stir in the flour. Add the milk and cook, stirring, until mixture comes to a boil. Add both cheeses and cook, stirring, until melted. Stir in the potatoes, salt, and black pepper. Reserve half for the Parsnip, Potatoes, and Leeks Au Gratin recipe.

Parsnip, Potatoes, and Leeks Au Gratin

1 cup peeled, sliced ($^1/_4$ inch) parsnip

Grease a 1-quart casserole.

Cook the parsnip in boiling water until tender, 7 minutes; drain.

In a medium bowl combine the cooked parsnip with the reserved half of the Base Recipe. Pour the mixture into the casserole. Sprinkle with the remaining half of the bread crumbs from the Base Recipe. Bake 20 minutes or until bread crumbs are browned and mixture is bubbly.

serves 2

totally Vegetarian

Double the Parsnip, Potatoes, and Leeks Au Gratin recipe and use the entire Base Recipe. Bake in a 2-quart casserole, topping the casserole with all of the Base Recipe bread crumb mixture.

Chicken with Potatoes and Leeks

1 tablespoon vegetable oil
Two 6-ounce skinless, boneless chicken cutlets

Grease a 1-quart casserole.

In a large skillet, heat the oil over medium-high heat. Add the chicken and cook, stirring, until lightly browned and cooked through, about 5 minutes. Slice the cooked chicken into strips and stir into the remaining half of the Base Recipe. Pour the mixture into the casserole. Top with the reserved half of the Base Recipe bread crumbs. Bake 20 minutes, or until bread crumbs are browned and mixture is bubbly.

serves 2

totally con Carne

Double the Chicken with Potatoes and Leeks recipe and use the entire Base Recipe. Bake in a 2-quart casserole, using all the Base Recipe bread crumb mixture.

Tempeh with Tomato-Leek Sauce
Flounder with Tomato-Leek Sauce

You can find tempeh, which is a "cake" made of fermented soybeans and/or grains, in the refrigerator case of any health food store.

BASE RECIPE

1 tablespoon olive oil
³/₄ cup sliced leek, rinsed thoroughly
1 clove garlic, minced
3 cups chopped tomato

In a 1¹/₂-quart saucepan, heat the oil over medium-high heat. Add the leek and garlic; cook, stirring, until softened, about 2 minutes. Add the tomatoes; bring to a boil. Reduce heat and simmer, uncovered, over medium heat 30 minutes, stirring, occasionally. Set aside ³/₄ cup for the Tempeh with Tomato-Leek Sauce recipe.

Tempeh with Tomato-Leek Sauce

Vegetable oil for frying
One 8-ounce package tempeh
¹/₂ teaspoon soy sauce
¹/₂ teaspoon sesame oil

Pour the oil to ¹/₂-inch deep in a large skillet and heat over medium-high heat until the oil sizzles when a small piece of tempeh is thrown in. Add the tempeh and cook until golden on each side, about 2 minutes per side; drain.

Add the soy sauce and sesame oil to the reserved Base Recipe. Serve over the tempeh.

serves 2

Flounder with Tomato-Leek Sauce

Two 6-ounce flounder fillets
1 tablespoon all-purpose flour
1 tablespoon olive oil
2 tablespoons white wine
1 teaspoon chopped capers
¹/₈ teaspoon salt

Dredge the flounder fillets in the flour. Heat the oil in a large skillet over medium-high heat. Add the flounder and cook until browned on both sides and cooked through, about 2 minutes per side. While the flounder is cooking, add the wine, capers, and salt to the remaining Base Recipe. Boil, serve over the flounder.

serves 2

chapter five

Italian

Linguine with Red Pepper–Tomato Sauce & Linguine with Red Clam Sauce

Although I use only chopped clams in this recipe, you can dress up the dish by steaming some fresh clams and serving them with the pasta. For the red pepper sauce, you can use jarred, roasted red peppers instead of starting from fresh, but you may want to add 1 teaspoon extra sugar to the recipe.

BASE RECIPE

1 tablespoon olive oil

1 cup chopped onion

3 cloves garlic, minced

One 14^1/$_2$-ounce can whole, peeled tomatoes, undrained

^{1}/$_3$ cup red wine

^{1}/$_4$ cup tomato paste

^{1}/$_2$ teaspoon dried oregano

^{1}/$_4$ teaspoon salt

^{1}/$_4$ teaspoon black pepper

12 ounces linguine

recipe tip:
Roast the red bell peppers before you start the Base Recipe. Let them cool while you prepare the Base Recipe. Also, while the pasta is cooking, prepare the tomato and clam sauces.

In a 3-quart saucepan, heat the oil over medium-high heat. Add the onion and garlic. Let cook, stirring, until softened, about 2 minutes. Stir in the tomatoes with their liquid, breaking them up with the back of a spoon. Stir in the wine, tomato paste, oregano, salt, and black pepper. Bring to a boil, reduce heat and simmer, uncovered, 10 minutes or until sauce is thickened. Reserve 1 cup for the Linguine with Red Pepper–Tomato Sauce recipe.

Cook linguine according to package directions; drain. Divide the pasta in half.

Linguine with Red Pepper–Tomato Sauce

1 red bell pepper

2 tablespoons water

$^1/_2$ teaspoon sugar

$^1/_8$ teaspoon dried thyme

Preheat the broiler.

Cut the bell pepper in half lengthwise. Discard the seeds and ribs. Place the bell pepper halves on a foil-lined pan and broil 4 to 6 inches from the heat until quite charred, 5 minutes. Turn and cook until second side is charred, 5 minutes more. Roll up the foil to form a package, seal the edges and set it aside to cool.

Peel and discard skin from the cooled bell pepper. Place the bell peppers, sugar, thyme, and reserved Base Recipe into a blender or food processor and purée until smooth.

Place the purée in a 1-quart pot. Cook over medium heat until heated through, about 5 minutes. Serve over half of the Base Recipe linguine.

serves 2 to 3

Linguine with Red Clam Sauce

One 6$^1/_2$-ounce can minced clams, undrained

Stir the clams and their liquid into the pot with the remaining Base Recipe. Return to boil; reduce heat and simmer 5 minutes. Serve over the remaining half of the Base Recipe linguine.

serves 2 to 3

Pasta with Mushroom-Tomato Sauce
Pasta with Sausage-Mushroom Sauce

Instead of using plain pasta, try a filled pasta such as tortellini, agnoletti, or ravioli,
but note that you will have to increase the amount of pasta to 16 to 20 ounces.

BASE RECIPE

1^1/$_2$ tablespoons olive oil

3 cups sliced, white mushrooms

1 cup chopped onion

3 cloves garlic, minced

4 cups chopped tomatoes

2 tablespoons tomato paste

2 tablespoons red wine, optional

^{1}/$_3$ cup chopped, fresh parsley

1 bay leaf

1 teaspoon dried oregano

^{1}/$_2$ teaspoon dried basil

^{1}/$_2$ teaspoon sugar

^{1}/$_2$ teaspoon salt

12 ounces medium pasta (such as penne, ziti, or rigatoni)

recipe tip:
Cook the sausage and pasta while the Base Recipe is simmering.

In a 3-quart saucepan, heat the oil over medium-high heat. Add the mushrooms, onion, and garlic. Let cook, stirring, until vegetables are softened, about 3 minutes. Stir in the tomatoes, tomato paste, wine, if using, parsley, bay leaf, oregano, basil, sugar, and salt. Bring to a boil, reduce heat and simmer, uncovered, 20 minutes or until sauce is thickened. Discard bay leaf from sauce. Set aside 1^1/$_4$ cups sauce for the Pasta with Sausage-Mushroom Sauce recipe.

Meanwhile, cook pasta according to package directions; drain and divide in half.

Pasta with Mushroom-Tomato Sauce

1 cup cooked peas

Add the peas to the remaining Base Recipe in the saucepan; cook over medium-high heat. Add half of the pasta and cook until heated through.

serves 2 to 3

Pasta with Sausage-Mushroom Sauce

8 ounces bulk or link Italian sausage

$^1/_3$ cup water

2 tablespoons tomato paste

Remove the sausage from casing, if necessary. Cook in a medium skillet over medium-high heat, until no longer pink, 3 to 4 minutes. Stir in the reserved $1^1/_4$ cups Base Recipe, water, and tomato paste. Cook, stirring, until thickened, about 3 minutes. Add the remaining half of the cooked pasta; cook, until heated through.

serves 2 to 3

Bulgur and Beans & Spaghetti and Meatballs

BASE RECIPE

1 tablespoon olive oil

1 cup chopped onion

3 cloves garlic, minced

One 14$^{1}/_{2}$-ounce can whole, peeled tomatoes, undrained

$^{1}/_{4}$ cup water

3 tablespoons tomato paste

$^{3}/_{4}$ teaspoon sugar

$^{1}/_{2}$ teaspoon dried oregano

$^{1}/_{2}$ teaspoon dried basil

$^{1}/_{4}$ teaspoon salt

$^{1}/_{8}$ teaspoon black pepper

recipe tip:
While the sauce is cooking, prepare the meatballs and cook the spaghetti.

In a 2-quart saucepan, heat the oil over medium-high heat. Add the onion and garlic; cook, stirring, until softened, about 1 to 2 minutes. Stir in the tomatoes with their liquid, breaking up the tomatoes with the back of a spoon. Stir in the water, tomato paste, sugar, oregano, and basil. Bring to a boil; reduce the heat and simmer, covered, 15 minutes or until thickened. Stir in the salt and black pepper. Reserve half of the Base Recipe for the Spaghetti and Meatballs recipe.

Bulgur and Beans

1 cup cooked bulgur

$^1/_2$ cup cooked (page xi) or canned, rinsed cannellini beans (white kidney beans)

$^1/_2$ cup chopped artichoke hearts

Add the bulgur, beans, and artichoke hearts to the remaining Base Recipe in the saucepan. Cook over medium-high heat, stirring occasionally, until heated through.

serves 2

Spaghetti and Meatballs

$^1/_2$ pound ground beef

1 tablespoon plain dry bread crumbs

$^1/_2$ teaspoon dried oregano

$^1/_4$ teaspoon salt

6 ounces spaghetti

In a medium bowl, combine the beef, bread crumbs, oregano, and salt. Form into 1-inch balls.

In a 2-quart saucepan, combine the reserved Base Recipe and meatballs. Bring to a boil over medium-high heat; reduce heat and simmer 5 to 7 minutes or until the meatballs are cooked through.

Meanwhile, cook the spaghetti according to package directions, drain. Serve the sauce and meatballs over the spaghetti.

serves 2

Pasta with Pesto and Sun-Dried Tomatoes &
Pesto Chicken and Vegetables

If you are in a hurry or, if fresh basil is not available, you can save time by using store-bought pesto instead of making the Base Recipe yourself. You will need $1/3$ cup of pesto.

BASE RECIPE

$1/2$ cup firmly-packed, fresh basil leaves

3 tablespoons olive oil

2 cloves garlic, minced

$1/3$ cup grated Parmesan cheese

> **recipe tip:**
> *Prepare the Pesto Chicken and Vegetables recipe while the pasta is cooking.*

Place the basil, oil, and garlic into the bowl of a food processor. Cover and process until basil and garlic are finely chopped. Stir in the Parmesan cheese. Set aside 3 tablespoons of the Base Recipe for the Pasta with Pesto and Sun-Dried Tomatoes recipe.

Pasta with Pesto and Sun-Dried Tomatoes

6 ounces penne pasta or any medium pasta

2 tablespoons pignoli nuts (pine nuts)

$1/4$ cup chopped sun-dried tomatoes packed in oil

Cook the pasta according to package directions; drain.

Meanwhile, toast the pignoli nuts in a dry skillet, stirring constantly, until slightly browned, about 2 minutes; set aside.

Place the pasta, pignoli nuts, tomatoes, and reserved Base Recipe into a serving bowl, toss to combine.

serves 2

Pesto Chicken and Vegetables

1 tablespoon olive oil

2 cups julienned yellow squash

$3/4$ pound skinless, boneless chicken breast, sliced $1/2$-inch thick

1 tablespoon white wine

Salt and pepper, to taste

In a large skillet, heat the oil over medium-high heat.

Add the squash and cook, stirring, until just tender-crisp, about 1 minute. Add the chicken and wine; cook, stirring, until chicken is cooked through and any liquid has evaporated, 7 to 9 minutes. Stir in the salt, black pepper, and remaining Base Recipe sauce.

serves 2 to 3

Penne with Arugula and Bean Sauce

Swordfish with Bean Sauce

You can substitute 2 cups of bite-sized escarole pieces for the arugula and any firm-fleshed white fish for the swordfish.

BASE RECIPE

2 tablespoons olive oil

1 bunch arugula (about 6 ounces)

3 cloves garlic, slivered

$1^1/_2$ tablespoons all-purpose flour

$^3/_4$ cup vegetable broth (page xii or store-bought)

$1^1/_2$ cups cooked (page xii) or canned, rinsed cannellini beans

$^1/_4$ chopped, sun-dried tomatoes, packed in oil

$^1/_8$ teaspoon black pepper

In a medium skillet, heat the oil over medium-high heat.

Add the arugula and garlic. Cook, stirring, until arugula is wilted, about 1 minute. Stir in the flour until absorbed. Stir in the vegetable broth and cook, stirring, until thickened. Stir in the beans, sun-dried tomatoes, and black pepper. Set aside 1 cup of the Base Recipe for the Swordfish with Bean Sauce recipe.

Penne with Arugula and Bean Sauce

6 ounces ziti or other medium pasta

2 tablespoons grated Parmesan cheese

Cook pasta according to package directions; drain.

Add pasta to the remaining Base Recipe in the skillet. Cook over medium-high heat, stirring, until heated through. Top with the cheese and toss to combine.

serves 2 to 3

Swordfish with Bean Sauce

Two 8- to 10-ounce swordfish steaks, about 1 inch thick

Preheat the broiler.

Broil the swordfish about 4 to 6 inches from the heat source, 2 to 4 minutes per side, until fish flakes easily with a fork or to desired doneness. Serve topped with the reserved Base Recipe.

serves 2

Penne Arrabisaya with Kalamata Olives & Penne Arrabisaya with Sausage

This is traditionally a spicy dish. If you prefer it mild, omit the crushed red pepper.
For the sausage, you can use sweet or spicy Italian sausage. You can slice it after you cook it,
or you can remove it from the casing and cook it that way.

BASE RECIPE

- 1^1/$_2$ tablespoons olive oil
- 1^1/$_2$ cups chopped onion
- 4 cloves garlic, minced
- 3 cups chopped tomatoes
- ^{1}/$_2$ teaspoon salt
- ^{1}/$_4$ teaspoon crushed red pepper flakes
- 12 ounces penne pasta

In a 2-quart saucepan, heat the oil over medium-high heat. Add the onion and garlic and cook, stirring, until softened, about 2 minutes. Add the tomatoes, salt, and crushed red pepper. Bring to a boil.

Reduce heat and simmer, covered, 30 minutes. Reserve 1 cup of the Base Recipe from the saucepan for the Penne Arrabisaya with Sausage recipe.

Meanwhile, cook the pasta according to package directions; drain and divide in half. Set aside.

Penne Arrabisaya with Kalamata Olives

$^1/_2$ cup halved Kalamata olives

$^1/_3$ cup chopped, fresh basil

Stir the olives and basil into the remaining Base Recipe in the saucepan. Add $^1/_2$ of the cooked pasta; cook over medium-high heat, tossing, until heated through.

serves 2 to 3

Double the Penne Arrabisaya with Kalamata Olives recipe and add to the entire Base Recipe. Toss with all of the pasta.

Penne Arrabisaya with Sausage

$^1/_2$ pound spicy or sweet Italian sausage

1 tablespoon tomato paste

In a large skillet, cook the sausage until no longer pink in the center, 3 to 4 minutes. Stir in the reserved Base Recipe and tomato paste. Simmer 10 minutes. Add half of the cooked pasta. Cook, tossing, over medium-high heat until heated through.

serves 2 to 3

Double the Penne Arrabisaya with Sausage recipe. Combine with the entire Base Recipe and all the pasta.

Baked Ziti with Eggplant
& Sausage Baked Ziti

Try the Base Recipe on page 138 for a homemade sauce.

BASE RECIPE

12 ounces ziti or other medium size pasta (such as penne)

3 cups marinara sauce (page 138 or store-bought)

2 cups shredded mozzarella

$1/4$ cup grated Parmesan

Preheat the oven to 350°F.

Cook pasta according to package directions; drain. Combine the cooked pasta, sauce, mozzarella, and Parmesan in a large bowl, mix to combine. Remove half of the mixture from the bowl for the Sausage Baked Ziti recipe.

Baked Ziti with Eggplant

$1^1/2$ tablespoons olive oil

2 cups cubed ($3/4$ inch) eggplant

$1/4$ cup water

$1/2$ cup shredded mozzarella

In a large skillet, heat the oil over medium-high heat. Add the eggplant and cook, stirring, until the oil is absorbed. Add the water and cook, stirring, until the eggplant is tender, about 3 minutes. Remove from the heat and add the remaining Base Recipe.

Spoon the mixture into an 8-inch square baking pan. Sprinkle with the mozzarella cheese. Bake 25 minutes or until cheese is melted and ziti are heated through.

serves 2 to 3

Sausage Baked Ziti

$1/2$ pound Italian sweet or hot sausage, casing removed

$1/2$ cup shredded mozzarella

In a medium skillet, cook the sausage over medium-high heat, breaking it into small pieces, until completely cooked and no longer pink, about 4 minutes. Add reserved Base Recipe to the sausage (with drippings). Spoon into an 8-inch square baking pan. Sprinkle with the mozzarella cheese. Bake 25 minutes or until cheese is melted and ziti are heated through.

serves 2 to 3

Cannellini Beans Italian-Style & Codfish Italian-Style

You might want to cook up some medium pasta, such as ziti, penne,
or rigatoni to serve with these dishes.

BASE RECIPE

1 tablespoon olive oil	2 tablespoons chopped, fresh parsley
1 cup chopped onion	1 bay leaf
2 cloves garlic, minced	$1/2$ teaspoon dried oregano
One $14^1/_2$-ounce can whole, peeled tomatoes, undrained	$1/2$ teaspoon sugar
	$1/4$ teaspoon dried thyme
$1/4$ cup water	$1/4$ teaspoon salt
3 tablespoons tomato paste	$1/8$ teaspoon crushed red pepper flakes

In a 2-quart saucepan, heat the oil over medium-high heat. Add the onion and garlic. Cook, stirring, until softened, about 2 minutes. Stir in the tomatoes with their liquid, breaking them up with the back of a spoon. Stir in the water, tomato paste, parsley, bay leaf, oregano, sugar, thyme, salt, and red pepper flakes. Bring to a boil, reduce heat and simmer, uncovered, 20 minutes or until sauce is thickened. Reserve $3/4$ cup Base Recipe for the Codfish Italian-Style recipe.

Cannellini Beans Italian-Style

$1^1/2$ cups cooked (page xi) or canned, rinsed cannellini beans

Add the beans to the remaining Base Recipe in the saucepan. Cook over medium-high heat, stirring, until heated through.

serves 2

Codfish Italian-Style

$3/4$- to 1-pound codfish fillet

In a $1^1/2$-quart saucepan, combine the codfish and reserved Base Recipe. Cover and bring to a boil over medium-high heat. Reduce heat and simmer, covered, about 3 to 5 minutes or until fish is cooked through and flakes easily with a fork. Break up fish into chunks with a fork.

serves 2

Cheese Manicotti & Beef-Filled Manicotti

If you can't find manicotti shells, you can make crêpes (page 122), to enclose manicotti fillings. Top with the sauce and mozzarella (as divided).

BASE RECIPE

1 tablespoon olive oil

1 cup chopped onion

2 cloves garlic, minced

One 28-ounce can crushed tomatoes

$^1/_3$ cup water

$^1/_4$ cup chopped, fresh parsley

1 bay leaf

$^1/_2$ teaspoon dried basil

$^1/_2$ teaspoon sugar

$^1/_4$ teaspoon dried thyme

$^1/_4$ teaspoon salt

$^1/_4$ teaspoon black pepper

8 manicotti shells

1 cup shredded mozzarella cheese

> **recipe tip:**
> *While the Base Recipe is cooking, prepare the fillings. Then cook the shells (or crêpes) and stuff and bake the manicotti.*

Preheat the oven to 350°F.

In a 3-quart saucepan, heat the oil over medium-high heat. Add the onion and garlic. Let cook, stirring, until softened, about 2 minutes. Stir in the tomatoes, water, parsley, bay leaf, basil, sugar, thyme, salt, and black pepper. Bring to a boil, reduce heat and simmer, uncovered, 20 minutes or until sauce is thickened; discard the bay leaf. Reserve $^1/_4$ cup of the Base Recipe for the Beef-Filled Manicotti recipe.

While sauce is cooking, prepare both fillings and cook the pasta according to package directions; drain. Fill 4 shells with the meat filling and 4 with the cheese. Place $^1/_2$ cup of the Base Recipe in the bottom of each of two 8-inch square pans. Lay the stuffed shells in each pan. Top each pan with half of the remaining Base Recipe. Sprinkle each with $^1/_2$ cup of the mozzarella. Bake for 20 minutes or until heated through.

Cheese Manicotti

1 large egg

$^2/_3$ cup ricotta cheese

$^1/_3$ cup shredded mozzarella cheese

3 tablespoons grated Parmesan cheese

$^1/_8$ teaspoon black pepper

In a medium bowl, beat the egg. Stir in the ricotta, mozzarella, and Parmesan cheeses, and black pepper. Use to fill 4 manicotti shells as instructed in the Base Recipe. Bake and top as directed in the Base Recipe.

serves 2

Beef-Filled Manicotti

$^1/_2$ pound beef

$^1/_4$ cup chopped onion

1 clove garlic, minced

$^1/_2$ teaspoon oregano

$^1/_4$ cup ricotta cheese

2 tablespoons Parmesan

1 tablespoon tomato paste

$^1/_4$ teaspoon salt

In a medium skillet, cook the beef with the onion, garlic, and oregano until the beef is no longer pink and is cooked through, about 4 minutes. Stir in the reserved Base Recipe, ricotta and Parmesan cheeses, tomato paste, and salt. Use to fill 4 manicotti shells as directed in Base Recipe. Bake and top as directed in Base Recipe.

serves 2

Cheese-Filled Rolled Eggplant
Beef-Filled Rolled Eggplant

When cooking the eggplant, instead of frying them in oil as I suggest here, feel free to brush the slices with olive oil and broil them instead, about 3 minutes per side. The cooking method does not really matter here, as long as they are completely cooked. Use homemade sauce (page 138) or store-bought.

BASE RECIPE

2 to 3 medium eggplants (about 7-inches long)

Salt

Vegetable oil for frying

2 cups marinara sauce (page 138 or store-bought)

$2/3$ cup shredded mozzarella, divided

> **recipe tip:**
>
> *If using homemade marinara sauce, prepare that first. Salt the eggplant first, while the eggplant drains, prepare the fillings. Then cook the eggplant slices and finish the Base Recipe.*

Preheat the oven to 375°F.

Cut the eggplants lengthwise into eight $1/8$ to $1/4$-inch-thick slices, discarding the end pieces that are mostly skin. Salt each slice lightly and place in colander to drain, about 10 minutes. Rinse the salt off each slice of eggplant; pat dry. Prepare the Cheese-Filled Rolled Eggplant and Beef-Filled Rolled Eggplant recipes.

Pour the oil to a depth of $1/4$-inch in a large skillet and heat over medium-high heat. Cook the eggplant slices, in batches, until slightly brown and cooked through, about 3 minutes per side. Add more oil, if necessary.

Place 3 tablespoons of the cheese filling on the thick end of half the eggplant slices; roll to completely encase the filling. Repeat the same procedure for the beef filling and the remaining eggplant slices.

Pour $1/2$ cup of the marinara sauce into the bottom of each of two 9 x 13-inch loaf pans. Place the cheese-filled rolls, seam side down, into one of the pans and the beef-filled rolls, seam side down, into the other. Top each set of eggplant rolls with half of the remaining marinara sauce. Sprinkle $1/3$ cup mozzarella over sauce in each pan. Bake 15 to 20 minutes, uncovered, or heated through.

Cheese-Filled Rolled Eggplant

$^3/_4$ cup ricotta cheese

$^1/_3$ cup shredded mozzarella cheese

2 tablespoons grated Parmesan cheese

1 tablespoon chopped, fresh basil

1 clove garlic, minced

$^1/_8$ teaspoon black pepper

In a medium bowl, stir together the ricotta, mozzarella, Parmesan, basil, garlic, and black pepper; use to fill half of the Base Recipe eggplant slices.

serves 2

totally Vegetarian

Double the Cheese-Filled Rolled Eggplant recipe using all the Base Recipe eggplant slices. Bake in a 9-inch square pan.

Beef-Filled Rolled Eggplant

$^1/_2$ pound ground beef

$^1/_3$ cup chopped onion

3 tablespoons marinara sauce

1 tablespoon chopped, fresh basil (or $^1/_2$ teaspoon dried)

1 tablespoon tomato paste

$^1/_4$ teaspoon dried oregano

$^1/_8$ teaspoon salt

In a small skillet cook the beef with the onion over medium heat, until the beef is cooked through and no longer pink in the center, about 4 minutes. Drain off any fat or cooking liquid. Stir in the marinara sauce, basil, tomato paste, oregano, and salt. Use to fill half of the Base Recipe eggplant slices.

serves 2

totally con Carne

Double the Beef-Filled Rolled Eggplant recipe and use it to fill all the Base Recipe eggplant slices. Bake in a 9-inch square baking pan.

Cheese-Stuffed Rice Balls
& Meat-Stuffed Rice Balls

This is excellent if you use Arborio rice (Italian medium grain white rice) instead of regular white rice. You can serve this with a marinara sauce if you like.

BASE RECIPE

$^1/_2$ cup water

$^1/_2$ cup vegetable broth (page xii or store-bought)

$^1/_2$ cup white rice

$^2/_3$ cup grated Parmesan cheese

$^1/_2$ cup shredded mozzarella cheese

$^1/_2$ cup shredded Fontina cheese

1 egg

1 teaspoon water

$^1/_2$ cup plain dry bread crumbs

Vegetable oil for frying

In a 1-quart saucepan, bring the water and broth to a boil. Add the rice and simmer, covered, until water has been absorbed, 20 minutes. Stir in all of the cheeses. Set the rice aside until cool enough to handle.

Divide the rice mixture into 12 parts; 6 for the Cheese-Stuffed Rice Balls recipe and the remaining 6 for the Meat-Stuffed Rice Balls recipe. Continue with the Cheese-Stuffed Rice Balls and Meat-Stuffed Rice Balls recipes.

Beat the egg with the water in a medium bowl; set aside. Roll the Cheese-Stuffed Rice Balls in bread crumbs, then dip in the egg, than re-roll in the bread crumbs. Repeat with the Meat-Stuffed Rice Balls.

Heat the oil in a large, heavy skillet over medium-high heat to 375°F or until oil bubbles when a few bread crumbs are dropped in. Fry the Cheese-Stuffed Rice Balls a few at a time until golden. Drain on paper towels before serving. Then repeat with the Meat-Stuffed Rice Balls.

Cheese-Stuffed Rice Balls

Six 1-inch squares Fontina cheese (3 ounces)

Wrap one portion of the Base Recipe rice mixture around one square of cheese, forming a ball. Repeat until all the pieces of cheese are used up. Bread and fry as directed in the Base Recipe.

serves 2

Meat-Stuffed Rice Balls

$1/4$ pound ground beef

$1/4$ cup shredded Fontina cheese

1 tablespoon minced onion

1 tablespoon tomato paste

1 clove garlic, minced

$1/4$ teaspoon dried oregano

$1/8$ teaspoon salt

In a 2-quart saucepan, bring water to a boil.

In a medium bowl, combine the beef, cheese, onion, tomato paste, garlic, oregano, and salt. Form the meat mixture into 6 balls. Cook the meatballs in boiling water for 3 minutes; drain.

Wrap one portion of the Base Recipe rice mixture around each meatball. Bread and fry as directed in the Base Recipe.

serves 2

Spinach Risotto & Risotto with Scallops

Risotto is a somewhat time-consuming dish, since you really have to stir fairly constantly while it cooks. The end result is a creamy, slightly al dente, piece of heaven. You must use Arborio rice, available in Italian and gourmet markets, for the creamiest risotto. It is worth the trip.

BASE RECIPE

2 cups vegetable broth (page xii or store-bought)

$1^{1}/_{2}$ cups water

$^{1}/_{4}$ cup dry white wine

1 tablespoon butter

2 tablespoons minced shallots

1 cup Arborio rice

In a 2-quart saucepan, heat the broth, water, and wine until simmering. Keep the broth mixture warm on low heat.

While broth is heating, melt the butter in a 3-quart saucepan over medium heat. Add the shallots, cook, stirring, 10 seconds. Add the rice and cook, stirring, until rice is coated with oil. Add $^{1}/_{4}$ cup of the warm broth mixture to the rice mixture, stirring constantly, until the rice has absorbed the liquid. Repeat until all of the broth mixture is used up, about 30 minutes. (You should make the next addition of liquid when you can draw a clear path on the bottom of the pot as you scrape through the rice with a wooden spoon. This will happen rather quickly at first and will take longer as you near the end of the cooking time.) Remove half of the Base Recipe to a 2-quart saucepan for the Spinach Risotto recipe.

Spinach Risotto

2 cups chopped, fresh spinach, lightly packed

$^1/_4$ cup chopped, fresh parsley

$^1/_4$ teaspoon dried thyme

$^1/_4$ cup grated Parmesan cheese

Stir the spinach, parsley, and thyme into the Base Recipe in the 2-quart saucepan. Cook, stirring, until the spinach is softened, about 3 minutes. Stir in the cheese and cook, stirring, until warmed through.

serves 2

Risotto with Scallops

2 cups water

6 to 8 ounces bay scallops

2 teaspoons fresh lemon juice

1 tablespoon snipped, fresh dill

1 tablespoon grated Parmesan cheese

In a 1-quart saucepan, bring the water to a boil over medium-high heat. Add the scallops, lemon juice, and dill and return to a boil; reduce the heat and simmer until scallops are opaque, 2 to 3 minutes. Drain, reserving 3 tablespoons of the cooking liquid.

Add the scallops with their reserved cooking liquid to the remaining half of the Base Recipe in the 3-quart saucepan. Stir in the cheese; cook, stirring, until heated through, 2 minutes.

serves 2

Spaghetti Squash Primavera

Stewed Turkey Balls with Vegetables

Use ground chicken instead of the turkey, if you like.

BASE RECIPE

1 tablespoon olive oil

1 cup julienned carrots

1 cup chopped onion

2 cloves garlic, minced

2 cups broccoli florets

1 cup julienned zucchini

One 28-ounce can crushed tomatoes

$1/2$ cup vegetable broth (page xii or store-bought)

1 teaspoon dried basil

$1/4$ teaspoon dried thyme

$1/4$ teaspoon salt, or to taste

$1/8$ teaspoon ground red pepper (cayenne)

> **recipe tip:**
> *Bake the spaghetti squash before you start the Base Recipe. Prepare the turkey balls while the squash is baking.*

While the spaghetti squash is baking: In a 3-quart saucepan, heat the oil over medium-high heat. Add the carrots, onion, and garlic and cook, stirring, until slightly softened, about 2 minutes. Add the broccoli and zucchini; cook, stirring, until just tender-crisp, about 2 minutes. Add the remaining ingredients and bring to a boil, reduce the heat and simmer 5 minutes. Reserve 3 cups of the Base Recipe for the Spaghetti Squash Primavera recipe.

Spaghetti Squash Primavera

1 spaghetti squash (about 3 pounds)

Preheat the oven to 350°F.

Place the spaghetti squash, whole, in a baking dish. Bake until tender when pierced with a fork, 45 minutes to 1 hour.

When the squash is cool enough to handle, cut it in half and discard the seeds. Using a fork, remove and separate the strands of squash from the shell (you should have about 4 cups). Toss the squash with the reserved 3 cups of Base Recipe. Serve hot.

serves 2 to 3

Use 2 medium spaghetti squash and all of the Base Recipe.

Stewed Turkey Balls with Vegetables

$3/4$ pound ground turkey

2 tablespoons plain dry bread crumbs

2 tablespoons minced onion

$1/4$ teaspoon dried basil

$1/8$ teaspoon salt, or to taste

In a medium bowl, mix together all the ingredients. Form the mixture into 1-inch round meatballs. Add the meatballs to the pot with remaining Base Recipe. Bring to a boil, and cook over medium heat until turkey balls are cooked through, 10 minutes.

serves 2 to 3

Double the Stewed Turkey Balls with Vegetables recipe and use all the Base Recipe.

Wild Rice and Kashi with Mushrooms &

Shrimp Scampi with Wild Rice and Kashi

Kashi is a grain mix that you can find in the hot cereal section of the supermarket or health food store. If you don't have Marsala, you can use Madeira or sherry instead. Do not confuse kashi with kasha, which is toasted buckwheat.

BASE RECIPE

1 tablespoon butter

$^1/_2$ cup chopped onion

$^1/_3$ cup finely chopped red bell pepper

$1^1/_2$ cups vegetable broth (page xii or store-bought)

1 cup water

$^1/_2$ cup wild rice

$^3/_4$ cup kashi (page xiii)

$^1/_4$ cup chopped, fresh parsley

In a 2-quart saucepan, melt the butter over medium-high heat. Add the onion and bell pepper and cook, stirring, until softened, about 4 minutes. Add the broth and water and bring to a boil. Add the wild rice and return to a boil; reduce the heat and simmer, covered, 35 minutes. Stir in the kashi, simmer 15 minutes more. Stir in the parsley. Set aside $1^1/_2$ cups for the Shrimp Scampi with Wild Rice and Kashi recipe.

Wild Rice and Kashi with Mushrooms

2 tablespoons butter

$^1/_2$ cup sliced leeks (white and light green part only), rinsed thoroughly

2 cups coarsely chopped portobello mushrooms

2 cups small white mushrooms, halved

$^1/_4$ teaspoon dried rosemary, crushed

2 tablespoons Marsala wine

In a medium skillet, melt the butter over medium-high heat. Add the leeks and cook, stirring, 10 seconds. Add both types of mushrooms and rosemary; cook, stirring, until cooked through, about 5 minutes. Stir in the Marsala, scraping up any brown bits on the bottom of the skillet. Stir in the remaining Base Recipe and cook, stirring, until heated through.

serves 2

Shrimp Scampi with Wild Rice and Kashi

2 tablespoon butter

2 cloves garlic, minced

$^1/_2$ to $^3/_4$ pound jumbo shrimp, peeled and deveined

1 tablespoon fresh lemon juice

In a medium skillet, melt the butter over medium-high heat. Add the garlic and cook, stirring, 10 seconds. Add the shrimp and cook, stirring, until no longer transparent, about 3 minutes. Stir in the lemon juice. Add the reserved Base Recipe and cook, stirring, until heated through.

serves 2

Lentil Escarole Stew & Lentil Sausage Stew

Serve this with brown rice and a salad for a hearty winter meal.

BASE RECIPE

2 teaspoons olive oil

1 cup chopped onion

1 clove garlic, minced

2 cups vegetable broth
(page xii or store-bought)

1 cup water

1 cup lentils

1 cup sliced celery

1 cup sliced carrot

1 bay leaf

$^1/_2$ teaspoon oregano

In a 2-quart saucepan, heat the oil over medium-high heat. Add the onion and garlic, cook, stirring, until onion is softened, about 2 minutes. Add the broth and water; bring to a boil. Add the lentils, celery, carrot, bay leaf, and oregano. Bring to a boil. Reduce heat and simmer, uncovered, 15 minutes. Discard the bay leaf. Remove 2 cups of Base Recipe from saucepan for the Lentil Sausage Stew recipe.

Lentil Escarole Stew

2 cups coarsely chopped escarole

2 tablespoons small shell or bow-tie pasta

$^1/_4$ teaspoon salt

$^1/_8$ teaspoon black pepper

Add the escarole, pasta, salt, and black pepper to the Base Recipe in the saucepan. Simmer, covered, until pasta is tender, 10 minutes.

serves 2

Lentil Sausage Stew

$^1/_2$ cup thinly sliced chorizo, kielbasa, pepperoni, or other cooked sausage

In a $1^1/_2$-quart saucepan, combine the reserved half of Base Recipe and the sausage. Simmer, uncovered 10 minutes.

serves 2

Pasta Puttanesca
Broiled Tuna with Puttanesca Sauce

Sun-dried tomato flakes are available in gourmet stores. If you can't find them, place sun-dried tomatoes (the drier the better) into a blender and process until the tomatoes become small flakes. If you are not a fish lover, this sauce is equally delicious over grilled chicken breasts.

BASE RECIPE

1 tablespoon olive oil

1 cup chopped onion

3 cloves garlic, minced

2 cups chopped tomato

1/3 cup red wine

2 tablespoons sun-dried tomato flakes

2 tablespoons tomato paste

1 tablespoon chopped capers

Pinch crushed red pepper flakes

1/3 cup chopped, fresh parsley

1/3 cup chopped black olives

1/3 cup chopped, stuffed green olives

In a 2-quart saucepan, heat the oil over medium-high heat. Add the onion and garlic, and cook, stirring, until softened, about 2 minutes. Add the tomatoes, wine, sun-dried tomato flakes, tomato paste, capers, and crushed red pepper. Bring to a boil; reduce heat and simmer, covered, 10 minutes. Stir in the parsley and the black and green olives. Simmer, covered, 5 minutes more. Reserve half of the Base Recipe for the Pasta Puttanesca recipe.

Pasta Puttanesca

4 to 6 ounces medium pasta
(such as ziti, rigatoni, penne)

Cook the pasta according to package directions; drain. Serve topped with the reserved Base Recipe.

serves 2

Broiled Tuna with Puttanesca Sauce

Two 6- to 8-ounce fresh tuna steaks, 1-inch thick

Preheat the broiler.

Broil the tuna about 4 to 6 inches from the heat source, 2 to 4 minutes per side, until fish flakes easily with a fork, or to desired doneness. Serve topped with the remaining Base Recipe.

serves 2

Eggplant Parmesan & Veal Parmesan

These are great favorites in any Italian restaurant. You can make the breaded cutlets (veal and eggplant) in advance and refrigerate them until you need them, then follow the Base Recipe, but you will have to bake them longer since they will have been chilled.

BASE RECIPE

2 cups marinara sauce,
   homemade (page 138) or store-bought

2 cups shredded mozzarella cheese

¹/₄ cup grated Parmesan cheese

> **recipe tip:**
> *Start by cooking the marinara sauce, if you are using home-made. Prepare the veal and eggplant recipes before you start the Base Recipe.*

Preheat the oven to 375°F. Have ready two 9-inch square baking pans.

Prepare both the Eggplant Parmesan and Veal Parmesan recipes.

Place the breaded eggplant and veal into each of the prepared baking pans. Top each with 1 cup of the sauce, spread to cover the slices. Sprinkle each recipe with 1 cup of the mozzarella and top each with 2 tablespoons of the Parmesan cheese. Bake, uncovered, until heated through and cheese has melted, 10 to 15 minutes.

Eggplant Parmesan

One ³/₄–1 pound eggplant

1 large egg

1 tablespoon water

2 tablespoons all-purpose flour

¹/₈ teaspoon salt, or to taste

¹/₃ to ¹/₂ cup plain or flavored dry bread
  crumbs

Vegetable oil for frying

Cut the eggplant into four 1-inch thick slices.

In a medium bowl, beat the egg with the water; set aside. On a piece of waxed paper, stir together the flour and salt and set aside. On a separate piece of wax paper, place the bread crumbs.

Dredge each slice of the eggplant into the flour mixture, then dip in the egg mixture, then coat with the bread crumbs.

In a large skillet, pour the oil to the depth of ¹/₄ inch. Heat the oil over medium-high heat until it bubbles when a few bread crumbs are tossed in.

Cook the eggplant, 2 slices at a time, until browned on bottom, about 2 minutes, then turn and cook on the second side, about 2 minutes more. Remove the eggplant from skillet and drain on paper towels. Repeat with the remaining two slices of eggplant, adding more oil if necessary. Use as directed in the Base Recipe.

serves 2

Double the Eggplant Parmesan recipe and use it with all of the Base Recipe. Cook in one large baking pan instead of 2 smaller ones.

Veal Parmesan

1 large egg

1 tablespoon water

2 tablespoons all-purpose flour

¹/₈ teaspoon salt, or to taste

¹/₃ to ¹/₂ cup plain or flavored dry bread
  crumbs

2 large or 4 small veal scallopini, sliced
  (total weight ¹/₂ pound)

Oil for frying

In a medium bowl, beat the egg with the water; set aside. On a piece of waxed paper, stir together the flour and salt and set aside. On a separate piece of wax paper, place the bread crumbs.

Dredge each slice of the veal into the flour mixture, then dip in the egg mixture, then coat with the bread crumbs.

In a large skillet, pour the oil to the depth of ¹/₄ inch. Heat the oil over medium-high heat until it bubbles when a few bread crumbs are tossed in.

Cook the veal, 2 slices at a time, until browned on bottom, about 3 minutes, then turn and cook on the second side, until veal is cooked through, about 3 minutes more. Remove the veal from the skillet and drain on paper towels. Repeat with the remaining two slices, adding more oil if necessary. Use as directed in the Base Recipe.

serves 2

Double the Veal Parmesan recipe and use it with all of the Base Recipe. Cook in one large baking pan instead of 2 smaller ones.

Polenta with Zucchini and Red Pepper Sauce

Sea Scallops in Red Pepper Sauce

Instant polenta is available in gourmet stores and Italian specialty markets, as well as in some supermarkets. If you can't find it, you can make polenta from scratch using regular cornmeal. Follow the package directions or consult an Italian cookbook for directions.

BASE RECIPE

2 large red bell peppers

1$^1/_2$ teaspoons olive oil

$^1/_2$ cup chopped onion

$^1/_2$ cup vegetable broth (page xii or store-bought)

2 tablespoons tomato paste

1 teaspoon red wine vinegar

1 small clove garlic, pressed

Preheat the broiler.

To roast the peppers:

Cut the bell peppers in half lengthwise and discard seeds and ribs. Place bell pepper halves in one layer on a large baking sheet. Broil, 4 inches from the heat, until quite charred, 5 minutes. Turn and cook until second side is charred, 5 minutes more. Place in plastic or paper bag and cool. Peel and discard the charred skin; set aside.

In a small skillet, heat the oil over medium-high heat. Add the onion and cook, stirring, until softened, about 2 minutes. Place bell peppers, onion, and remaining ingredients into a blender. Purée until smooth. Pour the purée into medium saucepan and heat just before serving. Reserve $^2/_3$ cup of the Base Recipe for the Sea Scallops in Red Pepper Sauce recipe.

Polenta with Zucchini and Red Pepper Sauce

1 tablespoon olive oil

2 cups sliced zucchini

$^1/_2$ cup sliced onion

$^1/_4$ teaspoon dried oregano

$1^1/_2$ cups water

$^1/_2$ cup milk

$^1/_4$ teaspoon salt

$^3/_4$ cup instant polenta

1 tablespoon butter, optional

In a medium skillet, heat the oil over medium-high heat. Add the zucchini, onion, and oregano. Cook, stirring, until tender, about 4 minutes. Stir the remaining Base Recipe into the vegetables.

In a $1^1/_2$-quart saucepan, bring the water, milk, and salt to a boil. Add the polenta and cook, stirring, until thick, about 4 minutes. Stir in the butter. Serve the vegetable mixture with the polenta on the side.

serves 2 to 3

Double the Polenta with Zucchini and Red Pepper Sauce recipe, using all the Base Recipe with the vegetables.

Sea Scallops in Red Pepper Sauce

$^1/_4$ cup water

$^1/_4$ cup white wine

1 tablespoon fresh lemon juice

$^1/_8$ teaspoon thyme

$^1/_8$ teaspoon salt

$^1/_2$ to $^3/_4$ pound sea or bay scallops

In a 1-quart saucepan, bring the water, wine, lemon juice, thyme, and salt to a boil. Add scallops and return to a boil. Reduce heat and simmer about 3 minutes or until scallops are opaque; drain.

Place $^1/_3$ cup of Base Recipe onto each of 2 plates. Top each with half of the scallops.

serves 2 to 3

Double the Sea Scallops in Red Pepper Sauce recipe and serve with all the Base Recipe.

Cornmeal Gnocchi with Butter Sauce

Cornmeal Gnocchi with Anchovy Butter

Five ounces chopped spinach may sound like an odd amount, but it's half of a 10-ounce package of frozen, chopped spinach.

BASE RECIPE

1 cup cold mashed potatoes

$^1/_2$ cup cornmeal

$^1/_3$ cup all-purpose flour

5 ounces chopped, frozen spinach, thawed and squeezed dry ($^1/_2$ of a 10-ounce package)

$^1/_2$ cup ricotta cheese

$^1/_3$ cup grated Parmesan cheese

$^1/_2$ teaspoon salt

In a large bowl, mix together, with your hands, all the ingredients to make a soft dough.

Divide the dough into fourths. On a floured board with floured hands, roll each quarter into a rope 12-inches long. Slice each rope into 15 pieces. After slicing, roll the dough between two forks to make ridges.

Bring a large pot of salted water to a boil. Add the gnocchi. (You may have to do this $^1/_3$ at a time, if your pot is smaller than 8 quarts.) Cook until the slices, or gnocchi, float to the top. Drain. Reserve half of the Base Recipe gnocchi for the Cornmeal Gnocchi with Butter Sauce recipe.

Cornmeal Gnocchi with Butter Sauce

3 tablespoons melted butter or margarine

1 tablespoon minced, sun-dried tomatoes, packed in oil

3 tablespoons grated Parmesan cheese

Preheat the broiler.

Place the reserved Base Recipe gnocchi into a 9-inch square baking pan. In a small bowl, combine the butter and sun-dried tomatoes. Pour the butter over the gnocchi and stir to completely coat. Sprinkle with the cheese. Broil the gnocchi 4 to 6 inches from the heat source until the cheese is browned, 2 to 3 minutes.

serves 2

totally Vegetarian

Double the butter and Parmesan cheese and use it with all of the Base Recipe gnocchi.

Cornmeal Gnocchi with Anchovy Butter

1 anchovy

$^1/_4$ cup butter, softened

3 tablespoons grated Parmesan cheese

Preheat the broiler.

Place the remaining Base Recipe gnocchi into a 9-inch square baking pan.

In a small bowl, mash the anchovy with the butter. In a small skillet, melt the anchovy butter over low heat. Pour over the gnocchi and stir to coat completely. Sprinkle with cheese. Broil the gnocchi 4 to 6 inches from the heat source until the cheese is browned, 2 minutes.

serves 2

totally con Carne

Double the butter and use it with all of the Base Recipe gnocchi.

Vegetable Pizza & Sausage Pizza

Use the pizza dough that you can find in the tubes in the refrigerator case of the supermarket, near the refrigerator biscuits. A pizza peel is a large, flat board used by commercial pizzerias to move pizzas in and out of the oven; they are available at kitchen supply stores.

BASE RECIPE

1 tablespoon olive oil

$^1/_2$ cup chopped onion

One 14$^1/_2$-ounce can whole peeled
   tomatoes, undrained

2 tablespoons tomato paste

$^1/_4$ teaspoon dried oregano

Cornmeal for sprinkling pizza peel

Two 10-ounce packages pizza crust

2 teaspoons garlic, minced

2 cups shredded mozzarella cheese

recipe tip:

Make one pizza at a time. While the first one is baking, prepare the second. Start with one vegetarian and one sausage. These pizzas are large enough for two to share the first pizzas, then you can go back to the kitchen to make the remaining two. Prepare the toppings while the Base Recipe simmers.

Preheat the oven to 450°F. Set the oven rack to lowest shelf setting; place large baking sheet on that shelf. (If your baking sheet has a lip, face it toward the back of the oven, with the flat edge toward the front.)

In a 1-quart saucepan, heat the oil over medium-high heat. Add the onion and cook, stirring, until softened, 1 to 2 minutes. Stir in the tomatoes, breaking them up with the back of a spoon. Add the tomato paste and oregano. Bring to a boil, reduce the heat and simmer 15 minutes.

Meanwhile, prepare both the vegetable and sausage toppings.

Place the simmered sauce in a blender or food processor and process until smooth.

Generously sprinkle a pizza peel, or large wooden cutting board, with cornmeal. Open one of the pizza crust packages and unroll dough. Divide the dough in half. Press each half into 5×7-inch rectangles. Sprinkle each crust with $^1/_2$ teaspoon of the minced garlic. Spread $^1/_3$ cup of the sauce over the garlic, to within $^1/_2$-inch of the edge of the dough. Sprinkle $^1/_2$ cup of the cheese over the each crust. (Don't be too generous with your sauce or cheese, or they will run off the pie onto the baking sheet). Top one of the crusts with half of the sausage topping and the other with half of the vegetable topping.

Slide the pizza off the pizza peel or wooden board onto the preheated baking sheet in the oven (this may require a slight jerking motion, especially if you did not sprinkle on enough cornmeal). Bake 7 to 10 minutes or until crust is browned and cheese is melted. To remove from oven, lift the baking pan out of the oven, remove pizza to serving plate and return baking sheet to oven to reheat. Repeat with remaining package of dough, sauce, cheese, and toppings.

Vegetable Pizza

$1/2$ cup green or red bell pepper rings

$1/2$ cup sliced mushrooms

One $1/4$-inch thick slice of onion, separated into rings

2 teaspoons olive oil

In a medium bowl, combine all of the vegetables; add the oil and toss to coat the vegetables. Use to top the Base Recipe pizza crusts.

serves 2

Sausage Pizza

$1/4$ to $1/2$ pound Italian sausage, casing removed

Cook the sausage in a small skillet over medium-high heat until sausage is no longer pink, about 3 minutes; drain off the fat. Use to top the Base Recipe pizza crusts.

serves 2

Caramelized Onion and Sun-Dried Tomato Strata & Bacon Strata

*A strata is a cross between bread pudding and crustless quiche.
It makes a really nice brunch and dinner entrée.*

BASE RECIPE

3 tablespoons butter, divided

3 cups sliced Bermuda, Spanish, or other sweet onion

$1/4$ teaspoon dried rosemary, crumbled

$1/8$ teaspoon dried thyme

4 large eggs

$1^1/2$ cups milk

$1/2$ teaspoon salt

$1/8$ teaspoon black pepper

5 cups cubed rye bread (about 8 slices)

1 cup shredded Swiss cheese

Preheat the oven to 350°F. Grease two 1-quart casseroles.

Heat 2 tablespoons of the butter in a large skillet, over medium-high heat. Add the onion and cook, stirring until softened, about 2 minutes. Stir in the rosemary and thyme, lower the heat and cook slowly, uncovered, until onions are golden, stirring occasionally, about 45 minutes. Place half of the remaining 1 tablespoon butter in each of the casseroles and place them in oven to melt, about 5 minutes.

In a large bowl, beat the eggs; beat in the milk, salt, and black pepper. Add the bread and toss; let stand 15 minutes, tossing once or twice. Add the onion mixture and cheese to the bread mixture, toss to combine. Reserve half of the Base Recipe for the Bacon Strata recipe.

Caramelized Onion and Sun-Dried Tomato Strata

$^1/_3$ cup chopped sun-dried tomatoes, packed in oil

Place the remaining Base Recipe in a medium bowl. Add the tomatoes and toss. Place the mixture into one of the greased casseroles. Bake for 35 minutes, or until a knife inserted in the center comes out clean.

serves 2

Double the Caramelized Onion and Sun-Dried Tomato Strata recipe and use all of the Base Recipe. Bake in one 2-quart casserole until a knife inserted in center comes out clean, 45 minutes.

Bacon Strata

6 slices bacon

In a medium skillet, cook the bacon until crisp. Drain on paper towels and crumble. Mix bacon into the reserved half of the Base Recipe. Place into one of the greased casseroles. Bake 35 minutes, or until a knife inserted in the center comes out clean.

serves 2

Double the Bacon Strata recipe and use all of the Base Recipe. Bake in a 2-quart casserole for 45 minutes, or until a knife inserted in the center comes out clean.

chapter six

Mexican and Spanish

Refried Bean Nachos Grande
Chicken Nachos Grande

To speed up this recipe you can use store-bought chips, guacamole, and canned refried beans instead of making homemade. Spanish beans are a seasoned bean product by Goya. If you cannot find them, any plain cooked beans will do.

BASE RECIPE

Tortillas:
- Six 5-inch corn or wheat tortillas
- Oil for deep frying
- Salt, optional

> **recipe tip:**
> *Prepare both the Refried Bean and Chicken Filling recipes before you prepare the Base Recipe.*

Guacamole:
- $^3/_4$ cup avocado pulp (1 small to medium avocado)
- 1 tablespoon fresh lime juice
- 1 tablespoon chopped scallion (white and green parts)
- 2 cloves garlic, minced
- 4 drops Tabasco sauce

Toppings:
- $^1/_4$ cup salsa
- 2 cups shredded Cheddar cheese
- 1 to 2 seeded jarred, marinated, jalapeño peppers, thinly sliced
- 2 to 3 tablespoons sour cream

Prepare the Refried Bean and Chicken recipes. Preheat the broiler.

Stack all six tortillas one on top of the other, and cut them into 6 wedges. You will have 36 wedges.

Pour oil to the depth of 1-inch into a deep, heavy skillet. Heat over medium high heat to 375°F, or until oil bubbles when a small piece of tortilla is dropped in. Add a few tortilla wedges into the oil at one time. Cook until wedges turn a slightly tan color, 1 to 2 minutes per side. Turn the wedges and cook until second side is tanned as well. Remove from skillet and drain on paper towels. Salt lightly, if desired. Repeat until all tortillas are fried.

To prepare the guacamole, mash the avocado with a fork in a medium bowl. Add the lime juice, scallion, garlic, and Tabasco sauce. Set aside.

Arrange half of the chips close together on a heat-proof platter or baking sheet. Arrange remaining chips close together on a second heat-proof platter or baking sheet. Top one set of chips with the chicken filling, top the remaining chips on second platter with the refried bean filling. Top both sets of chips with half of the salsa, Cheddar cheese, and jalapeño peppers, in that order.

Place both platters under the broiler until cheese is melted, 2–3 minutes. Garnish each dish with half of the guacamole and sour cream.

Refried Bean Nachos Grande

2 teaspoons olive oil

1¹/₂ tablespoons minced onion

1 clove garlic, minced

¹/₄ teaspoon ground cumin

One 15-ounce can Spanish pinto beans, slightly drained

Heat the oil in a medium skillet over medium-high heat. Add the onion and garlic and cook, stirring, until onion is tender about 1 minute. Stir in the cumin. Add the beans and mash with a fork. Cook until thick, about 5 minutes. Use as directed in the Base Recipe.

serves 2.

Chicken Nachos Grande

4 ounces skinless, boneless chicken breast

2 teaspoons olive oil

2 tablespoons chopped onion

1 clove garlic, minced

1 teaspoon chili powder

¹/₄ cup water

2 tablespoons tomato paste

¹/₄ teaspoon liquid from the jarred jalapeño peppers

¹/₈ teaspoon salt

Cut the chicken into thin strips. In a 1-quart saucepan, heat the oil over medium-high heat. Add the onion and garlic. Cook, stirring, until softened; about 1 minute. Add the chili powder and stir until the chicken is coated with the chili powder. Stir in the water, tomato paste, jalapeño liquid, and salt. Cook, stirring, until chicken is cooked and mixture is thickened. Use as directed in the Base Recipe.

serves 2

Bean and Cheese Tacos  Turkey Tacos

Tacos are a big crowd pleaser, especially at party time. These are easy to make and you can multiply the recipe easily for bigger groups. If you and your family usually eat more than two tacos per person, double the recipes.

BASE RECIPE

8 taco shells

1 cup shredded iceberg lettuce

$^1/_3$ cup finely chopped tomato

3 tablespoons minced onion

$^1/_4$ to $^1/_2$ cup salsa

> **recipe tip:**
>
> *Prepare the Cheese and Bean and Turkey Filling recipes before you prepare the Base Recipe.*

Preheat the oven to 350°F. Prepare the fillings.

Place the taco shells on a baking sheet and place in the oven to warm, 5 minutes.

In a medium bowl, combine the lettuce, tomato, and onion. Fill four of the tacos with the Turkey filling; fill the remaining shells with the Bean and Cheese filling. Top each taco evenly with the lettuce mixture and some salsa. Serve immediately.

Bean and Cheese Tacos

$^1/_2$ cup refried beans
(canned or homemade, page 179)
$^1/_2$ cup shredded Cheddar cheese

In a small saucepan, heat the beans with the cheese over medium heat, stirring often, until cheese has melted and is incorporated into the beans, 5 minutes. Fill the tacos as directed in the Base Recipe

serves 2

Turkey Tacos

$^1/_2$ pound ground turkey
2 tablespoons taco mix seasoning
3 tablespoons water
1 tablespoon tomato paste
1 tablespoon chopped, fresh cilantro, optional

In a medium skillet, cook the turkey over medium-high heat until cooked through, about 5 minutes. Stir in the taco mix until absorbed. Stir in the water and tomato paste. Cook, stirring, until mixture is thickened. Stir in the cilantro, if using.

serves 2

Rice and Bean Burrito
& Beef Burrito

If you can't find 10-inch tortillas, use the 7-inch ones and just make extra burritos, using less filling in each. You can use homemade guacamole (page 178) or store-bought.

BASE RECIPE

$^1/_2$ cup seeded, finely chopped tomato

$^1/_4$ cup minced onion

2 tablespoons minced green bell pepper

1 tablespoon minced, fresh jalapeño pepper, optional

Four 10-inch flour tortillas

1 cup guacamole

> **recipe tip:**
> *Prepare the fillings before you prepare the tortillas for the Base Recipe.*

Preheat oven to 350°F.

In a medium bowl, combine the tomatoes, onion, bell pepper, and jalapeño pepper, if using; set aside.

Prepare the fillings.

Wrap the tortillas in foil and place into oven until tortillas are warm and pliable, 5 to 10 minutes. Remove tortillas from the oven and place each one on a dinner plate.

Fill each of 2 of the tortillas with half of the Rice and Bean Burrito Filling; fill the remaining two tortillas with half of the Beef Burrito filling. Top each burrito equally with the guacamole and tomato mixture. Fold the burritos by wrapping two opposite sides inward, toward the middle, then fold the two open ends toward the center (it will look like a log); and eat.

Rice and Bean Burrito

1 cup cooked brown rice

$1/2$ cup cooked (page xvi) or canned, rinsed pinto beans

$1/4$ cup salsa (homemade page xii, or store-bought)

$1/2$ cup shredded Monterey Jack cheese

In a 1-quart saucepan, stir together the brown rice, beans, salsa, and cheese. Cook over low heat until heated through. Fill the tortillas as directed in the Base Recipe.

serves 2

Beef Burrito

2 tablespoons lime juice

2 tablespoons chopped, fresh cilantro

1 teaspoon vegetable oil

$1/4$ teaspoon ground cumin

$1/8$ teaspoon salt

$3/4$ pound London Broil, sirloin, or other tender boneless cut of beef

Preheat the broiler.

In a large bowl, combine the lime juice, cilantro, oil, cumin, and salt. Place the steak in the bowl and turn once to coat in the marinade. Let stand 10 minutes.

Broil the steak 4 inches from the heat source, turning once, about 5 minutes for medium-rare, depending on the thickness of the steak. Remove from the heat and let the steak rest for 5 minutes. Cut the steak into $1/4$-inch thick slices. Fill the tortillas as directed in the Base Recipe.

serves 2

Mexican Pizza with Beans
Mexican Pizza with Beef

These are a cross between pizza and nachos—favorites for the whole family;
and they're a cinch to make.

BASE RECIPE

4 regular-size pita breads
$^1/_4$ cup enchilada sauce
$1^1/_3$ cups shredded Cheddar cheese

recipe tip:
Prepare the toppings before
you begin the Base Recipe.

Preheat the oven to 375°F.

Prepare the toppings.

Place the pita breads on a large baking sheet. Top each with 1 tablespoon of enchilada sauce and spread to within $^1/_2$-inch of the pita bread edge. Spread the Bean topping on two of the pita breads, and spread the Beef topping over the remaining two pitas. Sprinkle $^1/_3$ cup of the Cheddar cheese over each of the pitas.

Bake 5 to 7 minutes or until the cheese is melted and the pizzas are heated through.

Mexican Pizza with Beans

$^1/_3$ cup refried beans, canned or homemade, page 179
1 tablespoon chopped, fresh cilantro, optional

In a medium bowl, stir together the beans and cilantro. Use as directed in Base Recipe.

serves 2

Mexican Pizza with Beef

$^1/_4$ pound ground beef
$^1/_2$ teaspoon chili powder

In a small skillet, cook the beef over medium-high heat, stirring, until no longer pink, about 2 minutes. Stir in the chili powder. Use as directed in Base Recipe.

serves 2

Mexican Cup-Of-Noodles with Beans
Mexican Cup-Of-Noodles with Chicken

I eat this for lunch at least twice a week. It's filling and easy to make. I usually use lo mein or thin Japanese noodles in this soup, but you can use angel hair pasta instead. You can also use shrimp instead of the chicken, and broccoli instead of the zucchini, if you prefer.

BASE RECIPE

6 cups vegetable broth (page xii or store-bought)

$^3/_4$ cup prepared salsa

One 8-ounce can corn kernels, undrained

1 teaspoon chili powder

$^1/_4$ teaspoon ground cumin

8 ounces thin noodles or angel hair pasta

In a 2-quart saucepan, bring the broth to a boil. Stir in the salsa, corn and its liquid, chili powder, and cumin. Return to a boil. Add the noodles and cook according to package direction; do not drain. Remove half of the broth and noodles to a $1^1/_2$-quart saucepan for the Mexican Cup-Of-Noodles with Chicken recipe.

Mexican Cup-Of-Noodles with Beans

1 cup cooked (page xi) or canned, rinsed kidney beans

$^1/_2$ cup chopped zucchini

Stir the beans and zucchini into the remaining Base Recipe in the 2-quart saucepan. Bring to a boil. Reduce heat and simmer, 5 minutes, until the zucchini is cooked and the beans are heated through.

serves 2

Mexican Cup-Of-Noodles with Chicken

$^1/_4$ pound chicken breast

2 tablespoons chopped, fresh cilantro

Slice the chicken breast into thin strips. Add to the reserved Base Recipe in the $1^1/_2$-quart saucepan. Stir in the cilantro. Bring to a boil. Reduce heat and simmer, until chicken is cooked through, 5 minutes.

serves 2

Cheese Enchiladas & Chicken Enchiladas

If you prefer, you can cook 8 scrambled eggs and use that to fill the vegetarian enchilada instead of or in addition to the cheese (you might even want to add some chopped chilies or chili powder to the eggs before scrambling).

BASE RECIPE

One 16-ounce can mild enchilada sauce;
  reserve 1 tablespoon for the Chicken Enchiladas
  recipe

Vegetable oil

12 corn tortillas

1 cup shredded Monterey Jack cheese

recipe tip:
Prepare the fillings before you prepare the Base Recipe.

Preheat the oven to 350°F. Grease two 8-inch or 9-inch baking dishes.

In a medium skillet, heat the enchilada sauce over low heat; keep warm.

Pour the oil to a depth of $1/4$-inch into a large heavy skillet and heat over medium heat. Add the tortillas, one at a time, and cook until pliable, about 1 minute. Be sure not to let them fry too long, because they will become too crisp. Dip each tortilla into the warm enchilada sauce, to coat both sides and stack them on a plate or piece of waxed paper.

Fill six of the tortillas with the Cheese Enchilada filling; fill the remaining six tortillas with the Chicken Enchilada filling. Roll up all of the tortillas and place them, seam side down, in the two baking dishes. Pour half of the remaining enchilada sauce over the cheese enchiladas, and the other half over the chicken enchiladas. Sprinkle $1/2$ cup of the cheese over the sauce in each pan. Bake until enchiladas are heated through and cheese has melted, 10 to 15 minutes.

Cheese Enchiladas

4 ounces Monterey Jack cheese

Shred cheese into a small bowl; set aside. Use to fill the enchiladas as directed in the Base Recipe.

serves 2 to 3

Chicken Enchiladas

1 tablespoon vegetable oil

$^1/_2$ to $^3/_4$ pound skinless, boneless chicken breast, thinly sliced

1 tablespoon enchilada sauce (reserved from Base Recipe)

1 tablespoon chopped, fresh cilantro, optional

1 teaspoon chili powder

In a medium skillet, heat the oil over medium high heat. Add the chicken and cook, stirring, until completely cooked through, about 3 minutes. Add the enchilada sauce, cilantro, if using, and chili powder. Use to fill the enchiladas as directed in the Base Recipe.

serves 2 to 3

Vegetable Fajitas & Turkey Fajitas

You can vary your choice of vegetables or meat. Use carrots, or rutabagas, green, yellow, or orange bell peppers. Substitute chicken, shrimp, or beef for the turkey.

BASE RECIPE

2 tablespoons lime juice

2 tablespoons chopped, fresh cilantro

1 tablespoon vegetable oil

1 teaspoon chili powder

1 teaspoon oregano

$1/2$ teaspoon ground cumin

2 large cloves garlic, minced

$1/8$ teaspoon salt, or to taste

2 cups zucchini sticks

1 cup red bell pepper strips

1 cup yellow squash strips

1 cup sliced onion

$1/4$ cup salsa (homemade page xvi, or store-bought)

> **recipe tip:**
> *Broil the vegetables for the Base Recipe and the turkey in the Turkey Fajita recipe at the same time.*

Eight 7-inch flour tortillas

Preheat the broiler. Grease a 9-inch square baking pan.

In a medium bowl, stir together the lime juice, fresh cilantro, vegetable oil, chili powder, oregano, cumin, garlic, and salt; reserve 1 tablespoon in a smaller bowl. Add all of the vegetables to the remaining mixture in the bowl, toss well.

Place the vegetables into the prepared pan and broil the vegetables until tender-crisp or desired doneness, about 5 minutes. Toss the cooked vegetables with the salsa. Reserve $1/2$ cup of the Base Recipe for the Turkey Fajitas.

Reduce the heat of the oven to 350°F. Wrap the stack of tortillas in aluminum foil. Place in oven to heat, about 3 minutes. Reserve 4 tortillas for the Vegetable Fajita recipe.

Vegetable Fajitas

$^1/_2$ cup shredded Monterey Jack cheese

Divide the reserved Base Recipe evenly onto each of the four tortillas. Top evenly with the cheese. Roll up and enjoy.

serves 2 (makes 4 fajitas)

Double the Vegetable Fajitas recipe, and use all of the Base Recipe.

Turkey Fajitas

$^1/_2$ pound turkey cutlets, sliced into strips

1 tablespoon vegetable oil

In a small bowl, combine the turkey with the reserved 1 tablespoon of the Base Recipe marinade and toss until the turkey is totally coated.

In a large skillet, heat the oil over medium-high heat. Add the turkey and cook, stirring, until completely cooked, about 4 minutes.

Stir in the $^1/_2$ cup of the reserved, broiled vegetables from the Base Recipe. Divide the Turkey Fajita filling evenly onto each of the remaining four tortillas. Roll up and enjoy.

serves 2 (makes 4 fajitas)

Double the Turkey Fajita recipe. Use 1 cup of the Base Recipe.

Mexican Stuffed Peppers with Corn
Mexican Stuffed Peppers with Veal

Feel free to substitute ground beef, chicken, or turkey for the veal, if you prefer.

BASE RECIPE

2 large, or 4 small, red or green bell peppers

1 tablespoon vegetable oil

1 cup chopped onion

2 cloves garlic, minced

$1/2$ teaspoon ground cumin

$1/8$ teaspoon ground red pepper (cayenne)

2 cups chopped, fresh tomatoes

$1/2$ cup water

$1/4$ cup lightly packed, fresh cilantro leaves

2 tablespoons fresh lime juice

$1/4$ teaspoon dried thyme

$1/4$ teaspoon salt, to taste

Preheat the oven to 350°F.

If using large bell peppers, cut them in half lengthwise. Discard the seeds and ribs. If using small bell peppers, cut off the top with the stem then remove seeds and ribs. Blanch the bell peppers in boiling water 4 minutes; drain and set aside.

In a medium skillet, heat the oil over medium-high heat. Add the onion and garlic; cook, stirring, until softened, 2 minutes. Stir in the cumin and red pepper. Add the tomatoes, cook, stirring, until softened, about 5 minutes. Add the water, cilantro, lime juice, thyme, and salt. Place the mixture in a food processor or blender; purée until smooth. Set aside half of the Base Recipe for the Mexican Stuffed Peppers with Veal recipe.

Mexican Stuffed Peppers with Corn

$^3/_4$ cup cooked corn kernels

$^1/_2$ cup cooked (page xi) or canned, rinsed kidney beans

$^1/_4$ cup chopped pimiento

2 tablespoons chopped scallion (white and green parts)

$^3/_4$ teaspoon chili powder

$^1/_8$ teaspoon salt

$^3/_4$ cup shredded Cheddar cheese

In a medium bowl, toss together the corn, beans, pimiento, scallions, chili powder, and salt. Add the cheese and toss again.

Spoon half of the corn mixture into each of two of the blanched bell peppers. Pour the remaining Base Recipe in a 9-inch loaf pan. Place the stuffed bell peppers over the sauce. Bake, covered, until heated through and cheese has melted, 45 minutes. Serve with any remaining sauce in the pan.

serves 2

Double the Mexican Stuffed Peppers with Corn recipe, using all of the Base Recipe. Bake in a 9-inch square baking pan.

Mexican Stuffed Peppers with Veal

$^1/_2$ pound ground veal

$^1/_3$ cup cooked corn kernels

$^1/_4$ cup cooked rice

2 teaspoons chili powder

$^1/_2$ teaspoon salt

In a medium bowl, combine all the ingredients. Spoon half of the mixture into each of two of the blanched bell peppers. Pour the reserved Base Recipe in a 9-inch loaf pan. Place the bell peppers in the sauce. Bake, uncovered, until the meat is cooked through, 45 minutes. Serve with any remaining sauce in the pan.

serves 2

Double the Mexican Stuffed Peppers with Veal recipe, using all of the Base Recipe. Bake in a 9-inch square baking pan.

Spaghetti Squash with Beans
Spaghetti Squash with Chicken

I find mild enchilada sauce spicy enough. If you like very spicy foods (and I do),
you can try medium or hot.

BASE RECIPE

1 spaghetti squash (about 3 pounds)

1 tablespoon vegetable oil

1 cup chopped onion

$^1/_2$ cup sliced zucchini

$^1/_2$ cup chopped red or green bell pepper

2 cloves garlic, minced

1 teaspoon chili powder

$^1/_2$ teaspoon ground cumin

$^1/_4$ teaspoon salt

One 8-ounce can stewed tomatoes

3 tablespoons mild enchilada sauce

recipe tip:
Prepare the sauce for the Base
Recipe while the squash cooks.

Preheat the oven to 350°F.

Place the squash in a baking dish and bake for 1 hour, until tender. Cut the squash in half and remove the seeds. Using a fork, pull apart the flesh, which separate like spaghetti strands. You should have 5 cups of squash.

In a large skillet, heat the oil over medium-high heat. Add the onion, zucchini, bell peppers, and garlic and cook, stirring, until softened, about 3 minutes. Stir in the chili powder, cumin, and salt. Stir in the stewed tomatoes and enchilada sauce and bring to a boil. Reduce heat and simmer, uncovered, 3 minutes. Stir in the spaghetti squash. Set aside 2 cups of the Base Recipe for the Spaghetti Squash with Chicken recipe.

Spaghetti Squash with Beans

- 1 cup cooked (page xi) or canned, rinsed pinto, black, small red, or kidney beans
- 1 tablespoon chopped green chilies
- 1 tablespoon enchilada sauce
- 2 teaspoons fresh lime juice
- $1/8$ teaspoon salt

Stir all the ingredients into the skillet with the remaining Base Recipe. Cook, stirring, over medium-high heat until heated through.

serves 2 to 3

Spaghetti Squash with Chicken

- $1/2$ pound skinless, boneless chicken breast, cut into strips
- 3 tablespoons enchilada sauce
- 1 tablespoon vegetable oil
- $1/8$ teaspoon salt

Combine the chicken and enchilada sauce in a medium bowl. Let stand at least 5 minutes. In a medium skillet, heat the oil over medium-high heat. Add the chicken with the sauce and cook, stirring, until cooked through, about 4 minutes. Add the reserved 2 cups of the Base Recipe and the salt. Cook, stirring, until heated through.

serves 2

Ragout with Kidney Beans
& Mexican Pork Stew

Tomatillos look like small green tomatoes in "paper." You can find them fresh in produce markets or canned in Hispanic markets. Green tomatoes are an acceptable substitute.

BASE RECIPE

1 tablespoon vegetable oil

1¹/₂ cups chopped onion

1 cup chopped green bell pepper

2 cloves garlic, minced

¹/₂ teaspoon ground cumin

¹/₄ teaspoon ground cinnamon

2 cups chopped tomato

1¹/₂ cups chopped, fresh pineapple

1 cup chopped tomatillo

3 tablespoons chopped, fresh cilantro

In a 3-quart saucepan, heat the oil, over medium-high heat. Add the onion, bell pepper, and garlic; cook, stirring, until softened, about 3 minutes. Stir in the cumin and cinnamon. Add the tomato, pineapple, and tomatillos; bring to a boil. Reduce heat and simmer 20 minutes. Stir in cilantro; reserve half of the Base Recipe for the Mexican Pork Stew recipe.

Ragout with Kidney Beans

1 cup cooked (page xi) or canned, rinsed kidney beans

¹/₄ teaspoon salt

Stir the kidney beans and salt into the Base Recipe still in the saucepan. Cook, over medium heat, until heated through, about 2 minutes.

serves 2

Mexican Pork Stew

2 teaspoons vegetable oil

¹/₂ pound boneless pork tenderloin, julienned

2 tablespoons tomato paste

¹/₄ teaspoon salt

Heat the oil in a medium skillet over medium-high heat. Add the pork and cook, stirring until cooked through, 3 to 5 minutes. Add the reserved Base Recipe, the tomato paste, and salt. Cook, stirring occasionally, until mixture is slightly thickened, 5 minutes. If you are serving only meat eaters, increase pork to 1 pound and tomato paste to ¹/₄ cup.

serves 2

Gazpacho Beans & Gazpacho Chicken

Gazpacho is traditionally a cold soup, perfect for the summertime.

BASE RECIPE

- 1 1/2 tablespoons olive oil
- 2 cups peeled, cubed cucumber
- 1 cup finely chopped, green bell pepper
- 1/2 cup sliced scallion
- 1 clove garlic, minced
- 2 cups tomato wedges
- 1 teaspoon red wine vinegar
- 1/4 teaspoon salt, or to taste
- 1/8 teaspoon ground red pepper (cayenne)

In a large skillet, heat the oil over medium-high heat. Add the cucumber, bell pepper, scallion, and garlic and cook, stirring, until vegetables are softened, about 2–3 minutes. Add the tomato and cook, stirring, until softened, about 3 minutes more. Stir in the vinegar, salt, and red pepper. Set aside 1 cup of the mixture for the Gazpacho Chicken recipe.

Gazpacho Beans

- 1 1/2 cups cooked (page xi) or canned, rinsed black beans

Stir the black beans into the remaining Base Recipe in the skillet. Cook over medium-high heat, stirring, until heated through, about 2 minutes. Cool in refrigerator 2 hours or until chilled; serve.

serves 2

Gazpacho Chicken

- 1 tablespoon olive oil
- 1/2 to 3/4 pound skinless, boneless chicken breasts, cut into 1/4-inch strips
- 1 tablespoon tomato paste
- 1 tablespoon chopped, fresh cilantro
- 1/4 teaspoon salt

In a medium skillet, heat the oil over medium-high heat. Add the chicken and cook, stirring, until chicken is cooked through, about 4 minutes. Add the reserved 1 cup of Base Recipe, tomato paste, cilantro, and salt. Cook, stirring, until heated through, 2 to 3 minutes. Cool in refrigerator 2 hours or until chilled; serve.

serves 2

White Kidney Beans & in Green Sauce

Turkey in Green Sauce

White kidney beans are also called cannellini. You can substitute chicken cutlets for the turkey here.

ళ ళ ళ ళ ళ ళ ళ ళ ళ ళ ళ ళ ళ ళ ళ ళ ళ ళ ళ

BASE RECIPE

1 cup fresh spinach, lightly packed

$^1/_2$ cup sliced scallion

$^1/_2$ cup fresh cilantro leaves, lightly packed

$^1/_2$ seeded jalapeño pepper

2 cloves garlic, minced

$^1/_2$ cup plain yogurt

1 tablespoon fresh lime juice

$^1/_4$ teaspoon salt

Place the spinach, scallion, cilantro, jalapeño pepper, and garlic into a food processor. Process until finely chopped. Set aside 5 tablespoons of the spinach mixture.

Add the yogurt, lime juice, and salt to the remaining mixture in the food processor; process until well combined. Set aside $^1/_3$ cup of the yogurt sauce for the White Kidney Bean in Green Sauce recipe.

Place the remaining yogurt sauce in a small saucepan over low heat, and heat until warm. Do not allow the sauce to come to a boil or it will separate.

ళ ళ ళ ళ ళ ళ ళ ళ ళ ళ ళ ళ ళ ళ ళ ళ ళ ళ ళ

White Kidney Beans in Green Sauce

1 tablespoon olive oil

1 cup coarsely chopped zucchini

$^1/_2$ cup chopped onion

$1^1/_2$ cups cooked (page xi) or canned, rinsed white
kidney beans

$^1/_4$ teaspoon salt

In a large skillet heat the oil over medium-high heat. Add the zucchini, onion, and 3 table-spoon of the reserved Base Recipe spinach mixture. Cook, stirring, until vegetables are tender, about 3 minutes. Add the beans, salt, and reserved $^1/_3$ cup Base Recipe yogurt sauce and cook, stirring, until heated through, about 2 minutes.

serves 2 to 3

Turkey in Green Sauce

1 tablespoon olive oil

$^1/_2$ pound turkey cutlets

In a large skillet, heat the oil, over medium-high heat. Add the remaining 2 tablespoons Base Recipe spinach mixture to the skillet. Add the turkey cutlets and cook about 2 min-utes per side or until the turkey is cooked through. Serve with the warmed Base Recipe yogurt sauce in the saucepan.

serves 2

Lentil Paella

Seafood Paella

*When preparing the Lentil Paella, you can use a full cup of cooked chickpeas (garbanzo beans)
or lentils instead of $^1/_2$ cup of each, if you prefer. Also, the artichokes called for can be
fresh cooked, frozen, or canned, but not marinated. Chorizo is a Spanish-style cooked sausage.
If you can't find it, pepperoni will do.*

BASE RECIPE

- 1 tablespoon vegetable oil
- 1 cup chopped onion
- 2 cloves garlic, minced
- 2 cups vegetable broth (page xii or store-bought)
- $^1/_4$ cup white wine or additional broth
- $^1/_4$ teaspoon saffron threads or ground cumin
- 1 cup converted white rice
- $^1/_2$ cup cooked peas
- $^1/_4$ cup chopped pimiento

In a 2-quart saucepan, heat the oil over medium-high heat. Add the onion and garlic
and cook, stirring, until softened, 1–2 minutes.

Add the broth, wine, and saffron and bring to a boil. Add rice; return to a boil.
Reduce heat and simmer, covered, 25 minutes or until the liquid is absorbed. Remove
from heat, stir in the peas and pimientos. Remove 2 cups of the Base Recipe from
saucepan for the Seafood Paella recipe.

Lentil Paella

$^1/_2$ cup cooked lentils (page xi)

$^1/_2$ cup cooked (page xi) or canned, rinsed chickpeas (garbanzo beans)

$^1/_3$ cup chopped, cooked artichoke hearts

Stir the lentils, chickpeas, and artichoke hearts into the Base Recipe in the saucepan. Cook, stirring until heated through.

serves 2

Seafood Paella

$^3/_4$ cup water

6 whole clams, rinsed thoroughly

$^1/_4$ pound sliced chorizo sausage

$^1/_4$ pound shrimp, peeled and de-veined

In a 1$^1/_2$-quart saucepan, bring the water to a boil. Add the clams and steam, covered, until all the clams have opened, about 3 minutes. Drain and discard any clams that did not open.

In a medium skillet, cook the chorizo over medium heat until heated through; remove from skillet. Add the shrimp and cook over medium heat until no longer pink, about 2 minutes. Add the reserved Base Recipe, chorizo, and clams to the skillet. Cook, stirring, until heated through.

serves 2

Kidney Bean Picadillo & Picadillo

This is a traditional Spanish beef dish, but it works excellently in its vegetarian version.

BASE RECIPE

1 tablespoon vegetable oil	1/8 teaspoon ground red pepper (cayenne)
1 cup chopped onion	One 14 1/2-ounce can whole, peeled
1/2 cup chopped green bell pepper	tomatoes, undrained
2 cloves garlic, minced	2 tablespoons tomato paste
1/2 teaspoon ground cinnamon	1 tablespoon packed brown sugar
1/4 teaspoon ground allspice	1/3 cup sliced pimiento-stuffed green olives
1/4 teaspoon ground cumin	3 tablespoons dark raisins

In a 2-quart saucepan, heat the oil over medium-high heat. Add the onion, bell pepper, and garlic; cook, stirring, until softened, about 2 minutes. Stir in the cinnamon, all-spice, cumin, and red pepper until absorbed. Add the tomatoes with their liquid, and stir, breaking up the tomatoes with the back of a spoon. Stir in the tomato paste and brown sugar. Bring to a boil; reduce heat and simmer 5 minutes. Stir in the olives and raisins. Remove 1 cup of the Base Recipe from the saucepan for the Picadillo recipe.

Kidney Bean Picadillo

1 1/2 cups cooked (page xi) or canned, rinsed kidney beans

Stir the kidney beans into the remaining Base Recipe in the saucepan. Cook over medium-high heat, stirring occasionally, until heated through, about 2 minutes.

serves 2 to 3

Picadillo

1/2 to 3/4 pound ground beef
1 tablespoon tomato paste
1/4 teaspoon oregano
1/4 teaspoon salt

In a medium skillet cook the beef over medium-high heat until no longer pink, about 3 minutes. Stir in the tomato paste, oregano, salt, and reserved 1 cup of the Base Recipe. Cook, stirring, until heated through.

serves 2

chapter seven

Middle East
and
Mediterranean

Moroccan Couscous with Curried Chickpeas & Moroccan Couscous with Lamb

You can use shoulder or leg steaks for the lamb recipe.

BASE RECIPE

$^1/_3$ cup slivered almonds

1 tablespoon vegetable oil

1 cup chopped onion

1 cup coarsely shredded carrot

1 teaspoon ground cinnamon

$^1/_2$ teaspoon ground tumeric

$^1/_2$ teaspoon ground ginger

One 8-ounce can whole, peeled tomatoes, undrained

$1^2/_3$ cups water

$^1/_2$ teaspoon salt

$^1/_2$ teaspoon sugar

1 cup couscous

$^1/_3$ cup raisins

Preheat the oven to 350°F.

Bake the almonds on a baking sheet for 10 minutes or until lightly browned. Set aside to cool.

In a 2-quart saucepot, heat the oil over medium-high heat. Add the onion and carrot; cook, stirring, until softened, about 2–3 minutes. Stir in the cinnamon, tumeric, and ginger until absorbed. Stir in the tomatoes with their liquid and break them up with the back of a spoon. Stir in the water, salt, and sugar; bring to a boil. Add the couscous, return to a boil. Reduce heat and simmer, covered, 7 minutes or until the liquid is absorbed. Stir in the raisins and almonds. Set aside 2 cups of the Base Recipe for the Moroccan Couscous with Lamb recipe.

Moroccan Couscous with Curried Chickpeas

2 teaspoons vegetable oil

$^1/_2$ teaspoon curry powder

1 cup cooked (page xi) or canned, rinsed chickpeas (garbanzo beans)

In a small skillet, heat the oil over medium high heat. Add the curry. Stir in the chickpeas and cook, stirring, until heated through, about 2 minutes. Add the chickpea mixture to the remaining Base Recipe in the saucepan. Cook over medium heat, stirring, until heated through.

serves 2 to 3

Moroccan Couscous with Lamb

$^3/_4$ pound lamb shoulder or steaks (1 inch thick)

Preheat the broiler. Cook the lamb, 4 to 6 inches away from the heat, 2 to 3 minutes per side for medium rare or until desired doneness. Cut into $^1/_4$-inch thick slices. Serve over the reserved Base Recipe.

serves 2

Barley-Stuffed Peppers
& Moroccan Stuffed Peppers

*I like to use red bell peppers for this recipe because I prefer the mild flavor; however,
green bell peppers provide a nice contrast in color to the sauce.*

BASE RECIPE

2 large or 4 small red or green bell peppers

1 tablespoon olive oil

$^1/_2$ cup chopped onion

2 cloves garlic, minced

3 cups chopped tomato

$^1/_2$ cup vegetable broth (page xii or store-bought)

> **recipe tip:**
>
> *Cook the barley before you
> start the Base Recipe. While
> the Base Recipe is cooking,
> prepare the fillings. Start
> baking the Moroccan Stuffed
> Peppers 20 minutes before you
> place the Barley-Stuffed Peppers
> into the oven so that both recipes
> will finish at the same time.*

Preheat the oven to 375°F.

If using large bell peppers, cut them in half through the stem, discard seeds and ribs;
or if using small bell peppers, cut off the top with the stem then remove seeds and
ribs. Blanch the bell peppers in boiling water 4 minutes; drain and set aside.

In a 2-quart saucepan, heat the oil over medium-high heat. Add the onion and garlic;
cook, stirring, 2 minutes or until softened. Add the tomatoes and broth. Bring to a
boil. Reduce heat and simmer 20 minutes. Transfer the sauce to a blender or food
processor. Purée until smooth. Reserve half the sauce for the Barley-Stuffed Peppers.

Barley-Stuffed Peppers

1 tablespoon vegetable oil

$^1/_2$ cup chopped onion

2 cloves garlic, minced

$1^1/_2$ cups chopped mushrooms

1 cup cooked barley

2 tablespoons snipped, fresh dill

$^1/_4$ teaspoon salt, or to taste

$^1/_8$ teaspoon black pepper

In a medium skillet, heat the oil over medium-high heat. Add the onion and garlic; cook, stirring, until softened about 2 minutes. Add the mushrooms; cook, stirring until softened, about 3 minutes. Stir in the barley, dill, salt, and black pepper.

Place the barley mixture evenly into two of the Base Recipe bell pepper shells. Place the reserved Base Recipe sauce into an 8-inch square baking dish. Place the bell peppers over sauce. Bake for 20 minutes or until heated through.

serves 2

Double the Barley-Stuffed Peppers recipe and use all the Base Recipe bell peppers. Place the Base Recipe sauce into a 9×13-inch baking pan. Place the bell peppers over the sauce and bake 20 minutes.

Moroccan Stuffed Peppers

$^1/_2$ pound ground lamb

$^1/_2$ cup cooked barley

$^1/_4$ cup chopped, dried apricots

$^1/_4$ cup chopped walnuts

2 tablespoons finely chopped onion

$^1/_2$ teaspoon crushed, dried mint leaves

$^1/_4$ teaspoon ground coriander

$^1/_4$ teaspoon salt

$^1/_8$ teaspoon black pepper

In a medium bowl, combine all the ingredients. Place the lamb mixture evenly into two of the Base Recipe bell pepper shells. Place the remaining Base Recipe sauce into an 8-inch square baking dish. Place the bell peppers over sauce. Bake for 40 minutes or until the filling is cooked through.

serves 2

Double the Moroccan Stuffed Peppers recipe and use all the bell peppers. Place the Base Recipe sauce into a 9×13-inch baking pan. Place the bell peppers over the sauce and bake 40 minutes.

Tangier Couscous with Chickpeas
Lamb Tangier Couscous

*You can use whole wheat couscous or rizcous for this recipe
instead of the regular couscous, if you like.*

∾∾∾∾∾∾∾∾∾∾∾∾∾∾∾∾∾∾∾∾∾∾∾∾∾∾∾

BASE RECIPE

1 tablespoon vegetable oil

1^1/$_2$ cups chopped onion

1^1/$_2$ cups sliced carrot

1 teaspoon ground ginger

^{1}/$_2$ teaspoon ground turmeric

^{1}/$_4$ teaspoon ground cinnamon

^{1}/$_4$ teaspoon salt

^{1}/$_8$ teaspoon ground red pepper (cayenne)

1^1/$_2$ cups diced (^{1}/$_2$-inch) butternut squash

1^1/$_3$ cups vegetable broth (page xii or store-bought)

^{1}/$_3$ cup light or dark raisins

> **recipe tip:**
> *While the Base Recipe is cooking, prepare the lamb balls.*

In a 3-quart saucepan, heat the oil over medium-high heat. Add the onion and carrot; and cook, stirring until the onion is softened, about 3 minutes. Stir in the ginger, tumeric, cinnamon, salt, and red pepper. Add the squash and broth; bring to a boil. Reduce the heat and simmer, uncovered, 10 minutes or until the squash is tender. Stir in the raisins. Remove half of the Base Recipe from the pot for the Tangier Couscous with Chickpeas recipe, making sure to divide the liquid (as well as the vegetables) evenly.

∾∾∾∾∾∾∾∾∾∾∾∾∾∾∾∾∾∾∾∾∾∾∾∾∾∾∾

Tangier Couscous with Chickpeas

1 cup cooked (page xi) or canned, rinsed chick-peas (garbanzo beans)

$^1/_2$ cup diced yellow squash

$^1/_3$ cup water

$^1/_2$ cup couscous

$^1/_8$ teaspoon salt

2 tablespoons chopped, fresh cilantro

Place the reserved Base Recipe in a 2-quart saucepan. Add the chickpeas, squash, and water. Bring to a boil; reduce the heat to low and simmer, covered, 5 minutes. Add the couscous and salt. Simmer, covered, 2 minutes; let stand 5 minutes. Add the cilantro and fluff with a fork.

serves 2 to 3

Lamb Tangier Couscous

$^1/_2$ pound ground lamb

1 tablespoon plain dry bread crumbs

1 tablespoon ground almonds

$^1/_8$ teaspoon salt

$^1/_4$ cup water

$^1/_2$ cup couscous

$1^1/_2$ tablespoons chopped, fresh parsley or cilantro

In a medium bowl, combine the lamb, bread crumbs, almonds, and salt. Form into 1-inch balls.

Add the lamb balls and water to the remaining Base Recipe in the saucepan. Bring to a boil over medium-high heat. Reduce the heat to medium and simmer, covered, 5 minutes. Add the couscous, simmer, covered, 2 minutes; let stand 5 minutes. Add the parsley and fluff with a fork.

serves 2 to 3

Black Bean Burgers & Lamb Burgers

My sister, Sherry, and friend, Bonnie Roche, both liked the bean burgers breaded with cornmeal, which made a crunchier coating. I preferred them coated in plain bread crumbs. Use whichever appeals to you. We all agreed on the fact that both recipes were really tasty.

BASE RECIPE

2 tablespoons tomato paste

2 tablespoons plain dry bread crumbs

2 tablespoons grated onion

2 cloves garlic, minced

1 teaspoon ground cinnamon

$^1/_2$ teaspoon crushed dried mint

$^1/_2$ teaspoon salt

$^1/_4$ teaspoon black pepper

In a medium bowl, combine all the ingredients. Set aside $1^1/_2$ tablespoons of the Base Recipe for the Lamb Burger recipe.

Black Bean Burgers

1¹/₂ cups cooked (page xi) or canned, rinsed
    black beans, mashed slightly

¹/₄ cup finely chopped red or green bell pepper

2 tablespoons plain dry bread crumbs

2 tablespoons chopped scallion (white and
    green parts)

¹/₂ teaspoon ground cumin

¹/₄ cup cornmeal or plain dry bread crumbs

Vegetable oil for frying

Add the beans, bell pepper, bread crumbs, scallion, and cumin to bowl with remaining Base Recipe. Form the mixture into four patties. Coat the patties in the cornmeal.

Pour the oil into a heavy skillet to a depth of ¹/₄-inch. Heat the oil to 375°F or until oil bubbles when a few bread crumbs are dropped in. Fry until browned on bottom, 2 minutes; turn and fry on second side until browned, 2 minutes more.

serves 2 to 3

Lamb Burgers

¹/₂ pound ground lamb

¹/₄ cup chopped, dried apricots

1¹/₂ tablespoons brown sugar

2 teaspoons currants

Preheat the broiler.

In a medium bowl combine the lamb, apricots, brown sugar, currants, and the reserved Base Recipe. Form into 4 patties. Broil the patties 4 to 6 inches from the heat, about 3 minutes per side for medium-rare or until cooked to desired doneness.

serves 2

Sweet Potato–Butternut Squash Kebobs

Swordfish Kebobs

In this recipe instead of my usual Japanese (Kikkomon), I use Chinese soy sauce (La Choy) for a more intense, saltier flavor. You'll need to use metal skewers for these kebobs, since the wooden ones aren't strong enough to pierce raw sweet potatoes. Serve both of these recipes with couscous.

BASE RECIPE

Marinade:

$^1/_3$ cup orange juice

1 tablespoon dark soy sauce

1 tablespoon mirin (rice wine) or dry sherry

1 tablespoon minced ginger

1 tablespoon honey

2 teaspoons sesame oil

1 teaspoon grated orange rind

$^1/_4$ teaspoon dried rosemary, crushed

> **recipe tip:**
>
> *Prepare the marinade in the Base Recipe, then marinate the swordfish and vegetables. While the kabobs are broiling, go back to the Base Recipe and cook the couscous. Cook the Sweet Potato Kebobs before the Swordfish Kebobs; the potatoes take more time.*

To Finish:

Water

1 cup couscous

$^1/_4$ cup thinly sliced scallion (white and green parts)

To prepare the marinade: In a 2-cup glass measuring cup, combine the orange juice, soy sauce, mirin, ginger, honey, sesame oil, orange rind, and rosemary. Place $1^1/_2$ tablespoons of the marinade into one medium bowl and 2 tablespoons of the marinade into a second medium bowl. Set aside remaining marinade.

Prepare the Sweet Potato–Butternut Squash and Swordfish recipes.

Five minutes before serving, add enough water to the reserved Base Recipe marinade to equal $1^1/_3$ cups. Place the liquid into a $1^1/_2$-quart saucepan and bring to a boil over high heat. Add the couscous and return to a boil. Reduce heat and simmer, covered, until liquid is absorbed, about 5 minutes. Divide evenly and serve with the kebobs.

Sweet Potato–Butternut Squash Kebobs

1 tablespoon brown sugar

1 large sweet potato, peeled and sliced $^1/_2$-inch thick

Three $^1/_2$-inch thick slices butternut squash, peeled and quartered

1 medium onion, cut into 8 wedges

Preheat the broiler or grill.

Stir the brown sugar into the bowl with the 2 tablespoons of the Base Recipe marinade. Add the sweet potatoes, squash, and onion and let stand 20 minutes, tossing occasionally. String the vegetables, alternately, onto skewers. Place the skewered vegetables on a broiler pan or a grill and cook, brushing occasionally with the marinade, until browned on one side, about 5 minutes. Turn and cook until cooked through, 5 minutes more. (While the kabobs are cooking, prepare the couscous in the Base Recipe.)

serves 2

Swordfish Kebobs

$^1/_2$ to $^3/_4$ pound swordfish steak, cubed

1 small onion, quartered

1 small green bell pepper, cut into eight pieces

Preheat the broiler or grill.

Add the swordfish, onion, and bell peppers into the bowl with $1^1/_2$ tablespoons of the Base Recipe marinade. Let stand 20 minutes, tossing occasionally. String the swordfish on two skewers and the vegetables on two skewers. Place the skewered vegetables on a broiler pan or grill and cook, brushing occasionally with the marinade, until browned on one side, about 5 minutes. Turn. Add the swordfish kebabs to the broiler or grill and cook 2 minutes. Turn swordfish and cook 2 minutes more or until cooked through. (While the kabobs are cooking, prepare the couscous in the Base Recipe.)

serves 2

Curried Chickpea Tzimmes
Curried Lamb Tzimmes

This dish is based on a traditional Jewish recipe, but with the very nontraditional addition of curry. You can use less ground red pepper for a milder version.

BASE RECIPE

1 tablespoon vegetable oil

$^3/_4$ cup chopped onion

1 tablespoon curry powder

1 teaspoon ground ginger

$^1/_8$ teaspoon ground red pepper (cayenne)

$^3/_4$ cup water

$^3/_4$ cup apple juice

1 tablespoon firmly packed brown sugar

2 cups peeled, cubed (1-inch) butternut squash

$1^1/_2$ cups peeled, cubed (1-inch) sweet potato

$^3/_4$ cup sliced carrots

$^1/_2$ cup pitted prunes

In a 3-quart saucepan, heat the oil over medium-high heat. Add the onion and cook, stirring, until softened. Stir in the curry, ginger, and red pepper until absorbed. Add the water, apple juice, and brown sugar; bring to a boil. Add the squash, sweet potatoes, and carrots. Return to a boil; reduce heat and simmer, uncovered, 15 minutes. Add the prunes and simmer, 10 minutes longer. Set aside 2 cups for the Curried Lamb Tzimmes recipe.

Curried Chickpea Tzimmes

$3/4$ cup cooked (page xi) or canned, rinsed chickpeas (garbanzo beans)

Add the chickpeas to the remaining Base Recipe and cook, covered, 3 to 5 minutes or until heated though.

serves 2

Curried Lamb Tzimmes

$1/2$ pound ground lamb

1 tablespoon plain dry bread crumbs

$1/4$ teaspoon ground cinnamon

$1/4$ teaspoon salt

In a medium bowl, combine the lamb, bread crumbs, cinnamon, and salt. Form the mixture into 1-inch balls. In a $1^1/2$-quart saucepan, combine the lamb balls and reserved Base Recipe and cook, covered, until the lamb balls are cooked through, about 5 minutes.

serves 2

Mediterranean Couscous with Vegetables
& Mediterranean Chicken

If you cannot find saffron, you can use $^1/_4$ teaspoon ground tumeric instead for the color, but the flavor will be slightly different.

ω ω ω ω ω ω ω ω ω ω ω ω ω ω ω ω ω ω ω

BASE RECIPE

1 tablespoon olive oil

1 cup chopped onion

$^1/_2$ cup sliced leek (white and light green parts only), rinsed thoroughly

2 cloves garlic, minced

$1^3/_4$ cups vegetable broth (page xii or store-bought)

2 cups chopped tomato

$^1/_3$ cup white wine

$^1/_2$ teaspoon grated orange rind

$^1/_4$ teaspoon dried thyme

$^1/_4$ teaspoon dried basil

Pinch saffron

1 cup couscous

$^1/_4$ teaspoon black pepper

> **recipe tip:**
> *Prepare the chicken and sautéed vegetables from the Mediterranean Couscous with Vegetables recipe before starting the Base Recipe.*

In a 2-quart saucepan, heat the oil over medium-high heat. Add the onion, leek, and garlic; cook, stirring, until softened, about 2 minutes. Add the broth, tomato, wine, orange rind, thyme, basil, and saffron. Bring to a boil. Reduce heat and simmer, covered, 10 minutes. Add the couscous and return to a boil. Reduce heat and simmer, covered, until the liquid is absorbed, 5 minutes. Stir in the black pepper. Reserve $2^1/_3$ cups for the Mediterranean Couscous with Vegetables recipe.

ω ω ω ω ω ω ω ω ω ω ω ω ω ω ω ω ω ω ω

Mediterranean Couscous with Vegetables

1 tablespoon olive oil

1 cup chopped carrots

1 cup chopped zucchini

$^1/_2$ cup chopped prunes

1 tablespoon fresh lemon juice

In a medium skillet, heat the oil over medium-high heat. Add the carrots and zucchini; cook, stirring, until softened, about 3 minutes. Add the prunes, lemon juice, and the reserved Base Recipe. Cook, stirring, until heated through.

serves 2 to 3

Mediterranean Chicken

1 tablespoon olive oil

8 ounces skinless, boneless chicken breast, sliced into $^1/_2$-inch strips

1 clove garlic, minced

1 teaspoon curry powder

1 tablespoon lemon juice

$^1/_4$ cup small, pimiento-stuffed green olives

$^1/_4$ teaspoon salt

In a medium skillet, heat the oil over medium-high heat. Add the chicken and garlic and cook, stirring, until cooked through, about 4 minutes. Stir in the curry powder. Add the lemon juice and cook, stirring, 1 minute. Add the olives, salt, and the remaining Base Recipe. Cook, stirring, until heated through.

serves 2

Sweet Potatoes and Chickpea Curry
Salmon with Mango Ginger Sauce

This is a really incredibly delicious way to serve salmon. The curry is delicious also, maybe perhaps a kind-hearted vegetarian will let their meat-eating family members have a taste. Make sure the mango is ripe (feels soft when gently squeezed and is aromatic) for this recipe.

BASE RECIPE

2 cups chopped mango

1¹/₂ tablespoons minced ginger

1 tablespoon minced jalapeño pepper

2 tablespoons chopped, fresh cilantro

Combine all of the ingredients in a 1-quart saucepan. Reserve ³/₄ cup of the Base Recipe for the Sweet Potatoes and Chickpea Curry recipe.

Sweet Potatoes and Chickpea Curry

1 tablespoon vegetable oil

$^1/_2$ cup chopped onion

2 cloves garlic, minced

1 tablespoon curry powder

$^1/_2$ teaspoon ground turmeric

$^1/_2$ teaspoon ground coriander

$^1/_2$ cup water

1 cup peeled, cubed sweet potato

1 cup sliced carrots

1 cup cooked (page xi) chickpeas (garbanzo beans)

2 teaspoons brown sugar

$^1/_2$ teaspoon salt

In a 3-quart saucepan, heat the oil over medium-high heat. Add the onion and garlic; cook, stirring, until softened, about 2 minutes. Stir in the curry, turmeric, and coriander. Stir in the water and reserved Base Recipe; bring to a boil. Add the sweet potato and carrots, return to a boil; reduce heat and simmer, covered, 20 minutes, stirring occasionally. Stir in the chickpeas, brown sugar, and salt. Simmer, covered, 5 minutes more.

serves 2

Double the recipe and use all of the Base Recipe, increase the water to $^3/_4$ cup.

Salmon with Mango Ginger Sauce

2 tablespoons orange juice

2 tablespoons lime juice

1 tablespoon brown sugar

2 salmon steaks (about 6 to 8 ounces each)

Preheat the broiler.

In a medium bowl, combine the orange juice, lime juice, and brown sugar. Add the salmon and let stand 10 minutes, turning once. Broil the salmon, 4 to 6 inches from the heat source, 2 to 3 minutes per side, or until desired doneness. While the salmon is cooking, heat the Base Recipe remaining in the saucepan, until mixture comes to a boil; serve over the salmon steaks.

serves 2

Double the Salmon with Mango Ginger Sauce recipe and use all of the Base Recipe as the sauce.

Yellow Rice with Zucchini and Chickpeas

Yellow Rice with Mussels

I find small mussels tender and tasty, and like to use them when I cook rather than the larger variety. Also, cultivated mussels will be easier to clean than those caught at sea. To clean mussels, scrub them and remove their beards. If the mussels do not open when they are cooked, discard them.

BASE RECIPE

1 tablespoon olive oil

1 cup chopped onion

2 cloves garlic, minced

$^1/_2$ teaspoon turmeric

1 cup converted white rice

1 cup water

1 cup vegetable broth (page xii or store-bought)

$^1/_8$ teaspoon saffron

In a 2-quart saucepan, heat the oil over medium-high heat. Add the onion and garlic and cook, stirring, until softened, 3 minutes. Stir in the turmeric. Add rice and stir until well-coated with the oil and turmeric. Add the water, broth, and saffron; bring to a boil. Reduce the heat and simmer, covered, until the water is absorbed, 20 minutes. Set aside half of the Base Recipe for the Yellow Rice with Mussels recipe.

Yellow Rice with Zucchini and Chickpeas

1 teaspoon olive oil

1 cup chopped zucchini

1 cup cooked (page xi) or canned, rinsed chickpeas (garbanzo beans)

$^1/_4$ cup chopped, pimiento-stuffed olives

2 teaspoons chopped capers

Heat the oil in a small skillet over medium-high heat. Add the zucchini and cook, stirring, until tender, about 3 minutes. Add the zucchini, chickpeas, olives, and capers to the remaining Base Recipe still in the saucepan. Cook, stirring, until heated through, 2 minutes.

serves 2

Yellow Rice with Mussels

$^1/_4$ cup water

2 tablespoons white wine, optional

30 small to medium mussels, scrubbed and debearded

$^1/_4$ cup chopped, fresh parsley

In a 3-quart saucepan, bring the water and wine to a boil over high heat. Add the mussels; cover and steam, about 3 minutes or until all the mussels have opened. Discard any unopened mussels. Drain. Add the reserved Base Recipe to the mussels in the saucepan. Stir in the parsley and heat over medium heat until warm.

serves 2

Imam Bayaldi  Beef-Stuffed Eggplant

Eggplant fans, this is the recipe for you. The flavor of the eggplant really shines through in this recipe.

BASE RECIPE

2 medium eggplants (about 1 pound each)

1 tablespoon olive oil

$1^1/_2$ cups chopped onion

3 cloves garlic, minced

2 cups chopped tomato

2 tablespoons chopped, fresh parsley

$^1/_4$ teaspoon black pepper

Preheat the oven to 350°F.

Cut each eggplant, on the diagonal, into $1^1/_2$-inch thick slices. Make a pocket in each slice by horizontally cutting each eggplant slice almost through so that the eggplant remains partially intact like a hot dog roll; set aside.

In a small skillet, heat the oil over medium-high heat. Add the onion and garlic and cook, stirring, until softened, about 2 minutes. Add the tomato, parsley, and black pepper. Reserve 1 cup of mixture for the Beef-Stuffed Eggplant recipe.

Imam Bayaldi

1 tablespoon olive oil

2 tablespoons pine nuts

1 teaspoon ground coriander

1 teaspoon fresh lemon juice

1 teaspoon sugar

$^1/_4$ teaspoon salt

Brush the outsides of the eggplant "hot dog" with some of the oil.

In a small bowl, stir together the nuts, coriander, lemon juice, sugar, salt, and the remaining Base Recipe. Stuff each eggplant evenly with the nut mixture (if there is some left over, that is okay), then brush with the remaining oil.

Place the stuffed eggplant in 9-inch baking pan, lined with greased aluminum foil. Spread any remaining nut mixture around the eggplant. Bake, covered, for 45 minutes.

serves 2

Beef-Stuffed Eggplant

$^1/_2$ pound ground beef

$^1/_4$ teaspoon ground cinnamon

$^1/_4$ teaspoon salt

1 tablespoon olive oil

In a medium bowl, combine the beef, cinnamon, salt, and $^1/_2$ cup of the reserved Base Recipe. Stuff each eggplant evenly with the meat mixture, brush top and bottom with olive oil.

Place the stuffed eggplant in 9-inch baking pan lined with greased aluminum foil. Sprinkle the remaining $^1/_2$ cup of the reserved Base Recipe around the eggplant. Bake, covered, for 45 minutes.

serves 2

Feta Frittata with Sun-Dried Tomatoes & Feta Frittata with Ham

This is a great brunch entrée. Start with glasses of fresh orange juice or mimosas, then serve the frittata with lovely crusty rolls and butter and a leafy salad.

BASE RECIPE

8 large eggs

4 large egg whites

$^1/_2$ teaspoon oregano

$^1/_4$ teaspoon salt, or to taste

$^1/_8$ teaspoon black pepper

One 10-ounce package chopped, frozen spinach, thawed and squeezed dry

1 cup crumbled feta cheese

$^1/_2$ cup sliced scallion (green and white parts)

$^1/_4$ cup chopped, fresh parsley

Preheat the broiler.

In medium bowl, beat together eggs, egg whites, oregano, salt, and black pepper. Beat in the spinach, feta cheese, scallion, and parsley. Set aside half for the Feta Frittata with Sun-Dried Tomatoes recipe.

Feta Frittata with Sun-Dried Tomatoes

2 tablespoons chopped, sun-dried tomatoes, packed in oil

$1^1/_2$ tablespoons butter

In a medium bowl, stir the sun-dried tomatoes and the reserved Base Recipe.

In a large heat-proof skillet, melt the butter over medium-high heat. Pour the egg mixture into skillet. Cook, stirring, until the eggs begin to set. Continue cooking until the top of the eggs are just slightly runny. Remove from heat, place under broiler 2 minutes until top is cooked.

serves 2 to 3

Double the Feta Frittata with Sun-Dried Tomatoes recipe using the entire Base Recipe. Prepare the recipe in two skillets or in one, using half of the mixture at a time.

Feta Frittata with Ham

$^1/_2$ cup diced ($^1/_4$-inch), cooked ham

$1^1/_2$ tablespoons butter

Stir the ham into the remaining half of the Base Recipe in the bowl.

In a large, heat-proof skillet, melt the butter over medium-high heat. Pour the egg mixture into the skillet. Cook, stirring, until the eggs begin to set. Continue cooking until the top of the eggs are just slightly runny. Remove from heat, place under broiler 2 minutes until top is cooked.

serves 2 to 3

Double the Feta Frittata with Ham recipe using the entire Base Recipe. Prepare the recipe in two skillets or in one, using half of the mixture at a time.

Curried Squash and Chickpeas
Curried Squash with Lamb Balls

Don't let the long list of ingredients discourage you; mostly they are spices that get stirred in at the beginning of the recipe. If you're missing one or two (as long as you do *have the curry), don't worry, the result will still be pretty good.*

BASE RECIPE

2 tablespoons vegetable oil

1 1/2 cups chopped onion

2 cloves garlic, minced

1 tablespoon curry powder

1 teaspoon ground cinnamon

1 teaspoon ground coriander

1/2 teaspoon ground ginger

1/2 teaspoon ground turmeric

1/2 teaspoon ground cardamom

1/4 teaspoon ground red pepper (cayenne)

1 cup water

3 cups cubed butternut squash

2 cups cubed sweet potato

1 cup chopped, peeled tart apple

1/3 cup golden raisins

1 teaspoon salt

In a 3-quart saucepan, heat the oil over medium-high heat. Add the onion and garlic; cook, stirring, until softened, about 2 minutes. Stir in the curry powder, cinnamon, coriander, ginger, turmeric, cardamom, and red pepper. Add the water and bring to a boil. Add the squash, sweet potato, and apple. Bring to a boil; reduce heat and simmer, uncovered, 20 minutes. Stir in the raisins, and salt.

Remove half of the Base Recipe from the pot for the Curried Squash with Lamb Balls.

Curried Squash and Chickpeas

1 cup cooked (page xi) or canned, rinsed chick-peas (garnbanzo beans)

Add the chickpeas to the curry remaining in the saucepan. Bring to a boil. Reduce heat and simmer, covered, 10 minutes.

serves 2 to 3

Curried Squash with Lamb Balls

$^1/_2$ pound ground lamb

3 tablespoons chopped walnuts

1 tablespoon plain dry bread crumbs

$^1/_8$ teaspoon salt

$^1/_8$ teaspoon ground cloves

In a medium bowl, combine the lamb, walnuts, bread crumbs, salt, and cloves. Form into 1-inch balls. Place the reserve Base Recipe and lamb balls in a $1^1/_2$-quart saucepan. Bring to a boil. Reduce heat and simmer, covered, 10 minutes.

serves 2

Vegetable Stew with Butter Beans
Vegetable Stew with Lamb

If you cannot find butter beans, chickpeas can be substituted.

BASE RECIPE

1 tablespoon vegetable oil

1¹/₂ cups chopped onion

3 cloves garlic, minced

1 teaspoon turmeric

1¹/₂ cups carrot chunks (1¹/₂-inch pieces)

1¹/₂ cups water

1 cup celery chunks (1-inch pieces)

3 tablespoons tomato paste

1 cup potato chunks (1-inch pieces)

¹/₂ teaspoon salt

¹/₄ teaspoon black pepper

recipe tip:
Prepare the lamb balls while the Base Recipe is cooking.

In a 3-quart pot, heat the oil over medium-high heat. Add the onion and garlic. Cook, stirring, until softened, 2 minutes. Stir in the turmeric. Add the carrots, water, celery, and tomato paste. Bring to a boil. Reduce heat and simmer, covered, 35 minutes. Add the potatoes, salt, and black pepper; simmer, covered, 10 minutes longer. Remove 2 cups of the Base Recipe from the saucepan for the Vegetable Stew with Lamb recipe, set aside.

Vegetable Stew with Butter Beans

1 cup cooked (page xi) or canned, rinsed butter beans

1 cup butternut squash chunks (1-inch pieces)

$^1/_3$ cup apple juice

1 teaspoon honey

Stir the butter beans, butternut squash, apple juice, and honey into the Base Recipe remaining in the saucepan. Bring to a boil. Reduce heat and simmer, covered, 20 minutes or until the squash and potatoes are tender.

serves 2

Vegetable Stew with Lamb

$^1/_2$ pound ground lamb

$1^1/_2$ tablespoons plain dry bread crumbs

1 tablespoon chopped, fresh parsley

1 clove garlic, minced

$^1/_4$ teaspoon salt

In a medium bowl, stir together the lamb, bread crumbs, parsley, garlic, and the salt. Form into 1-inch balls.

In a $1^1/_2$-quart saucepan combine the lamb balls and the reserved Base Recipe. Bring to a boil; reduce heat and simmer, covered, until the lamb is cooked through, 20 minutes.

serves 2

Fruit and Rice–Stuffed Acorn Squash
Lamb-Stuffed Acorn Squash

Acorn squash comes in dark green or yellow. It is almost a heart-shaped oval vegetable.
The flavor is mild and goes very well with sweet fillings.

BASE RECIPE

2 acorn squash (about $3/4$ pounds each)

$1/2$ cups chopped apple

$1/3$ cup chopped walnuts

$1/3$ cup chopped, dried apricots

$1/4$ cup chopped, dried dates

2 tablespoons raisins

2 tablespoons firmly packed brown sugar

Preheat the oven to 350°F.

Cut each acorn squash in half, through the stem. Discard the seeds. Place the squash in a baking dish and bake for 20 minutes; set aside. Do not turn off the oven.

In a medium bowl, stir together the apple, walnuts, apricots, dates, raisins, and brown sugar. Set aside $3/4$ cup of the Base Recipe for the Lamb-Stuffed Acorn Squash.

Fruit and Rice-Stuffed Acorn Squash

³/₄ cup cooked brown rice

Mix together the rice and the remaining Base Recipe. Fill two of the baked acorn squash halves evenly with the rice mixture.

Place the stuffed squash in an 8-inch square baking pan. Bake, covered, 35 to 40 minutes or until filling is heated through and squash is tender.

serves 2

Increase the chopped apple to 1¹/₂ cups, and double the amount of rice. Use this mixture to fill all four acorn squash halves.

Lamb-Stuffed Acorn Squash

¹/₂ pound ground lamb

¹/₄ teaspoon salt

In a medium bowl, combine the lamb, salt, and the reserved ³/₄ cup of the Base Recipe. Form into two balls. Place one lamb ball each into the two remaining acorn squash halves. Place stuffed squash in an 8-inch baking pan and bake 35 to 40 minutes or until the lamb is cooked through and the squash is tender.

serves 2

Reduce the apples in the Base Recipe to ¹/₂ cup, the walnuts to ¹/₄ cup, and omit the raisins. Increase to 1 pound of lamb, and ¹/₂ teaspoon salt. Form into 4 balls and fit one into each of the squash halves.

Curried Couscous with Chickpeas and Dates

Curried Couscous with Lamb and Dates

If you like mint, you can experiment with this recipe by adding chopped mint to either or both of the recipes.

BASE RECIPE

1 tablespoon vegetable oil

1 cup chopped onion

2 cloves garlic, minced

1^1/$_2$ tablespoons ground curry powder

^{1}/$_2$ teaspoon ground ginger

^{1}/$_2$ teaspoon ground cinnamon

1 cup vegetable broth (page xii or store-bought)

1 cup water

^{1}/$_2$ teaspoon salt

1^1/$_2$ cups cooked (page xi) or canned, rinsed chickpeas (garbanzo beans)

In a 2-quart saucepan, heat the oil over medium-high heat. Add the onion and garlic; cook, stirring, until softened, about 2 minutes. Stir in the curry powder, ginger, and cinnamon until absorbed. Stir in the broth and water, bring to a boil. Add salt and chickpeas; return to a boil. Reduce heat and simmer, uncovered, 10 minutes. Set aside half of the Base Recipe for the Curried Couscous with Lamb and Dates recipe.

Curried Couscous with Chickpeas and Dates

$1/_4$ cup apple juice

$1/_3$ cup couscous

$1/_2$ cup chopped, pitted dates

$1/_2$ cup chopped walnuts

Add the apple juice to the remaining Base Recipe in the saucepan. Bring to a boil.

Stir in the couscous; return to a boil. Reduce heat and simmer, covered, 5 minutes or until liquid is absorbed. Stir in the dates and nuts.

serves 2

Double the Curried Couscous with Chickpeas and Dates recipe and use all of the Base Recipe.

Curried Couscous with Lamb and Dates

$1/_2$ pound ground lamb

1 tablespoon plain dry bread crumbs

2 tablespoons finely chopped dates

$1/_8$ teaspoon salt

$1/_3$ cup couscous

2 tablespoons chopped, fresh cilantro

In a medium bowl, combine the lamb, bread crumbs, dates, and salt. Form into 1-inch balls.

Place the reserved Base Recipe into a $1^1/_2$-quart saucepan. Add the lamb balls and bring to a boil. Reduce heat and simmer, covered, 5 minutes. Stir in the couscous; return to a boil. Reduce heat and simmer, covered, 5 minutes or until liquid is absorbed. Stir in the chopped cilantro.

serves 2

Double all the ingredients of the Curried Couscous with Lamb and Dates recipe, except for the cilantro and use all of the Base Recipe.

Mediterranean Feta Cheese Tart & Mediterranean Lamb Tart

This recipe makes 2 tarts which can serve between 4 and 8 people, depending on their appetites. I use frozen, prepared crusts for this recipe, but if you are feeling ambitious, you can make your own homemade crust.

BASE RECIPE

Two frozen 6-inch tart crusts

1 tablespoon olive oil

$3/4$ cup chopped onion

2 cloves garlic, minced

$1^1/_2$ cups chopped tomato

2 large eggs

1 cup milk

$1/_2$ teaspoon dried oregano

$1/_8$ teaspoon black pepper

Preheat oven to 375°F.

Weigh down the pastry using pie weights or dried beans to prevent the crust from rising. Bake the tart crusts until just browned, 15 minutes. Remove the tart crusts from oven and remove weights. Lower the oven temperature to 350°F.

In a medium skillet, heat the oil over medium-high heat. Add the onion and garlic. cook, stirring, until onion is softened, about 2 minutes; stir in tomato. Reserve $3/4$ cup from the skillet for the Mediterranean Feta Cheese Tart recipe.

In a large bowl, beat the eggs lightly. Add the milk, oregano, and black pepper; beat until combined. Reserve one half of the egg mixture for the Mediterranean Feta Cheese Tart recipe.

Mediterranean Feta Cheese Tart

1 cup crumbled feta cheese (about 4 ounces)

$1/4$ cup sliced black olives

In a medium bowl, combine the feta cheese and olives with the reserved $3/4$ cup tomato mixture from the Base Recipe. Sprinkle the mixture into the bottom of one tart shell. Pour in the reserved half of the Base Recipe egg mixture. Bake 50 to 60 minutes or until puffy and slightly browned on top.

serves 2 to 4

Mediterranean Lamb Tart

$1/2$ pound ground lamb

$1/4$ teaspoon salt

Add the lamb and salt to the remaining Base Recipe in the skillet. Cook over medium heat, stirring, until no longer pink, 3 minutes. Sprinkle the lamb mixture into the bottom of one tart shell. Pour in the remaining Base Recipe egg mixture to cover the lamb filling in each tart. Bake 50 to 60 minutes or until puffy and slightly browned on top.

serves 2 to 4

Brown Rice Pilaf with Chickpeas
Brown Rice Pilaf with Sliced Lamb

I love sliced lamb that comes from cooked leg of lamb. But if you don't happen to have a whole leg of lamb available, you can cut the meat from shoulder of lamb or leg of lamb steaks.

BASE RECIPE

$1/2$ cup chopped almonds

1 tablespoon vegetable oil

1 cup chopped onion

1 cup vegetable broth (page xii or store-bought)

$1 1/2$ cup water

1 cup brown rice

$2/3$ cup chopped, dried apricots

$1/3$ cup raisins

$1/2$ teaspoon salt

Preheat the oven to 350°F.

Place the almonds in a shallow pan and bake for 10 minutes or until toasted; set aside.

In a 2-quart saucepan, heat the oil over medium-high heat. Add the onion and cook, stirring, until softened, about 2 minutes. Add the broth and water and bring to a boil; stir in the rice. Reduce the heat and simmer, covered, until liquid is absorbed, 45 minutes. Stir in the apricots, raisins, salt, and toasted almonds. Set aside 2 cups for the Brown Rice Pilaf with Sliced Lamb recipe.

Brown Rice Pilaf with Chickpeas

$^3/_4$ cup cooked (page xi) or canned, rinsed chickpeas (garbanzo beans)

1 tablespoon finely chopped, fresh mint

Add the chickpeas and mint to the remaining Base Recipe in the saucepan. Cook over medium heat, stirring, until heated through.

serves 2

Brown Rice Pilaf with Sliced Lamb

$^1/_2$ to $^3/_4$ pound lamb shoulder or leg steak, cut 1-inch thick

Preheat the broiler.

Broil the lamb 6 inches from the heat source 3 to 4 minutes per side for medium-rare or to desired doneness. Slice and serve over the reserved Base Recipe.

serves 2

Spaghetti Squash with Feta Cheese
Spaghetti Squash with Chicken

Spaghetti squash is a large, yellow, zeppelin-shaped winter vegetable. When cooked, the flesh becomes long and stringy, resembling spaghetti, hence its name. On the average, a medium squash will weigh about 3 pounds and should have a hard, blemish-free exterior.

BASE RECIPE

One 2^1/$_2$-pound spaghetti squash

2 tablespoons olive oil

^{1}/$_2$ pound coarsely chopped, fresh spinach

3 cloves garlic, minced

^{1}/$_4$ cup chopped sun-dried tomatoes packed in oil

^{1}/$_2$ teaspoon oregano

^{1}/$_4$ teaspoon salt

Preheat the oven to 375°F.

Place the squash, whole, into a baking pan and bake until tender, about 50 minutes. Cut the squash in half, discard seeds. Using a fork, pull out the center of the squash and place it in a bowl.

In a large skillet, heat the oil over medium-high heat. Add the spinach and garlic and cook, stirring until spinach is wilted, about 2 minutes. Stir in the sun-dried tomatoes, oregano, and salt. Add the squash. Set aside 2 cups for Spaghetti Squash with Chicken recipe.

Spaghetti Squash with Feta Cheese

$^1/_2$ cup crumbled feta cheese

Stir the cheese into the remaining Base Recipe in the skillet. Cook until heated through.

serves 2 to 3

Spaghetti Squash with Chicken

1 tablespoon olive oil

$^1/_2$ to $^3/_4$ pound skinless, boneless chicken breast, cut into strips

1 clove garlic, minced

1 tablespoon fresh lemon juice

$^1/_4$ teaspoon dried thyme

$^1/_4$ teaspoon salt

In a large skillet, heat the oil over medium-high heat. Add the chicken and garlic. Cook, stirring, until cooked through, about 3 to 4 minutes. Stir in the lemon juice and thyme. Cook, stirring, one minute more. Add the salt and the reserved 2 cups of the Base Recipe. Cook, stirring, until heated through.

serves 2 to 3

Vegetable Curry & Chicken Curry

Serve this "basic" curry with rice or a rice pilaf, and any chutney that you may have on hand.
You can also serve this with raita, a salad made with chopped cucumber, plain yogurt,
a little garlic, and fresh, chopped cilantro.

BASE RECIPE

1 tablespoon vegetable oil

1 cup chopped onion

1 tablespoon minced ginger

3 cloves garlic, minced

1 tablespoon curry powder

1 teaspoon ground turmeric

$^1/_2$ teaspoon ground cumin

$^1/_8$ teaspoon ground red pepper (cayenne)

2 cups sliced carrots

2 cups diced, raw potatoes

$^1/_2$ cup cooked peas

1 cup vegetable broth (page xii or store-bought)

> **recipe tip:**
> *Prepare the Chicken Curry*
> *before the Vegetable Curry.*

In a 3-quart saucepan, heat the oil. Add the onion, ginger, and garlic; cook, stirring, until softened, about 1 minute. Stir in the curry, turmeric, cumin, and red pepper. Add the carrots, potatoes, vegetable broth, and peas. Set aside half of the Base Recipe for the Vegetable Curry recipe.

Vegetable Curry

2 tablespoons vegetable oil

3 cups coarsely chopped cabbage

$^1/_3$ cup apple juice

$^1/_2$ teaspoon ground cinnamon

$^1/_2$ teaspoon ground coriander

$^1/_2$ teaspoon salt

2 cups cauliflower florets

$^1/_2$ cup tomato wedges

In a 3-quart saucepan, heat the oil. Add the cabbage and cook, stirring, until tender-crisp, about 2 to 3 minutes. Add the apple juice, cinnamon, coriander, and salt. Stir in the reserved Base Recipe, cauliflower, and tomato wedges. Bring to a boil. Reduce heat and simmer, covered, 20 minutes or until vegetables are tender.

serves 2

Chicken Curry

$1^1/_2$ to 2 pounds chicken legs, thighs, wings or breasts

$^1/_4$ teaspoon salt

Add the chicken to the remaining Base Recipe in the saucepan. Bring to a boil, reduce heat and simmer, covered, 10 minutes, and then 25 minutes, uncovered, or until the chicken is cooked through. Stir in the salt.

serves 2 to 3

Slightly Curried Cauliflower Stew with Pinto Beans
&
Slightly Curried Cauliflower Stew with Chicken

If you cannot find whole coriander seed, you can substitute 1 teaspoon ground coriander, but the flavor will be less distinct.

BASE RECIPE

1 tablespoon vegetable oil

1 cup chopped onion

1 cup chopped green bell pepper

3 cloves garlic, minced

1 tablespoon coriander seed, crushed

1 teaspoon curry powder

$^1/_2$ teaspoon ground cinnamon

$^1/_4$ teaspoon ground cumin

4 cups cauliflower florets

One 16-ounce can crushed tomatoes, undrained

$^3/_4$ cup water

1 teaspoon sugar

$^1/_4$ teaspoon salt, or to taste

In a 4-quart pot, heat the oil over medium-high heat. Add the onion, bell pepper, and garlic. Cook, stirring, until the vegetables are softened, 2 to 3 minutes. Stir in the coriander seed, curry, cinnamon, and cumin. Add the cauliflower, tomatoes, water, sugar, and salt.

Cook, covered, stirring occasionally, for 20 minutes or until vegetables are tender and liquid has thickened slightly. Transfer half of the Base Recipe to a 2-quart saucepan for the Slightly Curried Cauliflower Stew with Pinto Beans recipe.

Slightly Curried Cauliflower Stew with Pinto Beans

1 cup cooked (page xi) or canned, rinsed pinto beans

Add the beans to reserved Base Recipe in the 2-quart saucepan. Cook, stirring occasionally, 5 minutes or until heated through.

serves 2 to 3

Slightly Curried Cauliflower Stew with Chicken

8 ounces skinless, boneless chicken

2 tablespoons tomato paste

$^1/_4$ teaspoon salt

$^1/_4$ teaspoon Tabasco

Cut the chicken into $^1/_2$-inch thick slices. Add the chicken, tomato paste, salt, and Tabasco to the stew remaining in the 4-quart saucepan. Cook, uncovered, 5 minutes or until the chicken is cooked through.

serves 2

Cheese-Stuffed Eggplant
& Tuna-Stuffed Eggplant

*Although I suggest garlic, you can use any type of flavored crouton that appeals to you,
such as herb or cheese flavored.*

BASE RECIPE

1 large eggplant (about 1^1/$_2$ pounds)

2 tablespoons olive oil

1 cup chopped onion

3 cups chopped tomato

^{1}/$_4$ cup chopped, fresh parsley

^{1}/$_8$ teaspoon salt, or to taste

^{1}/$_8$ teaspoon ground red pepper (cayenne)

1^1/$_2$ cups garlic flavored croutons

Preheat oven to 350°F.

Cut eggplant in half lengthwise. Scoop out the flesh, leaving about ^{1}/$_4$-inch of flesh in the eggplant shell; dice the scooped eggplant flesh into ^{1}/$_2$-inch pieces (you should have 3 cups of the diced eggplant); set aside.

Place the eggplant shells in a baking dish and bake 20 minutes.

While the eggplant shells are baking, heat the oil in a large skillet over medium-high heat. Add the onion and cook, stirring, until softened, about 2 minutes. Add diced eggplant; cook, stirring, until vegetables are tender, about 3 minutes. Stir in tomato, parsley, salt, and red pepper. Cook, stirring, until tomato has given off liquid, about 3 minutes. Stir in the croutons. Reserve one-half of the Base Recipe for the Tuna-Stuffed Eggplant recipe.

Cheese-Stuffed Eggplant

$1/2$ cup shredded Gruyère cheese

2 tablespoons grated Parmesan cheese

Combine both of the cheeses with the remaining half of the Base Recipe in the skillet.

Fill one of the baked eggplant shells with the mixture. Place the filled eggplant on a baking sheet and bake, covered with aluminum foil, until heated through, 25 minutes.

serves 2

Double the Cheese-Stuffed Eggplant recipe and use the entire Base Recipe to fill both eggplant shells.

Tuna-Stuffed Eggplant

One $3^1/2$-ounce can solid white tuna, drained

2 tablespoons chopped, fresh basil

1 tablespoon fresh lemon juice

1 teaspoon chopped capers

In a medium bowl, break up the tuna. Stir in the basil, lemon juice, and capers. Add the reserved Base Recipe and toss. Fill one of the baked eggplant shells with the mixture. Place the filled eggplant on a baking sheet and bake, covered with aluminum foil, until heated through, 25 minutes.

serves 2

Double the Tuna-Stuffed Eggplant recipe and use all of the Base Recipe.

Bulgur with Tofu & Bulgur with Beef

Bulgur is cracked wheat that has been steamed, then dried. It come in three grinds: coarse, medium, or fine. I prefer medium or coarse grind for this recipe.

BASE RECIPE

1 tablespoon olive oil

1 cup chopped onion

3 cloves garlic, minced

2 cups water

$^1/_4$ cup tomato paste

1 cup bulgur, medium or coarse grind

$^1/_2$ teaspoon salt

recipe tip:
You can broil the beef while the bulgur is cooking.

In a 2-quart saucepan, heat the oil over medium-high heat. Add the onion and garlic; cook, stirring until softened, about 2 minutes. Add the water and tomato paste; bring to a boil. Stir in the bulgur; return to a boil. Reduce heat and simmer, covered, 20 minutes. Remove from heat. Using a fork, stir in salt; let stand, covered, 3 minutes. Set aside $1^1/_2$ cups for the Bulgur with Beef recipe.

Bulgur with Tofu

4 ounces baked or pressed tofu, diced

Add the tofu to the remaining Base Recipe in the saucepan. Cook, stirring over medium-high heat, until heated through.

serves 2

Bulgur with Beef

$^1/_2$ to $^3/_4$ pound boneless sirloin or London broil

Preheat the boiler. Broil the meat 6-inches from the heat source until desired doneness, about 2 minutes per side for medium-rare. Cut the beef into $^1/_4$-inch-thick slices. Add to the reserved Base Recipe and mix well.

serves 2

chapter eight

International Salad Entrées

Black Bean Taco Salad & Beef Taco Salad

You can buy taco boats packaged in the supermarket. If you can't find them, you can use tostada shells, but you'll need 6 tostada shells instead of the 4 taco boats.

BASE RECIPE

2 cups shredded iceberg lettuce

1 cup chopped tomato

3 tablespoons chopped onion

4 taco boats

$1/4$ cup salsa

$1/4$ cup sliced, pitted, black olives

1 tablespoon sliced marinated jalapeño pepper

recipe tip:
Prepare both the Black Bean Taco Salad and the Beef Taco Salad recipes before you prepare the Base Recipe.

Prepare both the Black Bean Taco Salad and Beef Taco Salad.

In a medium bowl, toss together the lettuce, tomato, and onion. Place $1/2$ of the Black Bean Salad into each of 2 of the taco boats; fill the remaining 2 boats with the Beef Taco Salad. Top each boat with $1/4$ of the lettuce mixture, 1 tablespoon of salsa, 1 tablespoon of sliced olives, and a few slices of jalapeño pepper, in that order.

Black Bean Taco Salad

2 teaspoons vegetable oil

$1/3$ cup chopped onion

$1/4$ cup chopped green bell peppers

1 cup cooked (page xi) or canned, rinsed black beans

$1/2$ cup water

$1 1/2$ tablespoons taco seasoning mix

In a 1-quart saucepan, heat the oil over medium-high heat. Add the onion and bell peppers and cook, stirring, until softened, about 2 minutes. Add the beans, water, and taco seasoning. Bring to a boil. Reduce heat and simmer 10 minutes, uncovered, stirring occasionally, until thickened.

Use as directed in the Base Recipe.

serves 2 as filling for taco boats or topping for 3 tostada shells

Beef Taco Salad

$1/2$ pound ground beef

$1/3$ cup chopped green bell pepper

$1/4$ cup chopped onion

$1/3$ cup water

$1 1/2$ tablespoons taco seasoning mix

1 teaspoon paprika

In a medium skillet, over medium high heat, cook the beef with the bell peppers and onions until the beef is no longer pink, about 3 minutes. Stir in the water, taco mix, and paprika. Bring to a boil. Reduce heat and simmer, uncovered, stirring occasionally, 10 minutes or until mixture is thickened. Use as directed in the Base Recipe.

serves 2 as filling for taco boats or topping for 3 tostada shells

Orzo Feta Salad & Orzo Beef Salad

Orzo is rice-shaped pasta. If you can't find it, or prefer to substitute, you can substitute 2 cups of cooked rice for the $^3/_4$ cup uncooked orzo.

BASE RECIPE

$^3/_4$ cup orzo

8 halves sun-dried tomatoes packed in oil

2 tablespoons olive oil

2 tablespoons vegetable oil

1 tablespoon red wine vinegar

1 clove garlic, minced

1 teaspoon dried oregano

$^1/_4$ teaspoon salt

$^3/_4$ cup diced red bell pepper

Cook the orzo according to package directions; drain. Rinse with cold water until cool. In a blender, place the sun-dried tomatoes, both oils, the vinegar, garlic, oregano, and salt. Cover and purée until the tomatoes are in very small pieces, about 30 seconds.

Place the orzo and bell peppers in a large bowl. Add the puréed mixture and toss until combined. Reserve $1^1/_4$ cups of the Base Recipe for the Orzo Feta Salad recipe.

Orzo Feta Salad

1 cup diced cucumber

$^3/_4$ cup crumbled feta cheese

$^1/_2$ cup sliced, pitted, black olives

In a medium bowl, combine the cucumber, feta cheese, olives, and the reserved Base Recipe. Toss.

serves 2 to 3

Orzo Beef Salad

$^1/_2$ to $^3/_4$-pound boneless meat, sirloin, or London broil

Cook steak under preheated broiler or on a heated grill until desired doneness. Cool, dice into $^1/_2$-inch pieces. Add the diced steak to the remaining Base Recipe in the bowl.

serves 2 to 3

Pasta Salad with Chickpeas
Pasta Salad with Proscuitto

For a heartier salad, substitute cheese tortellini for the cooked plain pasta, but increase the amount of pasta to 12 ounces. You can use sliced ham instead of proscuitto, if you prefer.

BASE RECIPE

8 ounces medium pasta (such as ziti or penne)

1 cup halved cherry tomatoes

One 6-ounce jar marinated mushrooms, drained

$^3/_4$ cup sliced zucchini

$^1/_2$ cup chopped green bell pepper

3 tablespoons chopped, fresh basil

3 tablespoons olive oil

1 tablespoon fresh lemon juice

1 tablespoon red wine vinegar

1 clove garlic, minced

$^1/_2$ teaspoon dried oregano

$^1/_2$ teaspoon sugar

$^1/_2$ teaspoon salt

$^1/_8$ teaspoon pepper

Cook pasta according to package directions, drain and cool. In a large bowl, combine the cooked pasta, cherry tomatoes, mushrooms, zucchini, bell peppers, and basil.

In a small bowl, stir together the olive oil, lemon juice, vinegar, garlic, oregano, sugar, salt, and black pepper. Pour over the pasta mixture and toss to coat. Place half of the Base Recipe into a second bowl for the Pasta Salad with Chickpeas recipe.

Pasta Salad with Chickpeas

$^1/_2$ cup cooked (page xi) or canned, rinsed chickpeas (garbanzo beans)

$^1/_3$ cup roasted red pepper strips

Add the chickpeas and roasted red pepper to the reserved Base Recipe; toss well and serve.

serves 2 to 3

Pasta Salad with Proscuitto

2 ounces sliced proscuitto, cut into $^1/_2$-inch strips

Add the proscuitto to the remaining Base Recipe; toss and serve.

serves 2 to 3

Caribbean Millet Salad with Squash
Caribbean Millet Salad with Beef

You can use 3 cups of cooked couscous if you don't want to use the millet
(of course, use the cooking directions for couscous if you're using the couscous).

BASE RECIPE

1 tablespoon vegetable oil

1 cup millet (page xiii)

2 cups boiling water

$^3/_4$ teaspoon salt

1 cup coarsely chopped cucumber

1 cup coarsely chopped red bell pepper

1 cup coarsely chopped mango

$^1/_2$ cup chopped red onion

2 tablespoons chopped, fresh cilantro

2 tablespoons lime juice

$1^1/_2$ tablespoons vegetable oil

1 teaspoon curry powder

$^1/_4$ teaspoon ground ginger

$^1/_4$ teaspoon ground coriander

$^1/_8$ teaspoon ground red pepper (cayenne)

> **recipe tip:**
> *Cook the millet, let cool. While the millet is cooling, cook the steak, then prepare the Base Recipe.*

Heat the oil in a 2-quart saucepan. Add the millet and cook, stirring, until some of the grains have browned and make crackling sounds, about 2 minutes. Add the water and salt; return to a boil. Reduce heat and simmer, covered, 30 minutes or until all the water has been absorbed. Set aside to cool.

While the millet is cooking, cook the steak for the Caribbean Millet Salad with Beef recipe.

In a large bowl, combine the cooled millet, cucumber, bell pepper, mango, red onion, and fresh cilantro. In a small bowl, stir together the lime juice, vegetable oil, curry powder, ginger, ground coriander, and red pepper. Pour the lime juice mixture over the millet mixture and toss. Set aside 3 $^1/_2$ cups for Caribbean Millet Salad with Beef recipe.

Caribbean Millet Salad with Squash

1 cup peeled, cubed butternut squash

2 tablespoons golden raisins

3 tablespoons plain yogurt

Cook the squash until tender (in a microwave for 5 to 6 minutes, or steam or boil until tender); cool.

Add the squash, raisins, and yogurt to the remaining Base Recipe. Toss and serve.

serves 2 to 3

Caribbean Millet Salad with Beef

8 to 12 ounces London broil or other tender boneless cut of beef, cut 1-inch thick

Salt and black pepper, to taste

$^3/_4$ cup coarsely chopped red bell pepper

Preheat broiler. Lightly salt and pepper the beef.

Broil 4 to 6 inches from the heat, about 4 minutes per side for medium-rare, or to desired doneness.

Add the bell pepper to the reserved Base Recipe; toss. Slice the cooked beef and serve warm or cold over reserved salad.

serves 2 to 3

Thai Tofu Salad & Thai Beef Salad

Although the dressing for this salad is very similar to the one for the Warm Thai Beef Salad, the end salads are extremely different. The steak is served warm or room temperature for the Beef Salad.

BASE RECIPE

Dressing:

1 jalapeño pepper, seeded and thinly sliced, optional

1/3 cup fresh lime juice

1 tablespoon soy sauce

2 cloves garlic, crushed

2 teaspoons sugar

1 teaspoon vegetable oil

> **recipe tip:**
> *Cook the steak before you start the Base Recipe.*

Salad:

6 cups bite-sized pieces romaine lettuce, rinsed well and patted dry

1 cup tomato wedges

1 cup cucumber slices

1/3 cup sliced red onion

To prepare the dressing:

In a small bowl, stir together all of the dressing ingredients until the sugar is dissolved.

To prepare the salad:

In a large bowl, toss together all of the salad ingredients. Add dressing to the salad and toss to combine. Set aside half of the Base Recipe in a second large bowl for the Thai Tofu Salad.

Thai Tofu Salad

$^3/_4$ cup diced ($^1/_4$-inch) baked or pressed tofu

3 tablespoons peanuts, chopped

Add the tofu and peanuts to the reserved Base Recipe. Toss and serve.

serves 2

Thai Beef Salad

$^1/_2$ to $^3/_4$ pound boneless beef, such as London broil or sirloin, 1-inch thick

Preheat the broiler.

Broil the steak 4 to 6 inches from the heat for about 3 minutes per side for medium-rare.

Thinly slice, then cut into bite-sized pieces; set aside while you prepare the Base Recipe.

Add to the remaining Base Recipe and toss.

serves 2

Thai Eggplant Salad
& Warm Thai Beef Salad

BASE RECIPE

$^1/_3$ cup fresh lime juice

2 tablespoons soy sauce

1 tablespoon vegetable oil

$1^1/_2$ tablespoons sugar

3 cloves garlic, minced

$1^1/_2$ cups cooked, long grain, white rice

$^1/_2$ cup chopped red onion

$^1/_2$ teaspoon crushed red pepper flakes

In a small bowl, stir together the lime juice, soy sauce, oil, sugar, and garlic.

In a large bowl, stir together the rice, onion, and red pepper flakes. Add the lime mixture and toss. Set aside half of the Base Recipe for the Warm Thai Beef Salad recipe.

Thai Eggplant Salad

1 tablespoon vegetable oil

2 cups finely diced eggplant

$^1/_4$ cup sliced scallion

3 tablespoons water

$^1/_2$ teaspoon sesame oil

1 cup shredded lettuce, rinsed well and patted dry

$^1/_2$ cup chopped cucumber

$^1/_2$ cup chopped tomato

In a medium skillet, heat the oil over medium high heat. Add the eggplant and scallion and cook, stirring until oil is absorbed. Add the water. Cooked stirring until eggplant is tender. Stir in the sesame oil. Add the remaining Base Recipe and cook, stirring, until heated through.

Place the lettuce on a plate, top with the cucumber, tomato, and serve the eggplant mixture.

serves 2

Warm Thai Beef Salad

$^1/_2$ pound ground beef

1 cup shredded lettuce

$^1/_2$ cup chopped cucumber

$^1/_2$ cup chopped tomato

In a medium skillet cook the beef over medium-high heat, until no longer pink. Stir in the reserved Base Recipe; cook until heated through. Place the lettuce on a serving plate. Top the lettuce with the cucumber and tomato; serve the beef mixture on top.

serves 2

Mediterranean Spinach Salad
Lamb and Spinach Salad

BASE RECIPE

1 pound fresh spinach

1 cup tomato wedges

1 cup sliced mushroom

$^1/_2$ cup scallion, cut into 1-inch pieces

$^1/_3$ cup sliced Kalamata olives

8 ounces crumbled feta cheese

$^1/_2$ cup plain yogurt

1 clove garlic, minced

$^1/_4$ teaspoon oregano

$^1/_8$ teaspoon pepper

Prepare the Mediterranean Spinach Salad recipe before you begin the Base Recipe.

While the chickpeas are cooking, in a large bowl toss together the spinach, tomato, mushrooms, scallion, and olives.

Place feta cheese, yogurt, 2 tablespoons of water, garlic, oregano, and black pepper into a blender or a food processor; cover and process until smooth. Set aside half of the Base Recipe for the Mediterranean Spinach Salad recipe.

Mediterranean Spinach Salad

1 tablespoon olive oil

2 cloves garlic, minced

$^1/_2$ teaspoon oregano

$^1/_8$ teaspoon dried thyme

$^1/_8$ teaspoon salt

1 cup cooked (page xi) or canned, rinsed chickpeas (garbanzo beans)

Preheat the oven to 350°F. In a medium bowl, stir together the oil, garlic, oregano, thyme, and salt. Add the chickpeas and toss. Place in a baking pan lined with aluminum foil. Bake, stirring occasionally, 40 minutes. Cool and serve with reserved Base Recipe.

serves 2

Lamb and Spinach Salad

$^3/_4$ pound boneless lamb steak, 1-inch thick

Broil the lamb 4 to 6 inches from the heat, 3 minutes per side for medium-rare, or until cooked to desired doneness. Cut into $^1/_4$-inch thick slices. Serve with the remaining Base Recipe spinach mixture and dressing; toss before serving.

serves 2

Potato Egg Salad & Potato Chicken Salad

You can dress up this salad by stirring in curry powder or by adding cooked peas to the salad or into the dressing, if you like. If I am using red bliss potatoes, I usually leave the skin on.

BASE RECIPE

2 cups diced, cooked potatoes

$1/2$ cup finely chopped celery

$1/4$ cup chopped, fresh parsley

$1/4$ cup mayonnaise

3 tablespoons yogurt

2 teaspoons spicy brown mustard

$3/4$ teaspoon salt

$1/2$ teaspoon grated onion

$1/4$ teaspoon black pepper

In a medium bowl toss the potatoes with the celery and parsley. In a small bowl, stir together the mayonnaise, yogurt, mustard, salt, onion, and black pepper. Add mayonnaise mixture to potato mixture and toss until combined. Set aside half of Base Recipe in another bowl for the Potato Egg Salad recipe.

Potato Egg Salad

4 hard-cooked eggs

Chop the eggs and combine with the reserved Base Recipe; toss well and serve.

serves 2

Potato Chicken Salad

8 to 12 ounces cooked, skinless, boneless chicken breast, diced

$1^1/2$ tablespoons mayonnaise

$1^1/2$ teaspoons distilled vinegar

Add the chicken, mayonnaise, and vinegar to the remaining Base Recipe; toss well and serve.

serves 2

Bulgur-Lentil Salad with Chickpeas & Bulgur-Lentil Salad with Chicken

BASE RECIPE

2 cups cooked bulgur

1 cup cooked lentils

$^1/_3$ cup chopped, fresh parsley

$^1/_3$ cup sliced scallion

$^1/_4$ cup chopped, sun-dried tomatoes, packed in oil

$1^1/_2$ tablespoons red wine vinegar

1 tablespoon olive oil

1 tablespoon vegetable oil

$^1/_4$ teaspoon salt

$^1/_4$ teaspoon pepper

In a large bowl, combine the bulgur, lentils, parsley, scallion, and sun-dried tomatoes. In a small bowl, combine the vinegar, both oils, salt and black pepper. Pour over the bulgur mixture and toss until combined. Set aside 2 cups for the Bulgur-Lentil Salad with Chicken recipe.

Bulgur-Lentil Salad with Chickpeas

1 cup cooked (page xi) or canned, rinsed chick-peas (garbanzo beans)

One 6-ounce jar marinated artichoke hearts, drained

Add the chickpeas and artichokes to the remaining Base Recipe and toss.

serves 2

Bulgur-Lentil Salad with Chicken

2 teaspoons balsamic vinegar

1 teaspoon spicy brown mustard

1 cup diced, cooked chicken

$^1/_2$ cup chopped red bell pepper

$^1/_4$ cup chopped cashews

In a medium bowl, stir together the vinegar and mustard. Add the chicken, bell pepper, and cashews, and toss. Add the reserved Base Recipe and toss.

serves 2

Curried Rice and Chickpea Salad
Curried Rice and Chicken Salad

To streamline your cooking time, you can use leftover chicken or even turkey for this recipe, or you can buy cooked chicken or turkey from the market, but have it cut into slices about $^3/_4$-inch thick.

BASE RECIPE

$^1/_3$ cup plain yogurt	1 cup chopped papaya
3 tablespoons mayonnaise	$^1/_2$ cup cooked peas
1 tablespoon curry powder	$^1/_2$ cup chopped celery
1 tablespoon chopped chutney	$^1/_3$ cup chopped cashews
$^1/_2$ teaspoon ground ginger	$^1/_3$ cup sliced scallion
$^1/_2$ teaspoon salt	(green and white parts)
2 cups cooked white or brown rice	3 tablespoons dark raisins

In a medium bowl, stir together the yogurt, mayonnaise, curry powder, chutney, ginger, and salt, reserve 2 tablespoons of the dressing for the Curried Rice and Chicken Salad recipe. In a large bowl, combine the rice, papaya, peas, celery, cashews, scallion, and raisins. Add the remaining dressing and toss. Set aside half of the Base Recipe for the Curried Rice and Chicken Salad.

Curried Rice and Chickpea Salad

$^1/_2$ cup cooked (page xi) or canned, rinsed chickpeas (garbanzo beans)

Stir the chickpeas into the remaining Base Recipe in the bowl. Toss to combine.

serves 2

Curried Rice and Chicken Salad

8 to 12 ounces cooked chicken breast, cubed

In a medium bowl, toss the chicken with the reserved 2 tablespoons of dressing. Add the reserved Base Recipe and toss to combine.

serves 2 to 3

Tomato and Black Bean Salad
Tomato and Tuna Salad

If you can't find hearts of palm (or don't like them), 1 jar of marinated artichoke hearts (drained) or $^1/_2$ cup halved black olives can be used instead.

BASE RECIPE

4 cups cubed tomatoes

1 cup sliced hearts of palm

$^1/_3$ cup sliced scallion (white and green parts)

1 tablespoon olive oil, preferably extra virgin

1 tablespoon red wine vinegar

$^1/_4$ teaspoon salt

$^1/_8$ teaspoon pepper

Combine all ingredients in a medium bowl. Remove $2^1/_2$ cups of the Base Recipe for the Tomato and Tuna Salad recipe.

Tomato and Black Bean Salad

1 cup cooked (page xi) or canned, rinsed, black beans

$^1/_2$ cup chopped avocado

2 tablespoons chopped, fresh cilantro

Add the black beans, avocado, and cilantro to the remaining Base Recipe in the bowl; toss.

serves 2

Tomato and Tuna Salad

One 6 $^1/_2$-ounce can tuna, drained

1 tablespoon red wine vinegar

2 teaspoons chopped capers

In a medium bowl, combine the tuna, vinegar, and capers with the reserved $2^1/_2$ cups of Base Recipe. Toss.

serves 2

Rice Salad with Black Beans
Rice Salad with Turkey

BASE RECIPE

¹/₄ cup mayonnaise	2 cups cooked, white or brown rice
¹/₄ cup plain yogurt	¹/₂ cup cooked peas
¹/₄ cup chopped scallion	One 6-ounce jar marinated artichoke
¹/₄ cup chopped, fresh parsley	hearts, drained and chopped
1 tablespoon red wine vinegar	¹/₃ cup sliced, black olives
1 teaspoon salt	¹/₄ cup chopped pimiento
¹/₄ teaspoon black pepper	

In a small bowl, stir together the mayonnaise, yogurt, scallion, parsley, vinegar, salt, and black pepper.

In a large bowl combine the rice, peas, artichoke hearts, olives, and pimiento. Add the mayonnaise mixture, and toss to combine. Reserve 2 cups for the Rice Salad with Turkey recipe.

Rice Salad with Black Beans

¹/₃ cup slivered almonds

³/₄ cup cooked (page xi) or canned, rinsed black beans

¹/₃ cup sliced, pimiento-stuffed green olives

2 tablespoons chopped, fresh cilantro

Preheat the oven to 350°F.

Bake the almonds on a baking sheet for 10 minutes, until lightly toasted; cool.

Combine all the ingredients with the remaining Base Recipe in the bowl. Toss and serve.

serves 2 to 3

Rice Salad with Turkey

1 cup diced cooked turkey breast

1 tablespoon chopped, fresh dill

In a medium bowl, add the turkey and dill to the reserved Base Recipe. Toss to combine.

serves 2 to 3

Red and White Bean Salad
& Tuna and White Bean Salad

*As with most recipes that use a fair amount of roasted red peppers, the quality of the recipe is
always better when you use homemade (see page 168) rather than the jarred variety.*

BASE RECIPE

1^1/$_2$ cups cooked (page xi) or canned,
   rinsed, small white beans

^{1}/$_2$ cup roasted red bell pepper slices

^{1}/$_3$ cup chopped, fresh parsley

^{1}/$_4$ cup chopped red onion

1 tablespoon olive oil

1 tablespoon vegetable oil

1 tablespoon fresh lemon juice

2 teaspoons cider vinegar

1 teaspoon Dijon mustard

^{1}/$_2$ clove garlic, minced

In a large bowl, combine the white beans, red pepper slices, parsley, and red onion.
In a small bowl, combine both the oils, the lemon juice, cider vinegar, mustard, and
garlic. Pour over the bean mixture and toss to combine. Set aside 1^1/$_4$ cups of the
Base Recipe for the Tuna and White Bean Salad Recipe.

Red and White Bean Salad

1 cup cooked (page xi) or canned, rinsed red
   or kidney beans

^{1}/$_2$ cup chopped celery

Add the beans and celery to the remaining
Base Recipe in the bowl. Toss.

serves 2 to 3

Tuna and White Bean Salad

One 6 ^{1}/$_2$-ounce can albacore tuna, drained

In a medium bowl, combine the tuna with
the reserved 1^1/$_4$ cups of Base Recipe. Toss to
combine.

serves 2

Bean and Corn Salad &
Salmon, Bean, and Vegetable Salad

You can serve these recipes as written, or add 4 cups of lettuce to each half and toss.

BASE RECIPE

1^1/$_2$ tablespoons vegetable oil

2 teaspoons cider vinegar

2 teaspoons lime juice

1 teaspoon spicy brown mustard

^{1}/$_4$ teaspoon black pepper

2 cups cooked (page xi) or canned, rinsed kidney beans

^{3}/$_4$ cup chopped green bell peppers

^{1}/$_2$ cup shredded carrot

^{1}/$_2$ cup chopped red onion

In a small bowl, stir together the oil, vinegar, lime juice, mustard, and black pepper.

In a large bowl, combine the beans, bell peppers, carrot, and onion. Add the dressing and toss. Set aside 1^1/$_2$ cups for the Salmon, Bean, and Vegetable Salad recipe.

Bean and Corn Salad

1 cup cooked corn kernels

1 tablespoon chopped, fresh cilantro

1 teaspoon chili powder

Add the corn, cilantro, and chili powder to the remaining Base Recipe in the bowl. Toss and serve.

serves 2

Salmon, Bean, and Vegetable Salad

One 6 ^{1}/$_2$-ounce can salmon, drained

2 tablespoons chopped fresh parsley

In a large bowl, combine the salmon, parsley, and the reserved Base Recipe. Toss and serve.

serves 2

Greek Salad & Salad Niçoise

You can dress up this recipe by substituting 6-ounce grilled tuna steaks for the canned tuna in the Salad Niçoise recipe.

BASE RECIPE

8 cups lightly packed, bite-sized pieces of romaine lettuce, rinsed well and patted dry

1¹/₂ cups tomato wedges

1 cup cucumber slices

1 large green bell pepper, sliced into 12 rings

3 tablespoons red wine vinegar

1 tablespoon vegetable oil

1 tablespoon olive oil

1 teaspoon fresh lemon juice

¹/₄ teaspoon dried oregano

recipe tip:
Prepare the ingredients for both salads before starting the Base Recipe.

In a large bowl, toss together the lettuce, tomato, cucumber, and bell pepper rings. In a small bowl, stir together vinegar, both of the oils, lemon juice, and oregano. Pour over salad and toss. Set aside half of the Base Recipe for the Greek Salad.

Greek Salad

4 ounces crumbled feta cheese

¹/₂ cup sliced radish

¹/₄ cup scallion (white and green parts), cut into 1-inch lengths

12 pitted, black olives

Add the feta cheese, radish, scallion, and olives to the reserved half of the Base Recipe. Toss and serve.

serves 2

Salad Niçoise

One 6-ounce can tuna, drained

2 to 3 boiling potatoes, cooked, cooled, and sliced

¹/₂ cup cooked or canned, drained sliced beets

12 whole green beans, cooked

1 hard-cooked large egg, cooled and sliced

¹/₄ cup sliced red onion

Arrange all the Salad Niçoise ingredients over the remaining Base Recipe.

serves 2 to 3

Caesar Salad sans Anchovies
&Caesar Salad

In the old days, when using raw eggs, we worried about contaminants on the egg shell and would quick-poach the egg to kill any culprits. Today, we worry about salmonella in the raw egg itself. I, personally, am willing to take the risk since contamination is rare. But, if you are not, or are cooking for very young or old family members, I suggest you skip this dressing recipe and substitute any store-bought anchovy-free Caesar salad dressing.

BASE RECIPE

1 large egg

2 tablespoons olive oil

2 cloves garlic, crushed

1 tablespoon fresh lemon juice

1 tablespoon red wine vinegar

$1/4$ teaspoon anchovy-free Worcestershire sauce

$1/4$ teaspoon salt, or to taste

$1/4$ cup grated Parmesan cheese

Place the egg in boiling water for 1 minute. Crack egg and discard egg white. Place yolk into a large salad bowl. Add the oil, and garlic. Whisk until combined. Add the lemon juice, vinegar, Worcestershire sauce, salt, and Parmesan cheese. Whisk until completely combined. Place 3 tablespoons of the Base Recipe into a small bowl for the Caesar Salad sans Anchovies recipe.

Caesar Salad sans Anchovies

- 6 cups loosely packed, bite-sized pieces romaine lettuce, rinsed well and patted dry
- 2 cakes baked or pressed tofu, sliced
- 1 tablespoon minced, sun-dried tomatoes, packed in oil
- 2 tablespoons grated Parmesan cheese
- Freshly ground black pepper, to taste
- $^1/_3$ cup croutons

Combine the lettuce and tofu in a large bowl. Add the sun-dried tomatoes and Parmesan cheese to the reserved Base Recipe in the bowl, mash with a fork until combined. Pour over salad and toss until dressing coats the lettuce. Grind some pepper over the salad; add croutons and toss again.

serves 2

Caesar Salad

- 6 cups loosely packed, bite-sized pieces romaine lettuce, rinsed well and patted dry
- 4 anchovies, minced
- Freshly ground pepper, to taste
- $^1/_3$ cup croutons
- Two 6-ounce skinless, boneless chicken breasts, broiled

Place the lettuce into a large bowl. Add the anchovies to the remaining Base Recipe, mash with a fork until combined. Pour over salad and toss until dressing coats the lettuce. Grind some pepper over the salad; add croutons and toss again. Serve topped with chicken breasts, cut into strips if you like.

serves 2

Mozzarella and Roasted Red Pepper Salad & Tuna and Roasted Red Pepper Salad

You can use jarred roasted red peppers, but homemade (page 168) are much better. Try fresh-made mozzarella cheese instead of packaged, or try using the mozzarella that comes floating in water. Use fresh grilled tuna in this recipe, too.

BASE RECIPE

2 red bell peppers

4 cups tomato wedges

$1/2$ cup chopped red onion

$1/2$ cup sliced, black olives

1 tablespoon olive oil

1 tablespoon red wine vinegar

$1/8$ teaspoon salt

$1/8$ teaspoon pepper

Preheat the broiler. Cut the bell peppers in half lengthwise. Discard seeds and ribs. Place bell peppers in one layer on a large baking sheet. Broil, 4-inches from the heat, 5 minutes or until quite charred. Turn and cook until second side is charred. Place in paper or plastic bag and cool. Peel and discard skin; cut into $1/4$-inch strips.

In a large bowl, combine the roasted red peppers, tomato, onion, olives, oil, vinegar, salt, and black pepper. Toss to combine. Set aside half of Base Recipe for the Mozzarella and Roasted Red Pepper Salad recipe.

Mozzarella and Roasted Red Pepper Salad

1 cup cubed mozzarella

2 tablespoons chopped, fresh basil

1 clove garlic, minced

In a medium bowl, combine the cheese, basil, and garlic with the reserved Base Recipe. Toss and serve.

serves 2

Tuna and Roasted Red Pepper Salad

One 6 $1/2$-ounce can tuna, drained

1 tablespoon fresh lemon juice

1 teaspoon chopped capers, optional

Add tuna, lemon juice, and capers to the remaining Base Recipe in bowl. Toss and serve.

serves 2

Index